LOVELL
OUR
DOGGE

About the Author

Michèle Schindler studied at Johann Wolfgang Goethe-Universität in Frankfurt am Main, Germany, reading English Studies and history with a focus on mediaeval studies. At the same time she worked as a language teacher, teaching English and German as a second language. In addition to English and German, she is fluent in French, and – crucially for this book – reads Latin.

LOVELL OUR DOGGE

THE LIFE OF VISCOUNT LOVELL, CLOSEST
FRIEND OF RICHARD III AND FAILED REGICIDE

MICHÈLE SCHINDLER

AMBERLEY

For Victoria

This edition published 2022

Amberley Publishing
The Hill, Stroud
Gloucestershire, GL5 4EP

www.amberley-books.com

British Library Cataloguing in Publication Data.
A catalogue record for this book is available from the British Library.

ISBN 978 1 3981 0339 9 (paperback)
ISBN 978 1 4456 9054 4 (ebook)

Typesetting by Aura Technology and Software Services, India.
Printed in the UK.

Contents

Francis Lovell's immediate family

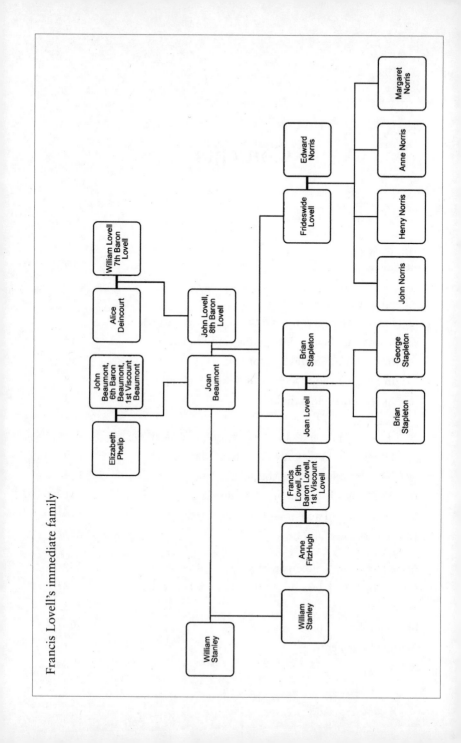

Lovell family tree

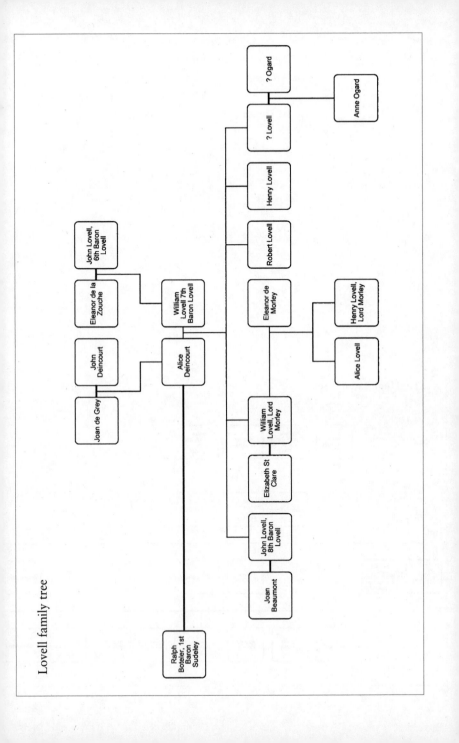

FitzHugh family tree

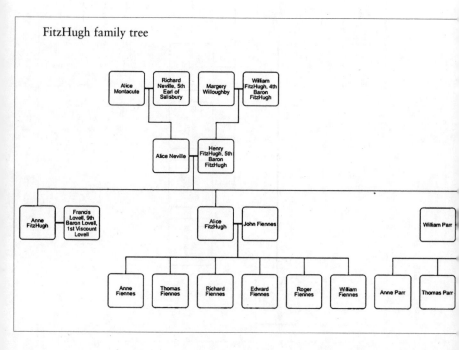

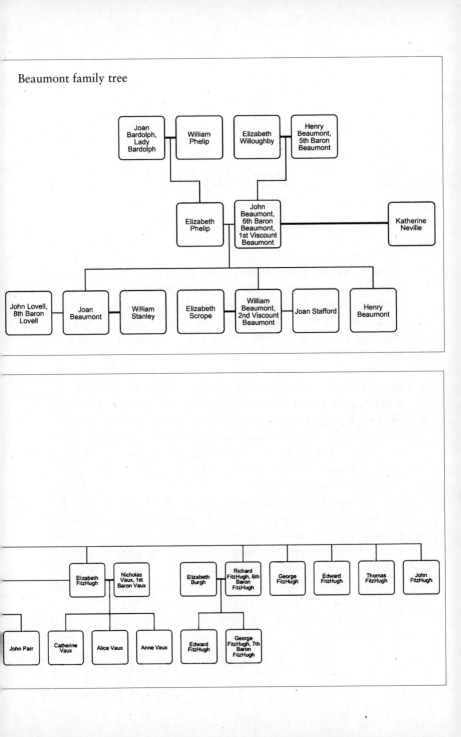

Beaumont family tree

Introduction

The boy and his twin sister were born at a tense time in history, into a country in turmoil. The series of conflicts now known as the Wars of the Roses had already begun, and periods of unrest would be a constant throughout their lives. Before long, the political situation would affect their own family and eventually even the twins themselves.

At the moment of their birth, however, the strife still seemed far away, and their arrival must have been a joyous occasion for their parents, John Lovell and Joan Beaumont. The couple, both scions of old and respected families, had been married for almost exactly ten years when the twins were born. The birth of the boy, whom they appear to have named after the saint honoured on his day of birth, St Francis of Assisi, must have been a particular relief for his parents. Though they could not have known it at the time of his birth, he was destined to be not only his father's heir one day, but also the heir of his rich grandmother Alice Deincourt. Even though he was not born to this position, his future must have seemed secure to his parents: a tranquil existence as a rich, respected baron's younger brother, living much as his ancestors and their siblings had for centuries.[1] Perhaps they also hoped that he would grow more influential than most of the Lovells had been in their time, taking instead after his maternal family, the more politically involved Beaumonts.

The future of the little girl, named Joan after her mother, may have seemed similarly certain: she could expect to marry a rich knight, as the Lovell daughters had for centuries.

Whether or not John and Joan had expectations for their children when they were born is of course impossible to say, but it seems very likely that they were very aware of their family history and would have wanted their children to continue the traditions and legacies of their forebears.

1

'The Lord Lovell ys son'

The Lovell Family

The Lovells and the Beaumonts were both rich, noble families, and over the centuries they had grown close. By the time of Francis's birth, the families had been of some importance for centuries; however, they had gained special distinction in the last generation.

Francis's paternal grandfather, William Lovell, was likely born in the year 1397. Aged nineteen at the time of his father's death, William became a ward of the king, as his grandson Francis later would as well. In the 1420s and 1430s, he served Henry V and Henry VI, holding among other roles a position of some importance in France.[1] His exact role in France is no longer known, but as Monika Simon points out in her dissertation about the Lovell family, the fact that his return to England is recorded in the Annals of St Albans suggests that it was a notable position.[2] After his return, William continued serving the king in various, if rather unremarkable capacities. He was appointed to commissions of oyer and terminer, to collect taxes and to keep the peace of the realm. He also held the constableship of Wallingford Castle and received an order to raise troops against the rebellion of Jack Cade in 1450.[3] Very little is known about William's actual activities in these commissions and jobs; it is even possible that the appointments were nominal. If not, William seems to have fulfilled his tasks quietly and discreetly, a quality his grandson Francis was to inherit.

It appears that after returning from France, William lived a mostly quiet life. Only once is he recorded to have caused trouble, this coming when he, together with several other men[4] including the Earl of Shrewsbury, refused to attend Parliament while Richard, Duke of York was Lord Protector during Henry VI's spell of insanity. For this transgression he received a written warning from the Duke of York, stating that 'if ye come not it shall give us cause to entreat you in such wise as shall be thought unto us by the advice of our said Council according to your disobedience.'[5] This was an empty threat, and William was eventually excused on the strength of his service to Henry V.

What William is most noted for in popular memory is in fact something completely unrelated to his political life: the reconstruction of his ancestral manor. Located in Minster Lovell, a village which got its name for its association with the local lords in the thirteenth century, and directly next to the River Windrush, the ruins seen today are those of a manor mainly built by William on the remains of an earlier structure. It has often been suggested that this manor reflected William's preference for a quiet life.[6] It was not built as a stronghold, nor did it have any defences. Instead, it is more likely it was a country home designed for comfortable living and the display of William's considerable wealth. The manor, built in the 1430s, was said to be large and impressive, if fairly conventional for the time. According to Anthony Emery, its one notable feature was an unusually high number of windows.[7]

It was probably mainly in this manor that William lived and raised his family. After his marriage in 1422 to Alice Deincourt, a rich heiress in her own right,[8] he had at least five children: one daughter, whose name is no longer known,[9] and sons John, William, Robert and Henry, of whom John was the eldest. William's inquisition post mortem records John as being twenty-two on his father's death in May 1455.[10] According to the inquisition, John Lovell's birth date was therefore 15 April 1433, meaning he was born over a decade after his parents' wedding. There is no explanation for the delay between adult marriage and offspring, which is unusual for the time; it might be that Alice did not accompany her husband during his service in France. It is also possible that they lost children before John's birth, though no such indication survives; nor is there any indication when John's surviving siblings were born.

Since William did not draw much attention during the 1430s and 1440s, nothing is known about his marriage and his relationship with his children, though what little evidence there is suggests he fulfilled all contemporary expectations by taking care of the family and working for their advancement. In around 1445, he married his second-eldest son, namesake William, to Elizabeth St Clare, daughter and, together with her sister, co-heiress of Thomas St Clare.[11] In the autumn of 1446, between 7 September and 4 November,[12] he married his eldest son John, then thirteen, to Joan Beaumont, the only daughter of John, Viscount Beaumont, and granted the couple some of his lands.[13] It seems that the young couple lived in his household from then on, but it is not definitely known.

William's will, which he made in March 1455 and to which he added two codicils in the week before his death, makes it clear that he did not yet have any grandchildren from his sons. More notably, the will also suggests problems between William and his eldest son.

While the will contained some grants for servants, as was usual for such documents, and also left some money to his granddaughter Anne Ogard, whom he describes as 'my daughter's daughter', it was William's sons who were the main focus of his will. William left quite a lot to his younger sons, perhaps in the knowledge that John would eventually be heir to his mother's[14] estates and wealth. Nothing about the provisions of the will appears out of the ordinary, and while it does not note what exactly was left to John, this is only a problem for modern researchers trying to find out what he owned. It would not have been too much of a problem at the time, as everything not explicitly bequeathed to his younger brothers or someone else would have fallen to him.

However, there are two notable features of the will and its codicils, both showing a curious distinction between William's treatment of his eldest son John and his three younger sons. While the will repeatedly names William, Robert and Henry, and they are clearly identified by William as 'sonne', John is never mentioned by name, and never identified as William's son. When mentioned, he is only 'my next heire', in stark contrast to the flowery and often repetitive language used in documents at the time and also elsewhere in the will. Secondly, William chose to leave a 'Bedd of

Bawdekyn with qwischens and thapparrell thereto' (a bed of bawdkin – silk brocade – with cushions and the apparel thereto), a valuable item, not to his firstborn as would have been the normal course, but to his second-born, William.[15]

While this could well be simply an oddity, explained perhaps by there being no need to mention John very often as his inheritance stood and did not need to be clarified, and he already being in possession of an equally valuable personal item as was left to William, this treatment of John is a notable aspect of an otherwise very conventional document, and as such gives rise to speculation.[16] Sadly, this document stands as our sole insight into any personal relationship between William senior and any member of his family.

William died on 13 June 1455,[17] shortly after the First Battle of St Albans, a key clash in the Wars of the Roses. Since William seems to have known or at least suspected his death was imminent by March 1455, when he made his will, it is probably not very surprising that neither he nor any of his sons were participants of this battle. Throughout what can be described as the run-up to the Wars of the Roses, William had shown his sympathy for the Lancastrian side,[18] represented by the incumbent Henry VI, and while it is by nature unprovable it seems likely that had he lived longer he would have fought for Henry VI. His sons certainly did, and so did Francis's other grandfather, John Beaumont.

William was fifty-eight years old when he died.[19] In his will, he requested a thousand masses for his soul to be read in the week after his death, a chapel to be founded where prayers were to be said for him in perpetuity, and for his body to be buried in Oxford. It is not known if the first two requests were followed; it seems that the last one was not. A still surviving tomb in St Kenelm's church, next to Minster Lovell Hall, which William had been involved in renovating, is assumed to be his. Though some have questioned this conclusion, most notably Monika E Simon,[20] the effigies, including weepers representing his wife and sister-in-law, suggest that it is indeed William's burial plot. It seems likely it was his wife, Alice Deincourt, who made the arrangements for the tomb.[21]

John Lovell officially entered into his inheritance in many counties on 21 October 1455,[22] the same day on which orders were issued for a dower to be assigned to his mother. We no longer have any knowledge of how these arrangements were made. All we know is that with his father's death John became Baron Lovell, and his wife Joan Beaumont his baroness.

The Beaumont Family

Like John, Joan was from a distinguished old family which had won greater fame in the previous generation. Her father, John Beaumont, was born on 14 August 1409 to Henry Beaumont and his wife Elizabeth. He became Henry V's ward at only four years old, after his father's death. Not much is known about John's early life, but it is a fact that in or around 1428 he was married to Elizabeth Phelip, only child of William Phelip, Lord Bardolph and his wife Joan.

Elizabeth and John had at least three children together, of whom Joan was probably the youngest. Approximately twenty-five years old when she died on 5 August 1466,[23] Joan was probably born in 1441, and therefore rather younger than her husband. Her brother Henry was likely born in 1434, and another brother, William, on 23 April 1438. It is unknown if there were any other children of John and Elizabeth; if there were, they had died by August 1441 as Henry, William and Joan were stated to be John's only issue at that time.[24]

During the 1430s, John Beaumont not only started a family but also established himself in Henry VI's government, starting with him joining Humphrey, Duke of Gloucester's expedition for the protection of Calais in 1436. His actions for the Crown appeared to earn him quite some respect, and certainly the king's gratitude, and over the years he was given many tasks and honours by the king. Most notably, on 12 February 1440, he was elevated from being a simple baron to the title of viscount, becoming the first man in England to hold the title.[25]

It is likely that personal connections to the king and royal advisers played a part in his preferment and, in view of his recorded actions, perhaps inordinate honours in comparison to others.[26] The nature of these connections is no longer possible to ascertain, but clearly they stood him in good stead, and naturally gave him cause to support Henry VI and his government instead of the Yorkists when the Wars of the Roses began.

Another perk John secured for himself and his family came after the deaths of his wife Elizabeth and her father William Phelip between June and August 1441, which saw him gain control over all lands his children inherited from the Phelip line, as well as the title of Lord Bardolph for his eldest son. The royal grant confirming this was made on 10 August of that year, stating that John was to have custody of the Phelip inheritance until the heirs came of age. Joan's brother Henry, then 'in his eighth year', was the first Phelip heir, followed by any heirs he might have; after him the line fell to her other brother William and his heirs. Finally, if they both died without issue, Joan and her heirs would inherit the Phelip lands.[27]

Elizabeth must have died only shortly before this announcement as she was still alive when her father died in June 1441 and the grant states that John was 'in no small way bereaved, and lost through death Elizabeth, lately his wife',[28] meaning she must have died in late June or in July 1441, perhaps as she gave birth to Joan. Only a year later, in December 1442, Joan's brother Henry also died. He was buried in Dennington, Suffolk.

John remarried in 1443, but despite the recent loss of his eldest son leaving him with only one son and one daughter, his choice of wife suggests a marriage aimed at fiscal and political gain rather than the creation of more heirs. By 25 August 1443 he had married Katherine Neville, sister of Cecily Neville. Katherine had been widowed twice before, the last time not quite a year before her marriage to John. In addition, she was some twelve years older than John. At approximately forty-six years of age, Katherine would have been thought unable to produce any more children, and indeed she did not. Instead, she brought him an interest in extensive lands from her previous marriages, especially her first to the Duke of Norfolk. Nothing is known about the personal relationship between John and Katherine, but the marriage lasted until John's death without ever causing any gossip.

As mentioned above, in 1446 John married the infant Joan, then around five years old, to the thirteen-year-old John Lovell, eldest son of William, Baron Lovell. Presumably, the marriage was arranged to re-establish an alliance made between the Beaumont and Deincourt families two decades before, when Joan's paternal aunt Elizabeth Beaumont married John Lovell's maternal uncle William Deincourt, a marriage that did not last long and produced no children.

Whether the marriage between John and Joan was arranged at short notice or long planned is not known, nor is it known why John chose to have his daughter marry at such a young age. Nevertheless, they were wed between 7 September 1446[29] and 4 November 1446.[30] In 1452, John also arranged a marriage for his son William. The boy, then fourteen, married another Joan, daughter of Humphrey, Duke of Buckingham, and niece of John's second wife Katherine.

The end of the 1440s saw a great deal of upheaval. England was losing the Hundred Years War with France, King Henry VI's marriage to Margaret of Anjou was revealed to involve handing sizeable territories on the Continent back to the French, and a power vacuum beckoned as influential courtiers like Humphrey, Duke of Gloucester and William de la Pole, Duke of Suffolk fell from grace and met their deaths – Gloucester dying while under arrest for treason, Suffolk being murdered while on his way to European exile. However, John managed to get through most of this chaos without suffering any loss of privileges, despite having been close to Suffolk and having been involved in the Gloucester's downfall.[31] It seems that during the late 1440s and early 1450s John tried to avoid open conflict with others. He accepted Suffolk's fall, even playing a part in his arrest,[32] and while he was opposed to the growing influence of Richard, Duke of York in 1452, he accepted York assuming control of the kingdom as Protector in 1453.

Though he was later to become an important supporter of the Lancastrian side during the Wars of the Roses, fighting for Henry VI, John remained aloof at first. Like Francis's other grandfather, John did not take part in the First Battle of St Albans in 1455;[33] however, while William Lovell was too sickly to fight, there is no obvious reason as to why John chose not to become involved. Perhaps he hoped to hedge his bets, or perhaps he didn't care whether a Lancastrian or a Yorkist sat upon the throne. Many who later turned against the Duke of York did initially sympathise with him, and it may well be that John had no interest in stopping the duke but kept his head down to evade the ire of the king's advisers.[34]

Regardless of his motivations, in the mid-1450s, at the time of his grandson Francis's birth, John Beaumont was not yet firmly associated with either side of the quarrel. His son-in-law John Lovell, meanwhile, was making his own way.

Francis's Parents

Upon becoming baron, it seems that John Lovell soon carved out a place as one of Henry VI's staunchest supporters, and also tried to form relationships that would benefit him and his family. He was soon handling a considerable workload for Henry VI's government,[35] but his attempts to build connections seem to have met with less success. Though associated with several men of power and influence, there is no indication John Lovell ever formed a lasting relationship with anybody of consequence, nor that any of them ever gave him a position of influence and power. Not even the fact that his mother, Alice, was at the very centre of the royal court, being the young Prince of Wales's nurse[36] and a rich and influential person in her own right, seemed to help. Whether John Lovell's lack of prominence was a matter of personal choice or a failure to network we do not know, as there is little extant information about his relationships; however, what does survive does not go in his favour.

Only two pieces of evidence survive to shed some light on John Lovell's connections outside his immediate family. One is a letter to his father-in-law John, Viscount Beaumont, written between 1455, when he became Lord Lovell upon his father's death, and 1460, when Viscount Beaumont died.[37] It is mostly a very formal missive, Lovell writing in response to a letter he received from Beaumont asking him to give the stewardship of the manor of Bagworth to one Thomas Everingham, Beaumont's second cousin. John agrees to this, couching his letter in conventionally deferential language. There is nothing surprising or unexpected about this, but it is notable that he almost presents himself as the supplicant. That he includes a plea to his father-in-law to remember him and do all he can for his 'worship or profit' supports this impression.

Most notable, however, is that he concludes the letter with the statement that 'my lady my mother recommended her unto your good lordship, in whom her most faith and trust is in, praying you ye will be [a] good brother unto her, for she hath taken you for her chief counsel.' Whereas Lovell humbling himself to his father-in-law in the letter is slightly overdone but is in itself hardly noteworthy, the inclusion of a plea for a good relationship between Beaumont and Alice Deincourt is more unexpected in a letter like this. From its tone, it appears that John was very eager either to establish or maintain a friendly relationship with his father-in-law, yet not entirely certain how this overture would be received. While Lovell's relationship with Beaumont does not appear to have been hostile at the time of the letter, nor does it seem to have been anything approaching a friendship.

It can be assumed that the aforementioned letter was written in 1455,[38] given that Alice Deincourt is apparently not at court at the time of writing despite being the Prince of Wales's nurse, and also given that she is said to have taken Viscount Beaumont 'for her chief counsel', which would be a natural thing to do just after her husband's death (William Lovell had died, of course, in 1455).

The second piece of evidence dates to 1456, and suggests that in the intervening period their relationship had clearly soured. In Beaumont's will, he includes the rather shocking statement that his daughter Joan 'is by the wrath of God, married to John my son'.[39]

We do not know why Beaumont condemned his son-in-law so strongly, but it could perhaps reflect Beaumont's anxiety after learning, shortly after William Lovell's death, that his son-in-law had already made his wife, Beaumont's daughter, pregnant. Lovell and his wife Joan had been married for almost nine years when William died and the young man inherited the title of baron, but Joan was still yet to turn fourteen. Most would have still considered her too young for consummation. John Lovell, however, clearly did not agree with this assessment. Though he and Joan were still childless when John became baron, Joan must already have been pregnant. Four months later at the most, possibly earlier, she gave birth to their first child, called John after his father. Soon afterwards, she became pregnant again. Fifteen months after becoming baron, John had three living children.

2

Francis's Early Years and the Wars of the Roses

Though there is no primary source in which his birthday is mentioned – estimates vary by as much as three years – Francis and his twin sister were likely born on 17 September 1456. As he requested in 1484 to have prayers said for himself and his wife on this day,[1] it can be assumed that the day meant something to him, and an explanation for this is found in the fact that 17 September is one of the minor feast days for St Francis of Assisi.

Francis was not a Lovell or Beaumont family name at all. There actually existed a rigid naming system for the sons of Lovell barons: the first boy was named John, the second William, and the third Robert. The Lovells had kept to this rule for three hundred years,[2] so there must have been a reason for his parents to subvert it; they seem to have named their son after the saint on whose day he was born. This would also fit with the evidence of the Calendar of the Patent Rolls, in which Francis is stated to be 'a minor' in February 1477[3] and fully of age by 6 November 1477,[4] and his father's inquisition post mortem, made in October 1465,[5] in which his age is given as nine years.

Little is known about Francis's early childhood, and most of what can be gleaned about it is based on knowledge about the customs of the day. In this way we can assume that Francis and Joan were christened within a few days of their birth. If they appeared sickly or were very small, which would have been likely for twins, it is even possible they were christened immediately after birth. As is often the case with Francis, we have no further information about this event; no indication who his and his sister's godparents were. In noble families it was typically relatives or close friends who were asked,[6] and with this in mind the likely candidates are William, Robert and Henry Lovell; William Beaumont; John Beaumont, their maternal grandfather; Beaumont's wife Katherine Neville; and Alice Deincourt, their paternal grandmother.

The fact of the birth producing twins, and their likelihood of being sickly, suggests another reason for Francis's unusual name, although his sister Joan's name was traditional for the family. We can only speculate, but perhaps Francis was thought to be likely to die while his twin sister seemed sturdier; if so, it might not have seemed such a transgression to give him an unconventional name. Perhaps it was simply a coincidence, and only a male saint was honoured on the day of the twins' birth.

If the Lovells followed conventions for people of their standing, then the babies were handed into the care of a wet nurse soon after birth, and their mother Joan did not breastfeed them. Even without evidence about their very early days, it is virtually certain that the day-to-day care for the babies was not carried out by the parents. Nicholas Orme, in his book *Medieval Children*, describes the way children of Francis's standing were typically cared for: in a nursery under the supervision of a nurse and at least one rocker, whose task was to rock the baby's cradle and do other menial work like changing the baby. Since Orme points out that '[t]he high rate of mortality seems to have been attributed, in part, to deficiencies in their milk,'[7] it is quite likely that the Lovells employed more than one wet nurse for their twin babies, so that the children were provided with sufficient milk from healthy women. Regardless, two babies would almost certainly have had more servants than one baby would have had. Since the babies' paternal grandmother, Alice Deincourt, was nursemaid to the Prince of Wales, some three years older than Francis and Joan, it is possible that she had connections and saw to the appointment of respected wet nurses for her grandchildren, and other servants such as the rockers.

As the children of a baron, and being the exact same age, Francis and Joan most likely would have spent their early years together, being looked after by the same people, together with their older brother John. Their upbringing and everyday life would not have differed much from that of other noble children. For the first years of their lives the wet-nurses were doubtless Francis and Joan's primary caregivers, not only feeding them but presiding over the nursery, supervising their routine and encouraging their development. There would have been servants to make certain they did not hurt themselves (or others), and also tutors to teach them the skills appropriate to their age.[8] Indeed, in their first years the routine was likely similar to that experienced by modern toddlers.

The household ordinances of the future Edward V, born fifteen years later, give an insight into how a highborn child would have spent his days,[9] and while there were certainly differences between the routine of the heir to the throne and the son of a baron, and the latter would have had less constant attention by physicians and priests, there would also have been a lot of similarities. Like Edward, little Francis, Joan and John would have been made 'to arise every morning at a convenient hour, according to [their] age'; the hour would have become earlier as they became older. They would have had someone to attend them as they were dressed, to watch them playing 'all such convenient disports and exercises as behoveth [their] standing', to supervise as they ate, and, doubtlessly, someone to instruct them at praying and religious doctrine.

The ordinances drawn up for Prince Edward suggest he heard Mass every morning. It is not known if the Lovell household also followed such a course, though it is certainly not impossible. Francis was later to become a pious man, which may have started in his childhood and been encouraged by his parents, for the choice of his name suggests that at least one of his parents, if not both, were, even for such a religious time, uncommonly pious. His grandfather, William Lovell, had been so as well, and we know that he, like Francis in his adult years, founded chapels and chantries and especially favoured St Christopher.[10]

Even if John and Joan's piety was entirely usual and not especially pronounced, religion doubtlessly played a big part in the lives of the toddlers, and they would have heard mass often. Potentially, like Edward V, they were encouraged or expected to 'offer afore the altar' on feast days. At the very least they would have heard sermons regularly, attended church on Sundays, Fridays and feast days, and been instructed in Christian doctrine.

As the twins grew older, they would have been given a sort of academic education. We do not know what exact shape it would have taken, but perhaps, like Edward's tutelage, it would have started early on with them being told 'such noble stories as behoveth [them] to understand and know'. As a baron's children, they would most likely have been expected to be literate, skilled in conversation, able to run a household and, in Francis's case, capable of fighting well.[11]

Whatever the nature of the teaching and education Francis and his siblings received in their early years, it was doubtlessly designed to help them in later life and probably reflected their parents' expectations and their worldview. If the focus of Francis's early education was martial, then it is likely his parents considered these skills more important for a baron than reading and writing.

The nursery and instruction therein during the early years of childhood were considered a woman's domain,[12] so that the twins and their older brother probably had more contact with their mother than their father. Indeed, John Lovell would have grown increasingly busy with matters of intrigue and warfare over the throne anyway, making him a distant figure. Soon his work away from the family was to bring tragedy upon them.

A Country in Turmoil

While Francis, Joan and John were growing up in Oxfordshire, tensions between the ruling elites of the kingdom were steadily worsening. Before long, their own family members had been drawn into the conflict. While none of their close kin had taken a part in what is today seen as the initial battle of what would come to be known as the Wars of the Roses, the first battle of St Albans in 1455, John Lovell and John Beaumont eventually supported the Lancastrian side of the conflict, represented by the ruling but mentally indisposed Henry VI, his wife Queen Margaret of Anjou and their only son, Edward, Prince of Wales.[13] John Beaumont in particular was known to have become close to Queen Margaret and Edward, Prince of Wales, in the second half of the 1450s.[14]

In July 1460, Francis was still two months shy of his fourth birthday. It is likely that he was still in the nursery and not yet under any proper tutelage. Even if he was already having lessons, they would have been simple affairs that a toddler could grasp. He would not yet have been instructed in fighting of course, nor in dancing and courtly arts, and history and mathematics would also have been studies for the future. Certainly, nothing he would have known at this age, whether taught by the mistress of his nursery or a tutor, would have helped him understand the nature and the consequences of the political situation of England at the time, which had become steadily more uncertain and violent over the preceding few years.

Francis and his sister Joan, and most likely also his brother John, though a year older, would not have understood why their father had left the household some weeks earlier, though in itself his absence would have been unremarkable. It was a normal part of their lives for one or both of their parents to leave for some time, and would not have affected their day-to-day routine. However, while neither Francis nor Joan could have known or expected it, this time John Lovell left to join the cause of King Henry VI against the approaching Yorkist lords,[15] as did their maternal grandfather John Beaumont, and the events that were to follow would have significant consequences for England, for the family and potentially even for the toddlers themselves.

By 1460 John Lovell had already established himself as a staunch Lancastrian, having fought against the Yorkist lords the year before; this service had seen him granted the office of master forester of Wychwood on 19 December 1459 'for good services against Richard, Duke of York, Richard, Earl of Warwick and Richard, Earl of Salisbury'.[16] Since that time, his sympathies had clearly remained unchanged, and in summer 1460 he joined with other Lancastrian lords such as the Earl of Kendall, Lord Scales and Lord Hungerford when they went to London to convince the city's aldermen and wider populace to hold out against some of the leading Yorkist lords, who were marching on the capital from Calais, where they had been in exile for the last few months. The three most prominent of those Yorkist lords were the Earl of Salisbury, the Earl of Warwick and the Earl of March. At first the Lancastrians seemed successful; however, the Londoners would soon change their minds and lend their support to the Yorkists.

An English Chronicle of the reigns of Richard II, Henry IV, Henry V and Henry VI, which was written within eleven years of the events, claimed that Lords Scales and Hungerford, identified by the writer as the leaders of the Lancastrian faction, 'would have had the rule and governance' of London but were thwarted in this because 'they of the city would not suffer them, saying that they were sufficient for to rule the city themselves.' This is possible, but the claim is somewhat contradicted by a statement made only a paragraph above, that 'the Earl of Salisbury, by common consent of the city was made ruler and governor of London,' the capital's people showing no urge for independence when assigning this office to the Yorkist man. Salisbury was to keep this office while the king and his enemies Warwick and March were absent, the two sides heading for a meeting at Northampton. There the king was accompanied, among others, by the Duke of Buckingham, John Beaumont and his son William.[17]

Seeing the city turn against their cause, the Lancastrian faction did not head north to swell the number of the king's men in Northampton, but instead retreated to the Tower of London on 2 July. The chronicler quoted above rather hilariously attributed this decision to Scales' and Hungerford's indignation at not having been allowed to rule the city, but it seems likely that the main factor, rather than any personal pride, was to keep the weapons still stashed in the stronghold in their hands.[18]

John Lovell chose to stay with Scales and Hungerford, and was prominently mentioned as one of the 'great men' doing so in the chronicle: 'lord Vessy, lord Lovell, lord Delaware, lord Kendall à Gascony, Sir Edmund Hampton, knight, Sir Thomas Brown, knight, shire of Kent, John Bruyn of Kent, Sir Gervase Clifton, knight, treasurer of the king's house, Sir Thomas Tyrell, knight, the Duchess of Exeter, and many others'.[19]

In holing up in the Tower, the plan was not only to deny the rebels those arms which were kept there but also to wait the rebels out, maintaining a supply of fresh food through the Tower's access to the river. In this, however, they were thwarted, for while most Yorkist rebels marched on to meet the king and his army, the aforementioned Earl of Salisbury remained in London and together with Lord Wenlock set up a blockade on the river, besieging the fortress 'by land and by water'.[20]

The Lancastrian lords inside the Tower retaliated, perhaps rather excessively, by attacking the besiegers with wildfire, a weapon which has been described as a medieval version of napalm. This of course carried the risk of hurting not only enemies but also innocent bystanders, and the chronicle states, probably correctly, that its use indeed 'burned and hurt men and women and children in the street'.[21] The besiegers retaliated by bombarding the Tower both from the water as well as the land, badly damaging some of its walls, though not badly enough to create a breach.

It is unclear why the Lancastrian lords decided to risk harming the population of London. It could have been out of desperation, since they were running out of food, but equally it could be that they hoped to push the citizens of London to reconsider their support for the Yorkists. If it was the latter, it was a miscalculation; the more the city was damaged and its people injured, the more they turned to the Yorkists and offered them support, making the situation of the besieged party in the Tower more and more untenable.

What part John Lovell played in these events is impossible to say. Quasi-contemporary chroniclers like the one quoted above mention him prominently but do not credit him with greater power than the other lords, nor do they single him out for any blame. It is likely that he completely supported the decisions of the Lancastrians in the Tower, but more cannot reasonably be said about his role in the siege.

What is known, however, is that John Lovell fixed his name under a letter written by the besieged lords to the Mayor of London, complaining of their treatment. It is a remarkable missive, lacking almost completely in the customary politeness of the day, and assigning all blame for the situation to the besiegers:

> Sirs, it is you [who] are saying that you are the king's true liegemen and so are we, wherefore we will desire of you to write the cause why you make us war. And that we may understand how you may join your sayings and your deeds together, and also what should be the cause that you take prisoners and we should not defend us against you, and of this above-said we pray of you an answer for we cast us no more to encumber you with our writing, etc.[22]

The reply that they got cannot have left them in doubt that the city had by now turned completely against them:

> Like it your lordshippes to understand and with for certain that according to our saying, we have ever been, now we are, and ever will be the king's true subjects and humble liegemen. And where you by your bill desire of us to write the cause why we make you war etc. Thereto we answer and say that you and your fellowship have begun and made war by divers assaults, shooting of guns and otherwise by which the king's true liege people as well as the inhabitants of this city, men, women and children have been murdered, maimed, slain and mischieved in sundry wise. And so that as has been done by us is only of your occasion in our defence. And such as we take for prisoner been for the attempted occasions and assaults done by them as aforesaid in breach of the king's peace and for despoiling of the king's true people of their vitals and goods without due contract or payment had in that behalf contrary to the good equity and all law etc.[23, 24]

Though the lords may have been alarmed by this letter, it cannot have come as a surprise. Since the letters are undated, it cannot be said with certainty how long the siege lasted after this exchange, and therefore we cannot know if this answer had any effect on the besieged in the Tower. It is possible but very unlikely that it made a great deal of difference; though negotiations were underway for the Lancastrian lords' surrender by 16 July,[25] it is more likely that their resistance was broken by lack of food and the arrival of news from the north.

The Yorkist lords who marched north had met the king and his men at Northampton on 10 July. Along with John Beaumont, Henry VI was accompanied not only by his wife and son but also by the Duke of Buckingham, the Earl of Shrewsbury and others. While they had all been named as 'mortal and extreme enemies' by the Yorkists in the previous year,[26] Buckingham was perhaps their most bitter enemy, and the enmity between him and March and Warwick was the most personal.

Humphrey, Duke of Buckingham, was Edward of March's uncle through his marriage to Anne Neville, older sister of March's mother Cecily Neville, but there is no indication that there had ever been a cordial relationship between them. Buckingham was a staunch supporter of the king, as was his wife. After the battle of Ludlow in autumn 1459, March's mother Cecily, younger sister Margaret and younger brothers George and Richard had been captured by the Lancastrians and sent to Anne Neville's household after York, Salisbury, Warwick, March and March's younger brother Edmund of Rutland had fled,[27] and the captives remained there in July 1460. It is on record that Cecily Neville needed 'many a great rebuke'[28] and made clear her distaste about her and her children's enforced stay with her sister. The presence of the captive Yorkists would have been foremost in the minds of Buckingham and March as their confrontation drew near.

Under these circumstances, Buckingham's behaviour when the two armies met at Northampton was even more dangerous than it would have been in any case. While the Yorkist lords March and Warwick made overtures of politeness, Buckingham made it clear that he had no interest in finding a peaceful solution. When Warwick sent messengers to the king asking for an audience, Buckingham made sure he was rebuked in no uncertain terms, and even threatened Warwick with death.[29] It is not known if the messengers reached the king or if Buckingham intercepted them beforehand, although the latter seems more likely. It is interesting to consider what Shrewsbury and Beaumont thought of their ally's behaviour; their later actions, when battle broke out at Northampton, suggests they supported Buckingham and agreed with his decision not to let Warwick see the king.

Buckingham's responses to Warwick may seem rather intense, and certainly unhelpful in defusing the situation, but his reactions were understandable to a certain extent. By 1460, Buckingham had seen Henry VI forgive the Yorkist lords several times, sometimes under coercion and other times of his own free will, only for them to turn against him once more. He would have also known that the Earl of Warwick, though only around half his age, was extremely eloquent and had repeatedly talked people into joining him and his cause.[30] Allowing him and March to see Henry VI may have therefore been potentially risky, especially if he feared punishment once Warwick and March were in control.

The Yorkists, of course, had their own good reasons to feel aggrieved. Richard of York's long years of loyal service to the king had seldom been rewarded, and he came to feel that his power was being transferred to the queen's favourites. At first his complaints had been supported even by those very close to the king, such as his half-brother Jasper Tudor.[31] However, the two camps developed as the situation escalated, and by the time the Yorkists and Lancastrians met at Northampton, York and his sons, as well as Salisbury and Warwick, were actually attainted traitors.[32] York, together with his second son Edmund, Earl of Rutland, had fled to Ireland to escape execution, and there they remained in July 1460.[33] Warwick, Salisbury and March had only recently returned from their own exile in Calais to seek out some power before trying to open a dialogue with the king. They would have been aware that their failure likely meant execution.

Both parties knew what was at stake when they met in Northampton, and both would have been aware that whoever held the king had the upper hand. It is perhaps unsurprising, then, that Warwick's attempts to see the king and prevent a battle were in vain. Though Buckingham could have been less hostile and provides an obvious scapegoat for the violence that followed, both for the Yorkists of the time and centuries of historians, it is hard to see how a battle could have been avoided without him giving in and abandoning his advantage, possibly with disastrous consequences for himself.

It has also been speculated that the Yorkists' professed wish to see the king was a smokescreen, and that they would have attacked regardless.[34] After all, they had brought heavy weaponry from London,[35] and men of their faction were already engaged in armed conflict with the Lancastrian lords back at the Tower of London. However, by presenting themselves as peace-seekers who were rebuffed by hostile Lancastrians they could present themselves as being in the right, more victim than aggressor.

The truth may, in fact, lie somewhere in between. March, whose mother, sister and younger brothers were in Buckingham's control, may have wanted to engage in armed conflict, but Warwick, who was older and more experienced, was likely more reluctant, In bringing heavy weaponry he may simply have been preparing for the worst; it could very well be argued that it would have been foolish of the Yorkist lords not to bring heavy weapons when the Lancastrian side had them.

If it had been Warwick's intention to avoid battle, he changed his mind when he was denied an audience with the king. After his envoy to Henry VI had come back for the second time, bearing the message that he would not be allowed to see the king and would die if he attempted to do so, he is said to have responded that he would see the king 'two hours after noon' or die on the field.[36]

Unsurprisingly, the Lancastrian lords did not cave in to this ultimatum. At two o'clock, Warwick therefore followed through on his threat. He and March commanded their men to attack the Lancastrians and get through to the king, and the lords around the king prepared to deny them. The chronicler, who is very pro-York, reports the battle as follows:

> Then on the Thursday the 10th Day of July, the year of our Lord 1460, at 2 hours after noon, the said earls of March and Warwick let cry throughout the field that no man should lay hand upon the king nor on the common people, but only on the lords, knights and squires: then the trumpets blew up and both hosts centred and fought together half an hour.[37]

The battle did not last longer because it soon became clear that the Lancastrians were at a disadvantage. They had been in their position longer and had placed their weapons for the possibility of warfare several days before fighting erupted, and this proved disastrous. Due to the heavy rain over the ensuing days, the cannons had become waterlogged and could not be fired, easing the Yorkists' way through the muddy field. As the chronicler put it: 'The ordenance of the king's guns availed not, for that day was so great rain, that the guns lay deep in the water, and so were quiet and might not be shot.'[38] It also appears that was there little danger from the Lancastrian archers, as the persistent rain made the act of loosing arrows a slower affair.

However, this was not the primary reason for the Yorkist victory. If they had critically wounded or killed one of the enemy commanders, the Lancastrian lords may still have caused enough confusion to prevent the Yorkists from reaching the king. However, one of their number, Sir John Grey of Ruthyn, turned traitor and allowed the Yorkists to pass, giving command over his men over to the youthful Earl of March:

> The lord Grey, that was the king's vanguard, broke the field and came to the earl's party, which caused cessation of many a man's life: many were slain, and many were fled, and were drowned in the river.[39]

This treason meant the high-born Lancastrians guarding the king's tent, John Beaumont among them, found themselves surrounded by Yorkist fighters and with no hope of relief. They must have realised then that they had only two options: surrender and allow Warwick and March to pass, throwing themselves on the Yorkist lords' doubtful mercy, or fight and die in the doomed attempt to keep Henry VI from them.

John Beaumont, as well as the Duke of Buckingham, Lord Egremont and the Earl of Shrewsbury, all chose the latter option. Surrounded by Kentishmen who had pledged their support to the Yorkist cause, with Warwick and March drawing closer and defeat inevitable, they bravely fought on – until death. All of them fell in hand-to-hand combat. The chronicler, who writes the deaths of Yorkist casualties with praise for their bravery, reports the Lancastrian losses in colder tones:

> The Duke of Buckingham, the earl of Shrewsbury, the lord Beaumont, the lord Egremont were slain by the Kentishmen beside the king's tent, and many other knights and squires.[40]

With the deaths of the chief Lancastrian fighters, the way to Henry VI was clear. The Yorkist lords found King Henry VI in his tent and treated him with all due respect, assuring him they were loyal to him and had only objected to being treated badly by his advisors, the very men now lying dead in front of the tent in the rain on the muddy battlefield.[41]

The deaths of the Lancastrian lords dealt the king's party a heavy blow. Though few other fighters had lost their lives,[42] a lot had rested on the Duke of Buckingham, on the earls of Shrewsbury and Egremont and on John Beaumont. There was nobody who could have filled their positions. Buckingham's heir, his grandson Harry, who would later gain fame and notoriety for his mysteriously slippery loyalties, was only four years old. Of the men, only John Beaumont left an heir who was old enough to take up the fight and don his father's armour: his son William, who had turned twenty-two less than three months before the battle.[43]

The power vacuum created by the deaths of these lords would have been clear to the Lancastrian party as soon as they learnt of it, and they knew their position to be drastically weakened. The Yorkist faction, meanwhile, were doubtless emboldened by the victory and lost no time in making for the capital, where John Lovell and his fellow fighters were still holed up in the Tower. Just six days after the battle of Northampton, on 16 July 1460, the Yorkist lords arrived in London with Henry VI.[44]

It is probably not a coincidence that this is the day on which the Lancastrians agreed to surrender the Tower.[45] The Londoners would have expected the Lancastrian lords to know that their situation was now hopeless. The Lancastrians may well have indicated a willingness to negotiate when word of the battle's outcome first reached them. While this was not the end of the conflict, at this moment the Lancastrian faction appear to have focussed on damage control.

We do not know how the besieged party in the Tower learnt of events at Northampton. Given that Salisbury and Wenlock had built a pretty thorough blockade around the stronghold, it seems likely that they learnt about it from their enemies, perhaps gloating from the siege lines. For John Lovell, and likely others, the news would not only have been politically devastating but also personally painful; his father-in-law was dead, slain in battle.

It is reasonable to think that the news of Beaumont's death made Lovell reconsider his stand in the Tower; in the face of defeat, improving relations with the victors might have seemed wise. At the same time, however, he may well have thought of revenge. We do not know whether he was one of those who pushed for a surrender; it could have been Scales or Hungerford or any of the other lords who first suggested quitting the Tower. Regardless, negotiations were begun, perhaps encouraged by the not-at-all-vengeful agreement of 16 July 1460, as recorded by the Common Council:

> Be it remembered that we, William Hulyen, Mayor of the City of London, and the aldermen and the commons of the same, agree us by this present to hold firm and stable and to perform every point in that that in us shall be all such appointments touching the giving over the Tower of London by the Earl of Kendall, the Lord Scales, the Lord Lovell, the Lord Hungerford and Sir Edmund Hampton and others now being within the same Tower, and the receiving of the Tower aforesaid by the Earl of Salisbury to the king's use as be made by the same earl [or] his deputies on that one party, and the said Earl of Kendall, lord Scales, lord Lovell, lord Hungerford, and Sir Edmund Hampdon and others [of] that other party. In witness whereof to this same present we have put our common seal. Written at London aforesaid, the 16th day of July, the 38th year of the reign of King Henry VI [1460].[46]

Three days later, the Lancastrian lords surrendered.[47] It appears that Lord Scales and Hungerford were given safe conducts to leave the city, but the rest the aforementioned lords, including John Lovell, were arrested.[48] Lord Hungerford's safe conduct saw him out of the city unscathed, but Lord Scales was not so lucky. Aware that the citizens hated him for his use of the wildfire, he tried to steal away under cover of darkness but was recognised and killed by the boatmen he employed to row him to safety.[49]

The other men who had surrendered were tried at Guildhall, but only six, of comparatively little standing, were pronounced guilty and suffered a traitor's death. The other men were freed, and attempts were probably made to persuade the lords to come over to the Yorkist cause by the leniency of their judgement.[50] This worked on Lord Delaware and the Earl of Kendall but did not win over Lord Hungerford or John Lovell, who continued fighting for Lancaster.

While all of this was going on, Francis and his sister were almost certainly with their mother in Oxfordshire, continuing their lives as before, most likely unaware that anything dangerous was going on.

However, the death of Francis's grandfather John Beaumont may have been the boy's first experience of the dynastic and political quarrels affecting his own young life. Even if he did not know his grandfather well, he and Joan would very likely have seen a change in their mother when she learnt of the news. Perhaps inexplicable to their young minds, her grief was a harbinger of things to come, when the civil war would finally reach the world of the two toddlers.

Perhaps their father returned home immediately after being released by the Yorkist victors, but it seems that he had more on his mind than taking close care of his children. For one thing, he tried unsuccessfully to seize some of his late father-in-law's estates.[51] Perhaps he was justified in this, as he tried to claim them in his wife's name,[52] though it does seem like a rather strange time to insist on this right, as both he and his brother-in-law William, Beaumont's heir, whom he tried to take them from, were mainstays of the Lancastrian cause – quarrels between them could only hurt the cause.

Though the Yorkist faction was firmly in charge for a few months after the Battle of Northampton and the siege of the Tower, they appeared to seek accord with at least some of the Lancastrians. William Beaumont was treated well and faced no repercussions for his father's choice to die fighting for the Lancastrian cause, nor for his own support of it. In fact, while he had to prove his age to get his inheritance, as was standard, there is no evidence of any cruelty in his treatment despite the hostilities between the Yorkist lords and his father, which had been going on for some time. In September 1460, William was found to be twenty-two years old, having been born on 23 April 1438, and therefore old enough to inherit, and was allowed all his late father's estates and possessions.[53] John Beaumont's will, made in 1456, was also obeyed. Since it was made some months before the birth of Francis and Joan, they were not mentioned in it. However, their mother Joan, whom John rather touchingly referred to as 'my daughter Lovell, my life' in the will, inherited the sizable sum of 1,500 marks from him. Joan's oldest son, John, was to inherit '990 shillings […] 10 years after his birth'. Joan's husband John Lovell inherited nothing, and none of the family received any of John Beaumont's personal items.[54]

We do not know if John and Joan were hurt by their relatively minor inclusion in John Beaumont's will. Nevertheless, whatever their feelings on the matter, there would have been little time to dwell on it. John Lovell was soon involved in the political strife of the kingdom once more.

It seems probable that he, like his brother-in-law William, was present in London when Richard of York returned from his exile in Ireland in October 1460 and entered the city in triumph. However, it is unlikely that his family was present with him. Francis, who had recently turned four years old, would have heard nothing save a censored, simplified version of the news considered fit for children.

As autumn turned to winter, the tentative peace gained from Northampton failed once more. Though a compromise had been reached, whereby Henry VI remained on the throne until his death but made Richard, Duke of York, his heir,[55] it was not one that was very popular with the king's men. John Lovell was among those unhappy with this compromise, and when hostilities broke out again Lovell joined the Lancastrian cause once more. Most likely his mother Alice supported him in this, and perhaps so did his brothers, though there is no indication of their movements at this time.

In the few months between the battle of Northampton and the outbreak of further hostilities in the winter, John Lovell tried to establish several claims on lands, even settling some with violence. The only record we have of these incidents is in the Calendar of Patent Rolls of later years, where several men John ousted are listed as being reinstated in their positions.[56] There was nothing particularly out of the ordinary in highborn men and women of some power solving arguments about property and possessions with violence, it is just that John chose to do so at a rather inconvenient time, with the country in the midst of a civil war. On the other hand, perhaps it was these very circumstances that allowed John to succeed with his claims, and maybe he hoped that a Lancastrian victory would see him confirmed in possession of the manors he had seized as a token of gratitude for his help in defeating the Yorkists, or so as not to risk losing his support. Even if he did not think that far, he would have had every reason to continue supporting the Lancastrian side, and he did. When the conflict reignited once more, John Lovell once more fought for the Lancastrians.

It seems that neither he nor his brothers, nor William Beaumont, were present at Wakefield when a battle took place between the Yorkists and the Lancastrians, in breach of a ceasefire, on 30 December 1460. Nevertheless, they would surely have been pleased by the news that the Duke of York and the Earl of Salisbury were both dead. They were probably less pleased, however, to hear of the death of seventeen-year-old Edmund of Rutland, the Duke of York's second son. Not only was his death seen as murder by everybody, but the suggestion that it was vindictive and unnecessary meant that March and Warwick would become yet more vindictive, more intractable in their opposition to the Lancastrians.

The next major battle was the second battle of St Albans, which happened on 17 February 1461 as the victors of Wakefield headed south to London. Warwick attempted to block the Lancastrian approach at St Albans but was outflanked. The Yorkists were driven away and the king fell back into Lancastrian hands. None of the Lovells nor William Beaumont are recorded as having been present at this battle, nor are they mentioned as being present at the inconclusive battle of Ferrybridge on 28 March, at which battle the Yorkists openly fought for the throne itself, with the Earl of March now being named King Edward IV.

Just one day after Ferrybridge, however, the huge, famous battle at Towton took place. Both John and William, if not John's brothers, were noted to be present then, so it is reasonable to assume that they also both were involved at the precursor Ferrybridge, though neither of them appears to have made much of an impression.

It would be interesting to know if they fought side by side, or if they did not see each other at all during the fight. The latter is quite possible, especially if they did not arrive together, both perhaps having gathered men to bring, as the Battle of Towton was a massive one. In fact, it has been called the bloodiest battle ever fought on English soil, and the casualties have been estimated to lie between 20,000 and 40,000 men. Fought on Palm Sunday 1461 in a snow storm, it lasted for several hours. The Yorkists, heavily outnumbered, turned the tide by using the strong winds in their favour, their archers firing upon the Lancastrian positions while remaining out of range of enemy bowshot. Bolstered by this and the arrival of reinforcements under Norfolk, they routed the Lancastrians. Many were killed fleeing the field, and some prisoners were executed.

Both William Beaumont and John Lovell survived the battle. Many others did not, but with the defeat of their side and the terrible carnage around them, it is hard to believe either felt very lucky about their survival. In fact, if possible, the situation became even worse for William Beaumont. Not leaving the battlefield quickly enough, he was taken prisoner by the Yorkist soldiers. John Lovell could have been captured too, but if so he was quickly released. He was stripped of his possessions for fighting for Henry VI but kept his freedom.

1461 to January 1465

Presumably, John was dispossessed in Edward IV's first parliament; certainly by 8 August 1461 he had lost his lands, as an entry in the Calendar of Patent Rolls dated to that day records two men, Ralph Wolseley and John Crafton, appointed 'as receivers of all moneys from all manors and lands of which John, lord of Lovell, knight was seised, or anyone else for his use, in the counties of Cambridge, Salop, and Essex'.[57] However, even at the time, it seems that the king had a possible rapprochement with John Lovell in mind, for the grant is explicitly said to last only 'as long as they remain in the king's hands'.

John did not have to wait long. On 27 December that year, he was granted back his lands and possessions by the new government, as for that day, the Calendar of Patent Rolls record '[r]atification of the estate which John Lovell, knight, has in the manor of Swavesey and Fulbum and the advowson of the priory of Swavesey, county of Cambridge, the manors of Great Hohind, county of Essex, Snodesbury, Wykebumell and Russelhall, counties of Worcester and Stafford, and Peccheford, county of Salop, and the manor of Broughton and lands in Weston, Redgrave and Aylesbury, county of Buckingham, of which he is seised in his demesne as of fee tail, as appears by fines levied in the courts of the king's progenitors'.[58]

It is not known when exactly he was given back his lands, but by December at the latest John had accepted Edward IV as king. He was never involved in conflict with him again.

His brother-in-law William was not so lucky. He remained imprisoned until November 1461, when he managed to flee into exile,[59] likely joining Margaret of Anjou and her son, Edward, formerly Prince of Wales. Why he was imprisoned for so long when Edward usually favoured a more inclusive political style, at least at the beginning of his reign, is unknown. Perhaps Edward, like Henry VII with Thomas Howard in later years, was trying to teach him a lesson and use him as an example to others. William might have refused to accept Edward as king, or might have been found to be in contact with Margaret of Anjou and remained imprisoned for that.

Whatever the reason for his imprisonment, and however he managed to flee, it is clear that after March 1461 William Beaumont never again saw his sister Joan, his brother-in-law John, or their oldest son. Almost a decade would pass before he was able to make contact with his little niece and younger nephew.

It is unclear whether little Francis and his siblings were close to their uncle William. Given that their father had been in a quarrel about lands with him, it is perhaps likely that he was a remote figure, at least after 1460. Because of this, his exile may have had little impact upon them.

What is far more definite, however, is that their father's dispossession, short though it was, made an impact on their lives. Accustomed to a wealthy lifestyle, the family would have suddenly been reliant on the charity of others, probably their relatives. They would still have been living in comparative luxury, but the children would have been able to sense the unease in the household.

It is probable that the family was forced to live with a relative while John was dispossessed. One possible host would have been John's mother Alice Deincourt, who, despite her high standing at the Lancastrian court, had not suffered dispossession under the Yorkists. However, John's ancestral home, where the family mainly appears to have stayed, was part of his wife's dowry[60] and as such would probably have been exempt from any punishment meted out to John.

Though Edward IV forgave John within a year and had given him back his lands and possessions at some point before late December 1461, the family had to get used to living in straitened circumstances. We can only guess how this affected the children. By 1462, John Lovell was deeply in debt. In the summer of that year, he is recorded to have owed 1,000 marks to two men named Richard Quartermayns and Richard Foweler, and another 1,000 marks to John and William Crofton.[61] His situation only became worse. By the next year he was clearly struggling to maintain his baronial lifestyle while making ends meet, and saw himself forced to sell two manors to a merchant named William Luster,[62] and another one to a merchant named Thomas Stoke.[63] Regardless of whether this was done to raise money or to settle debts, it suggests a degree of desperation.

It could well be that the little twins and their brother suffered under their father's financial difficulties, but it is by no means certain. Perhaps their way of living had been more lavish during their very first years, or perhaps their circumstances remained the same while their parents tightened the purse strings in other ways. However, even with their father in financial difficulties, they would have enjoyed a certain standard of living and it is unlikely they wanted for necessities.

Whatever their lives were like after Edward IV's accession, it stands to reason that, as far as the family's circumstances permitted, they would have followed the same program of education they had before. One thing we can be sure of is that they would have seen more of their father then than they had before.

It is possible that, having the time and leisure for it, John began influencing the children's education more than he had before Edward IV's accession, involving himself more in their upbringing. The conventions of the day suggest he probably didn't teach them anything himself, but it is quite possible that he himself first introduced them to the world beyond the cloistered life of the nursery they inhabited as toddlers.

Their first view of this wider world may well have come when they were five years old, when their paternal grandmother Alice Deincourt remarried, choosing as her second husband Ralph Butler, Lord Sudeley, who had been a man of some standing in the Lancastrian government. Despite their Lancastrian sympathies, both Alice and Ralph had been allowed to keep their wealth; indeed, they may have married primarily to combine their assets, although it is equally possible it was a love match between the nearly sixty-year-old Alice and the nearly seventy-year-old Ralph Butler.

The licence for their marriage, for which Alice paid £100, was recorded on 8 January 1463,[64] and it stands to reason that the wedding took place soon afterwards. Whether it was a grand celebration or simply a small ceremony is now sadly lost to history, but it is easy to imagine that at least their closest family attended the wedding, and perhaps Alice's eldest son John brought his children with him.

If Francis and Joan did come along it would have been an exciting event for the youngsters, their first time taking part in a celebration involving strangers of high standing. This sort of experience would have made for a valuable learning opportunity, as networking was a vital skill for a baron's son and heir, and it was just as important for a baron's second son, as well as for his daughter, who would in time be expected to make a good marriage. Even if the twins did not attend their grandmother's wedding, as they grew older they would have attended other ceremonies to learn how to behave in public, and how to navigate such events.

It is quite possible that the development of such social graces was personally encouraged by the twins' parents, practised rather than taught as mere theory by tutors. Doubtlessly noble but shorn of their political importance in the new Yorkist regime, John and Joan would have been ideally placed to teach their children themselves, as they were no longer in demand on matters of state.

In fact, there is no evidence whatsoever that John tried to work his way up in Edward IV's new government. This is significant in a man who had successfully involved himself in Henry VI's government as soon as he became baron, eventually taking up a key role during the conflicts in the last years of Henry's reign. We do not know if John stayed away of his own volition or was frozen out, but he is only recorded to have been given a single task in Edward IV's government, being named on a commission of oyer and terminer in April 1464.[65]

In the same year, Francis and Joan's younger sister was born. Like her brother Francis, she received an unusual name in honour of a saint, in her case the patron saint of Oxford, Frideswide. There was a significant age gap – eight years – between Frideswide and the twins, but there is no indication there were other, short-lived, children between the births of the twins and Frideswide. This could indicate that little Frideswide was born after the twins' older brother John died, in an attempt by John and Joan to have another spare. This, however, is pure speculation. It is not known when John Lovell Jnr died, only that it was after 1456, and before his father's death in January 1465.

By the time Frideswide was born in 1464, Francis had already passed his seventh birthday, perhaps even his eighth. By this age he might have left the nursery to be taught by a male tutor, while his sister Joan would have learnt tasks considered more suited to a woman of noble birth. Francis's education would have involved swordsmanship and other martial arts, while Joan would have learnt how to run a household. Both, however, would have been taught how to read and write, some basic mathematics, plus dancing and the courtly arts.

The family's straitened circumstances might have meant they couldn't afford separate tutors. They also might have begun to learn of current events in the kingdom at this time, being considered old enough to grasp the fundamentals of politics.

It may have been in this way, or perhaps through gossip, that Francis and Joan, and if he was still alive their older brother, heard news of the king's surprising marriage to a Lancastrian widow, a woman who was Lady Grey before her marriage to Edward IV but whom history remembers by her maiden name: Elizabeth Woodville. The news might not have meant much to the twins, but it is very likely that they would have been old enough to be expected to show an interest in such information, and to keep up with what was happening in the kingdom. Most of their days, however, would have been spent not listening to gossip or forming opinions on current events, but in lessons.

It is, in fact, possible that Francis and Joan were not given a particularly thorough education in their parents' household. Certainly, it is notable that Francis's handwriting as an adult resembled Richard of Gloucester's closely, indicating they were taught by the same tutor, which could only have happened later in Francis's life when they were both in the household of Richard Neville, Earl of Warwick. This indicates that Francis's parents either laid no particular stress on him being able to write, or else that he had only just begun to learn when something happened that would affect the course of his entire life.

'... during the minority of the said Francis'

Francis's life changed drastically when, apparently unexpectedly, his father John died on 9 January 1465 at the age of just thirty-one. It is not known how John died, only that his death appears to have been sudden. There is no indication he even left a last will and testament. This suggests he died of an illness so abrupt he could not even dictate a will on his deathbed, or met his end in an accident. Sadly, we do not know which it was.

On 14 January 1465,[1] a writ of Diem Clausit Extremum was issued, an acknowledgement from the king of his death initiating the division of his estates. Why this was issued five days after his death rather than the next day, as happened when his father William died, is unclear. It may have been that the January weather made travel difficult for any messenger bearing news of the death, or perhaps the king's men took their time reacting to the news. It is also possible, though unlikely, that John's death was not immediately discovered; for instance, if he died in a hunting accident it is possible he was only found later.

Francis was eight years and four months old when his father died, and he became the 9th Baron Lovell. Among his first duties would have been leading his father's funeral as his chief mourner, a task which could be done even by children that young.

John's funeral would have most likely taken place within a few days of his death. His body would have been laid out in the nearby church, St Kenelm's (where his father lay buried), and surrounded by candles until it was time to bury him, presumably after his mother and perhaps his brothers had arrived to attend the funeral.

While nothing is recorded of his actual funeral, it is a definite oddity that John was not given a sarcophagus or even a tombstone, or any marker at all, for his grave. While we know that he had financial difficulties in the years before his death, and that his widow, whose father was dead by this point and her brother attainted, may not have been able raise the money to mark his burial plot, it is certainly strange that neither his mother Alice, who was still wealthy, nor his surviving brothers Henry and William arranged for a tombstone at the very least. It is even stranger, and quite telling, that Francis, who grew up to be very rich, never saw to it that John's tomb was marked.[2]

Francis appeared close to his sisters as an adult, suggesting they had built a good relationship in their early years, though Francis cannot have got to know Frideswide well before their father died, as she was only a baby at the time. However, he showed signs of favouring her when they were both adults, which presumably means he had some strong family feeling for her. His sister Joan would die before he rose to prominence and therefore less about her and about their relationship is known, but he seems to have been just as close to her. Clearly, it was not a lack of family feeling that lay behind Francis's decision to neglect his father's grave.

This suggests that it was John himself who was not popular with his small son, or the rest of his family, and there are more indications for this. One is the fact that his older daughter, Francis's twin sister Joan, chose not to name a son after him despite the fact that she followed family tradition in giving her first son her husband's name, Brian; if somebody is willing to honour this tradition, it would be expected that they would follow the custom through to naming the second son after their father. This in itself is not direct evidence of a rift; perhaps Joan simply disliked the name John for aesthetic reasons, or named her second son, George, after a saint in thanksgiving instead. However, in the light of how John's family otherwise treated him and his memory, it is certainly interesting. However, it is not as shocking and telling as Francis's behaviour.

While not giving him a marker for his tomb despite his later wealth could in itself be seen as a clear indication of what Francis thought of his father, he went further than that. Later in his life, in early 1484, we know of two arrangements he made for prayers to be read. One was part of the foundation for a fraternity, for which he received permission together with John, Duke of Suffolk and John Russell, Bishop of Lincoln on 20 February of that year.[3] One of the tasks of this new fraternity was to read services for the 'good estate' of the founders and their families, yet Francis chose to have prayers said for his grandfather William and not for his father. It therefore seems that he was not averse to remembering his family members, so this is not a matter of burying his Lancastrian pedigree. It appears to have been the person of his father he shunned.

This impression is solidified by the second arrangement for prayers he made in 1484 when he sold the Hospital of St John and James, which had belonged to his family for over a century, to William Waynflete, Bishop of Worcester, to be annexed to Magdalen College, Oxford. Part of the deal included prayers to be said for Francis and his wife annually on 17 September.[4] While there is nothing unusual in such a request, it is curious that despite the fact that the hospital was the resting place of some of his distant Lovell ancestors, Francis did not, as would once more have been the traditional and expected course of action, request prayers to be said for his father and those ancestors. Most definitely, when selling a hospital that had been in his family for so long it would have been expected of him at least to include his closest ancestors, such as his parents, in the prayers.

While this, on the face of it, is less of an attack on his father specifically than the other request of prayers, it would have been very nearly impossible for Francis to have prayers said in the hospital for all his ancestors save for the one he had inherited it from. Since his request for prayers for his grandfather William that year shows he was not opposed to remembering members of his paternal family, it seems like his primary motivation, once again, was to deny his father prayers.

The obvious conclusion is that John Lovell's twin children, but especially Francis, wanted nothing to do with him and his memory, wanted to do nothing to assist him in any way, even after death. It is possible to speculate on why this might be. It is clear that shame over their Lancastrian heritage did not play a role, at least for Francis, as William was marked by these as much as John, yet Francis still had prayers said for him. There is also the fact that William himself seemed to dislike John – recall how he refused to call John his 'sonne' in his last will and testament.

It is possible that John was an irresponsible gambler, who lost money and gave little thought to the needs and the well-being of his family. This could have definitely caused some resentment in his father, as well as his children, though not having prayers said would be a very harsh and rather unusual punishment for such a transgression. Sadly, more likely is that he was violent and abusive towards his family. This would also explain his father-in-law's harsh words in his will.

If Francis and Joan were victims of such treatment, it could explain the lasting hatred their actions suggest, even to the point of Francis living to subvert his father's expectations. The adult Francis was pious, and caring for the souls of the departed by arranging for prayers to be said was not only seen as a traditional Christian duty but also good for the soul of whoever ordered it. By medieval understanding, Francis's soul would have profited from John being remembered in death. Surely, then, there would have been a good reason not to do it, one that would negate the benefits of treating his father's soul kindly. John having committed many sins Francis found abhorrent, like adultery – or, worse at the time, adultery with a man – would not have been such a reason. On the contrary, it would have been a cause to have more masses read for him so he could eventually be absolved. If John had committed abhorrent sins that personally hurt Francis and his sister and mother, however, it might have seemed unpalatable, indeed unexpected, to have prayers said for him.

Naturally, during a time in which corporal punishment was standard and marital rape did, by law, not exist, John's behaviour would have to have been excessive for Francis and Joan to exhibit such hatred, beyond mere distance and neglect of memory. If this was the cause for their behaviour, it would almost have to mean John became so violent towards them and their mother that he put their lives at risk, or else, horribly, that he committed sexual violence against them. This could explain the deep hatred his children felt, as well as the fact that none of his family wanted anything to do with him.

This is, of course, mere speculation. Perhaps the twins' hostility towards their father, unusual though it was, had another explanation. We only know that it existed, and that in light of his later actions, the young Francis may have been happy or at least relieved when his father died. However, we do not know his immediate reaction to his father's death. Certainly, whatever had happened in the family to sow such discord, John's death marked a huge change in the Lovell household.

Marrying Anne FitzHugh

It must have been within days of his father's funeral that Francis, just eight years old, was informed that he, now a ward of the king, would have to leave his mother and sisters to live with a man the king had chosen for the task of seeing to his education.[5]

Having to live among strangers in the care of a man very close to the king may have been a daunting prospect for young Francis, even though it was of course quite normal for rich heirs who had lost their father. It may also be that he was excited. Most likely, the changes in his life happened so quickly he had little time to reflect on them.

It appears that Edward IV initially kept Francis's wardship, thereby taking control of all incomes from the Lovell lands and possessions. He did not exercise his ability to choose a bride for Francis, however, granting that decision to his cousin Richard Neville, Earl of Warwick. The earl appears to have lost no time in finding the young Francis a wife, though rather than marrying the boy to his younger daughter Anne – an outcome many believe the king hoped for – Warwick decided to wed him to his niece Anne FitzHugh.

Anne was the youngest daughter of the earl's sister Alice, Lady FitzHugh, and her husband Henry FitzHugh, Baron FitzHugh. Probably born in 1460,[6] Anne had two older sisters, Alice and Elizabeth; an older brother, Richard, born around 1459;[7] and four younger brothers named George, Edward, Thomas and John.[8] Through her mother, she was related to some of the highest and mightiest in the realm; she was even kin to the king. This was certainly a good match for Francis.

A letter from John Wykys to John Paston dated to 'the Monday next after Saint Valentine' informs the recipient of two weddings which had recently taken place:

Item, the Earl of Arundel's son has wedded the Queen's sister.

Item, the Lord Lovell's son has wedded my Lady FitzHugh's daughter.[9]

The 'queen's sister' was Margaret Woodville, one of Elizabeth Woodville's younger sisters, and her new husband was Thomas FitzAlan, the eldest son and heir of William FitzAlan, Earl of Arundel. Through his mother Joan, Thomas was a nephew of the Earl of Warwick. Interestingly, this means he was a first cousin of the other bride mentioned in Wykys's letter, Lady FitzHugh's daughter, Anne. The bridegroom, of course, was Francis.

It is curious that Wykys identifies Francis as 'Lord Lovell's son', despite the fact that his father was dead at that point and Francis himself, despite his youth, was therefore Lord Lovell. It may be, however, that this was because John Lovell had only very recently died; though traditionally it is assumed that this letter was written in 1466,[10] this is almost certainly untrue; it was in fact composed on 20 February 1465.

The argument for 1466 is mainly based on three facts: first, that the letter cannot have been written earlier than 1465, as Edward had only married Elizabeth Woodville in spring 1464 and announced the marriage in September 1464; secondly, that it cannot have been written later than 1466, as Paston's father died in May 1466 and is referenced as still alive in the letter; and thirdly, that in February 1465 Francis's father had been dead for just a month and the inquisition into his death had not even been made. This happened only in autumn 1465, but these things were often delayed by some months, and more so when the heir was a minor, as Francis was. These facts could have been a hindrance, and speak against a day in February 1465 as their wedding date. However, these problems could have been overcome, and there are more powerful arguments speaking for a February 1465 marriage.

As mentioned above, Wykys's reference to Francis as 'Lord Lovell's son' rather than 'Lord Lovell' could be a hint, but hardly a conclusive or even a very telling one. A far better argument is the fact that on 11 February 1466, King Edward IV's first child, Princess Elizabeth, was born, and her birth celebrated with much pomp. While it is conceivable that the baby's aunt Margaret was married during the celebrations, it is not likely Francis and Anne were. The Earl of Warwick was in attendance in London when the princess was born. He stood as her godfather and played a prominent part in the queen's churching a few weeks later.[11] Francis and Anne, as well as Anne's parents, were not noted to be in attendance, though.

It follows, therefore, that the Earl of Warwick was busy in London in February 1466, not having his ward and his niece married elsewhere. Since the marriage was arranged by Warwick, Francis would not have been married without his presence, and it is unlikely in any case that Warwick would have scheduled such an event at the same time as the birth of a royal heir; indeed, had the birth turned out to be that of a boy, this would have been the arrival of the new prince. A wedding could very easily have been scheduled for a month before or after the expected birth, so a February 1466 wedding makes very little sense.

Therefore, it seems Francis and Anne were married in 1465. Despite the wedding taking place so soon after John Lovell's death, there would have been no organisational problems; the children were not related within the prohibited degree, so no dispensation was required from Rome. All that would have been needed was their presence and the king's agreement. Even the fact that no inquisition had been made into Francis's inheritance yet would not necessarily have been a problem, since he was only eight years old in any case and would not enter into his inheritance for well over a decade.

It is interesting to note that in his letter to John Paston, Wykys does not specify which of Lady Alice FitzHugh's daughters had married Francis. Since all three of her daughters, Alice, Elizabeth and Anne, were still unmarried at this point, it was far from self-evident. It is, however, possible that Wykys was not certain which of the FitzHugh daughters had been Francis's bride, or was uncertain about their names.

In fact, it is rather curious that Francis was married to Anne, the youngest, rather than to one of her older sisters, Alice or Elizabeth, as it was rather out of the ordinary for a younger sister to be married before a match for her older sisters had been arranged. Alice, then around eighteen, was only married in November 1466, and then only to Sir John Fiennes, the heir to a barony and therefore of lesser status compared with Anne's youthful husband. Perhaps the FitzHughs decided that while age gaps in arranged marriages were hardly out of the ordinary, they preferred to marry Alice to Sir John, who was her age, and Anne to a boy only four years older than her, rather than marry Alice to a boy eight years her junior and Anne to a man twelve years her senior. Perhaps, despite the fact that he was already a baron and stood to inherit lots of land in due time, the FitzHughs also saw that Francis had inherited massive debts from his father and considered him less of a prospect than Sir John. Perhaps it was a mixture of these reasons, or something else entirely. It is all speculation, as is any explanation for why Elizabeth, the second sister, was apparently not considered for either match, and was only married years later, to Sir William Parr.[12]

Anne and Francis were likely married either at Middleham, which was the Earl of Warwick's favourite castle, or Ravensworth, which was the FitzHughs' ancestral keep, but we do not know for certain, and Wykys's letter gives no hint. Nor does he give any indication on what day exactly the wedding took place, though it was probably in mid-February 1465 and definitely before 20 February 1465.

Nothing is known about the actual celebration, though speculations can be made, going by similar events, such as the wedding of Edward IV's second son Richard, Duke of York, and Anne Mowbray. The latter, as a royal wedding, would have been far grander and more splendid than the wedding between a fatherless baron and a baron's daughter, but it stands to reason there would have been some similarities, if only in the way that the children were led by adults. Like little Anne Mowbray, Anne FitzHugh would have been led to the church or chapel in which the ceremony was to take place by a male relative. In the case of Anne Mowbray, this was the adolescent cousin of her young groom, John de la Pole, Earl of Lincoln;[13] in the case of Anne FitzHugh, it most likely would have her father. Presumably, the Earl of Warwick would have acted in the place of Francis's father.[14]

It is possible, even likely, that Francis and Anne's wedding ceremony was followed by a banquet and some celebrations. The Earl of Warwick and his brother-in-law Henry FitzHugh must have been present at any such event, as without them the wedding could not have taken place. If it was conducted in Middleham Castle, then almost certainly his wife Anne Beauchamp, Countess of Warwick, and their daughters, thirteen-year-old Isabel and eight-year-old Anne, would have been present. If it happened in Ravensworth then it is less likely that Warwick's wife and daughters would have been there, but on the other hand the bride's siblings are more likely to have been present. Whether anybody from Francis's family attended is even more unclear. His sister Frideswide, at only a few months old, was naturally too young, but it is possible his mother and sister Joan travelled with him to be present as he was married. It is unpleasant to imagine Francis having to experience such a life-changing event alone among strangers.

In the Earl of Warwick's Household

Either shortly before or shortly after his marriage, Francis was likely sent by the king into the Earl of Warwick's household to be educated there. While it appears that Edward held Francis's wardship, as he was still making payments from its revenues in 1466,[15] it seems he employed his cousin Warwick to be responsible for the little boy's education. This is not a complete certainty, however, for in 1465 Francis's mother was still alive, so it is possible that Francis continued living with her after his marriage. It is between these two scenarios: there is no indication Francis ever lived at court or was raised in a royal household. Maybe it did not matter much to Edward IV whether the eight-year-old boy was raised in the household of one of his men, like Warwick, or in his mother's household, but this is guesswork. Given the Lancastrian pedigree of the Beaumont family, Edward IV may not have wished to risk giving Joan Beaumont the chance to instil such loyalties in her son and decided instead to have him raised by a loyal Yorkist.

The latter speculation is somewhat supported by what happened to other fatherless little boys of a Lancastrian background, such as Francis's later enemy Henry Tudor, Earl of Richmond. When Henry's Lancastrian guardian, his uncle Jasper Tudor, fled into exile after Edward IV's accession, the young Tudor was not allowed to live with his mother but instead given into the care of the Herberts, a noble Yorkist house.[16] It stands to reason that Edward IV would have made a similar decision for Francis, who was only four months older than Henry Tudor and whose circumstances were not dissimilar.

In fact, Edward IV may have granted Warwick power over Francis's education and marriage as a way to kill two birds with one stone. First, it would establish the little boy in a Yorkist household so he could learn loyalty to Edward; at the same time, however, it might have been a concession to his cousin. Letting Warwick pick a bride for the little boy could have been compensation for Edward marrying his sister-in-law Margaret Woodville to Warwick's nephew Thomas FitzAlan. It is well recorded that Warwick opposed the Woodville family and was angry about the many marriages they had made with his family, and Edward may have hoped that Francis's marriage would act as a sweetener for his nephew's marriage, with the control Warwick was given over the little boy's education a sign to him that he was still a trusted and favoured advisor.

This theory is supported by the fact that a grant of £1,000 to the Earl of Warwick, for 'costs and expenses incurred by him on behalf of the Duke of Gloucester, the king's brother, and for the exhibition and marriage of the son and heir of the Lord Lovell',[17] exists from the year 1466. While Warwick could have been compensated for the costs of the children's wedding without this meaning Francis lived with him, the fact that 'exhibition' was included suggests that he was also responsible for his education and upbringing as a lord, with all that entailed.

The grant is also interesting in that the £1,000 sum was in fact taken from revenues that were part of Francis's inheritance,[18] which clearly shows Edward, not the Earl of Warwick, controlled the Lovell finances at this point, and that the right to arrange Francis's marriage had been granted to the earl in isolation, not as part and parcel of receiving custody of Francis and his lands. The fact that Edward reimbursed Warwick for his brother Richard's upbringing in the same grant supports the theory; if he entrusted his own brother to Warwick for a good upbringing then it is likely that he was happy to send Francis there too.

While naturally interested in Francis and his future, Edward appears to have shown no interest in the boy's sisters Joan and Frideswide, and they appear to have continued living with their mother. It is tempting to imagine that Joan wrote letters to her brother and informed him of all that was happening in their household, but no such letters have survived. However, if she did not tell him, Francis would still have learnt of news affecting his family.

One such piece of news would have been the marriage of his grandfather John Beaumont's second wife, Katherine Neville, to the much younger John Woodville, brother of the queen. Whether Francis was personally very interested in this is up for speculation, but it was something that caused a scandal. The age gap was immense even by the standards of the time, and the widespread assumption was that the marriage was only made to increase the Woodvilles' wealth; because of this, the match was known at the time as 'the diabolical marriage'.[19] Since the bride was not only Francis's grandmother by marriage but also the Earl of Warwick's aunt, it is almost certain that this wedding would have been a subject in the earl's household and that Francis would have heard of it.

Even if he had no personal feelings about it at the time, the settlement made by the king for this marriage included a grant that would have certainly interested Francis in his adult life; in addition to Katherine Neville's massive dower lands, especially from her first marriage, Edward IV declared her the rightful owner of some lands held by her stepson William Beaumont, Francis's uncle.[20] However, since William had been attainted, these lands should have been either in the king's hands, subject to grants, or, if declared exempt from the attainder, held by his wife Joan or his sister and heiress, Francis's mother.

It is doubtful if the young Francis understood the significance of this fact, or even heard about this aspect of the marriage. Regardless, the news would have soon been followed by another development that would have affected him more.

Whether he found out through letters from his family or simply through court gossip, in late 1465 Francis would have definitely been informed in some way that, only ten months after his father's death, his mother was to marry once again. His new stepfather was to be Sir William Stanley, younger brother to Sir Thomas Stanley, 2nd Baron Stanley. The upcoming marriage was recorded in the

Calendar of Patent Rolls on 12 November 1465, in a grant of 'the castle, manor and lordship of Skipton in Craven and the manor of Marton in Craven, county York, with all the towns, townships, hamlets, lands, rents, services, reversions, knights' fees, advowsons, farms, offices, franchises, liberties, mines of coal and lead and all other possessions and appurtenances' to both[21] 'the king's servant William Stanley, knight, and Joan late the wife of John Lovell, knight, lord Lovell, whom he will shortly marry'.[22]

Sir William, unlike his brother Sir Thomas, had been staunchly on the Yorkist side throughout the recent conflicts. It is possible that this is why Joan chose to marry him, to, as J. M. Williams puts it, 'join the new connection'[23] and rid herself of all association with her Lancastrian background. It is, however, also possible that she had more personal reasons. This is suggested by the fact that just barely nine months after William was to 'shortly marry' her, she gave birth to his son, a child that may have either been slightly premature or else conceived shortly before their wedding. However, things were to take yet another turn.

Joan Beaumont died either in childbirth or shortly afterwards of complications, on 5 August 1466, at the age of twenty-five, leaving William a widower, their son without a mother and her Lovell children full orphans, with neither father nor mother left to take charge of their upbringing.

It was not recorded at the time where Joan and Frideswide lived in the immediate aftermath of their mother's death. The king did not seem to consider them important enough to officially assign their care to anyone, but evidence indicates that Joan and Frideswide were raised in the household of Alice and Henry FitzHugh from August 1466 onwards. They were later recorded as being there, together with Francis, in 1470, their inclusion suggesting that they had not just newly arrived there but were considered established members of the FitzHugh household and extended family.[24]

It is, of course, possible that Joan and Frideswide only arrived at the FitzHugh household when their brother Francis's complete wardship was granted to the Earl of Warwick in 1467, but there is no obvious reason to assume this was so. The only other households they could have likely stayed at after their mother's death would have been that of their paternal grandmother Alice Deincourt and her husband Lord Sudeley, or that of their stepfather Sir William Stanley together with their younger half-brother William.[25] Both Alice Deincourt and her husband, as well as Sir William, were apparently still in good health and financially secure, allowing them to take care of the children well after 1467.[26]

Though Francis, if he still lived with the girls, would have been forced to leave to join Warwick's household when his custody was granted to the earl, there would have been no compulsion (and no reason) for his sisters to join him. It is unlikely anyone would have seen cause for them to leave either the Stanley or the Sudeley households when he did, or really at any time between their mother's death and 1470 when they are registered with the FitzHughs, which suggests they never were in those households. Most likely, they stayed with Sir William only until he had contacted their relatives and found willing carers for the girls. He would presumably have contacted the king and the Earl of Warwick, as well as the nearly ten-year-old Francis, to tell them of his wife's death, probably by sending a messenger.

It is recorded that in the summer of 1466 Henry FitzHugh spent some months at Middleham as the Earl of Warwick's guest.[27] It is possible that Alice FitzHugh and some of her children joined him there; after all, Alice was Warwick's sister. Given that their daughter Anne was already married to one of Warwick's wards, it may be that they decided to have them spend some time in the same household so the children had a chance to get to know each other a little more closely, as sometimes happened with such matches.

Whether or not his wife and children were present, it seems likely that Henry FitzHugh learnt of Joan Beaumont-Stanley's death while visiting Warwick. He, and possibly his wife, may have decided then and there that they would take in the Lovell daughters and give them a proper upbringing. Since they had children of the same age, this might not have been too difficult to arrange, nor would it have been the first time they took in children. In fact, Alice had often acted *in loco parentis* for children whose parents were dead or unavailable to take care of them. Therefore, making similar arrangements for the upbringing and education of Joan and Frideswide Lovell may have seemed like the obvious decision.

Joan was around Elizabeth FitzHugh's age, while Frideswide was likely around two and therefore similar in age to the youngest

FitzHugh sons. If Alice and her children joined Henry FitzHugh at Middleham, it was likely there that Joan and Frideswide joined the household, and first met Francis's in-laws. It would also have been the first time Francis and his sisters had seen each other in over a year. Frideswide would have been too young to remember him, and it is quite possible that during her years in the FitzHugh household she grew closer to the FitzHugh boys than to her own, much older brother, though it appears that eventually they would come to share a close relationship.

It is quite likely that Anne Lovell got to know her sisters-in-law far better than her husband at this time, as while she might have seen him during occasional visits he did not live in the same household. This probably wasn't a major issue for Francis and Anne; at their young age, neither was likely to have been too interested in the other. There would have been other issues for both of them to worry about. They were too young for their marriage to have any consequences for their day-to-day life, which would have been consumed with their respective educational regimes, aimed at shaping them into the proper nobleman and noblewoman they were expected to become.

Francis's education at the Earl of Warwick's household would have been very similar, if not identical to, the one Edward IV's brother Richard of Gloucester received there. As Paul Murray Kendall points out, there would have been lessons

> ...in 'the schools of urbanity and nurture of England'. After rising early and hearing Mass, they broke their fasts with a mess of meat, bread, and ale. Studies followed under the direction of a learned clerk or chaplain: some Latin, more French, a smattering of law and of mathematics, music, penmanship. More important still was the subject of knightly conduct. The boys were taught 'to have all courtesy in words, deeds, and degrees [and] diligently to heed rules of goings and sittings'. They conned a variety of tracts on courtly behavior and Christian doctrine, treatises of knighthood and of war, the accepted code for challenges and the *Acts of Arms*, allegories such as *La Forteresse de Foy*, *Froissart's Chronicles*, *The Government of Kings and Princes*.[28]

All of this, and more, would have been enough to keep Francis occupied without worrying too much about anything else, and it is likely he soon became used to his situation. Whether these lessons were a continuation of what he had learnt in his father's household or whether they would have been new to him is something else we cannot know. However, as mentioned above, due to his young age when his father died, the bulk of his education would have been provided by the Earl of Warwick.

Another important, if less formal, skill he would have learnt at Middleham would have been socialising and networking. He would have met important people, and at some point in his first year in Warwick's care he would have made the acquaintance of his fellow student, King Edward IV's youngest brother, Richard of Gloucester.

Some four years older than Francis, Richard arrived in his cousin Warwick's care at the age of twelve in 1465.[29] Despite their age difference, Francis and Richard would have been taught together and learnt all the aforementioned skills side by side, but how much they socialised at this point is a mystery. It is often assumed, on the strength of their friendship as adults, that the two boys became close in the years they spent together as Warwick's wards,[30] but it is only that: an assumption. Perhaps it was so; they may have bonded over the similarities in their lives, as they had both lost their fathers at a very young age and Francis, we think, went through some sort of trauma in his father's household, which Richard, who himself went through several traumatising events in his childhood, might very well have understood. It is equally possible that the difference in age between them meant they were uninterested in one another, and that the differences in their lives, with Richard a prince in line for the throne and Francis a mere baron, were more important than their similarities.

Francis met others in Warwick's household who would prove to be of great importance in his later life. Sir Robert Percy, who would also become a close friend of Richard's and would eventually serve in his government with Francis, was also present in the household when Francis was there. He was, however, a young adult of approximately twenty years by 1465, more than twice Francis's age, and it is doubtful whether anything more than a passing acquaintance developed between the two at the time. Equally, Francis would have met Warwick's daughters: Isabel, later to become the Duchess of Clarence, and Anne, who later became Richard's wife and eventually queen. Though it is often assumed that Francis was close to Anne Neville in later life,[31] there is absolutely no evidence for it, and no conclusions can be drawn about their relationship as children.

It is interesting to speculate as to Francis's thoughts about the political developments around him as he grew old enough to understand them. Perhaps he had already developed the tendency he showed in later life of judging situations emotionally rather than logically. If so, his tutors likely attempted to educate this trait out of him. What can be said with reasonable certainty is that Francis's life would have had a regularity in those years that it likely never had again in his adult years.

It is unlikely that anything changed for Francis when Edward IV granted Warwick his complete wardship on 13 November 1467. As was common for such grants, it included the 'custody of all lordships, manors, lands, rents, services and possessions with advowsons, knights' fees, franchises, liberties, warrens, courts leet and other commodities late of John Lovell, knight, deceased, tenant in chief, or Joan his wife or any ancestor of Francis, his son and heir during the minority of said Francis', as well as his 'marriage without disparagement'.[32]

Since Francis was already married and, as explained above, also seems to have already lived in Warwick's household, this would not have affected him much. It profited Warwick a lot, however, and was presumably an attempt by Edward IV to stop the rapid deterioration of his relationship with him. Though it ostensibly affected Francis most of all, in practice it would have made the least difference to him of all those involved.

The Earl of Warwick officially held Francis's wardship until his death in the Battle of Barnet in early 1471, but the boy, by then in his early teenage years, had not stayed put at Warwick's household. Perhaps as early as 1469, but most definitely by autumn 1470,[33] Francis was instead living in the FitzHugh household, together with his wife and his sisters.

4

In the Lord FitzHugh's Household

It is not known exactly when Francis arrived at the household of his in-laws, though it is likely he was sent there to keep him away from the political issues once more blighting the realm – the Earl of Warwick had rebelled against Edward IV. Even in his father-in-law's household, however, Francis still would have experienced the consequences of this strife. He may have already left Warwick's household when the earl married his daughter Isabel to the king's young brother George, Duke of Clarence, against Edward IV's wishes,[1] but by now he was old enough to have understood the gravity of the act. The marriage was followed by Clarence and Warwick rebelling in 1469, killing the king's father-in-law Richard Woodville and brother-in-law John Woodville and capturing the king himself.[2] Nearly thirteen years old now, not only was Francis old enough to understand all that was happening, but he would have understood what it meant for Edward IV and his reign.

It would be very interesting to know what Francis thought of this rebellion, and especially of the deaths of Richard and John Woodville. Though they were killed for pretty much no more good reason than Clarence and Warwick's hatred for their family and their support of the king against them, Francis may not have felt too sorry for them. He grew into a man who was slow to forgive, and if he had taken a dim view of John Woodville's marriage to his step-grandmother then he may have felt that the killings were a kind of rough justice. On the other hand, he may have thought that Warwick and Clarence had committed an unforgivable crime by going against the king. We do not know his feelings at this early stage, but when he was old enough to pick his friends he continued a close association with the FitzHugh family, who would go on to support Warwick and Clarence; this suggests that, at the very least, Francis held nothing against the rebel noblemen.

Whatever his thoughts, it is not hard to imagine that like most others, Francis watched with interest as the situation between the king and his brother and cousin developed. Perhaps he was disappointed when the rebellion and the king's capture eventually came to nothing, but it is possible that either he, or someone informing him of what was happening, was canny enough to realise the seeds of discontent had been sown, and that the 1469 uprising was not the end of hostilities.

It is unlikely that the renewed unrest in the country changed much in Francis's life. The only major change would have been his leaving Warwick's household for his in-laws', an event which we cannot place in time with any precision; since Francis was not included in the pardon given to Warwick and Clarence's men after the uprising of 1469, it seems most likely he was gone before then.

Once in the FitzHughs' household, Francis must have been faced with a daily routine of lessons and learning similar to the one he had known in Warwick's household. It is possible that, living together with his sisters, he made an effort to get to know the by then five-year-old Frideswide and reconnected with the older Joan. It is also possible that he tried to establish some sort of relationship with his young wife, getting to know her a little better, though as she was only nine years old and he was thirteen, they would not have had much in common. At best, they would have had a sibling-like friendship.

The FitzHugh Rebellion

It is hard to imagine that Francis was worried about the nature of his relationship with his wife at this point. He would have been distracted by other matters, not simply his own daily life but presumably, as the months passed, the political conflict that was brewing once more.

Within less than a year of Clarence and Warwick receiving pardons for their uprising of 1469, there was more unrest in the country, especially in the north. Small rebellions broke out again,[3] and this time Francis's father-in-law Henry FitzHugh was significantly involved. In summer 1470, after their new uprising was crushed, Warwick and Clarence fled the country with Warwick's wife Anne Beauchamp and daughters Anne and Isabel, the latter being Clarence's wife.[4] Their original plan had been to reach Calais, which was still an English territory, but they were turned away by those who held the town for Edward IV.[5] This must have been an unexpected blow, but Warwick and Clarence did not give up, instead changing plans and going to the French king's court to meet up with Henry VI's wife Margaret of Anjou and his son Edward of Lancaster in the hopes of coming to an agreement with them.[6] While this was happening, aggrieved citizens and Warwick's adherents in the north, led by Henry FitzHugh, rose against the king.

Though this rebellion has been often dismissed as insignificant over the centuries,[7] Edward IV clearly did not share this view. Indeed, his concern may have been entirely justified as the rebellion appeared much more dangerous at the time than it does in hindsight. In fact, on 5 August 1470, John Paston wrote a letter to his brother, confusingly also named John, reporting rumours circulating in London about this uprising, saying that '[t]her be many ffolkes uppe in the northe so that [Henry] Percy not able to recyst them'.[8] Edward IV had only recently returned to Henry Percy the family's birthright, the earldom of Northumberland, at the expense of Warwick's brother John Neville. Neville had held the earldom from 1461, when it had been stripped from the Percy family as punishment for fighting on the Lancastrian side in the earlier conflicts. Since Percy was a powerful magnate in the north, by reappointing him it is clear that Edward IV hoped to gain some support in that part of the country, which was traditionally more Lancastrian and moreover loyal to Warwick. The news that Percy had failed to quell the rebellion must therefore have been shocking and unwelcome news, and Edward clearly thought he needed to show his strength. His reaction was to travel north immediately to see to the rebellion in person.[9]

It is possible that the rebels were not prepared for a confrontation with the king, or perhaps that their purpose had only been to distract the king from Warwick's plotting in France. Whichever it was, the rebellion fizzled out within days of Edward arriving in the north.[10] Edward, probably hoping to win over his dissatisfied subjects with leniency, pardoned all involved in the uprising, which would become known as the FitzHugh Rebellion. These pardons were recorded in the Calendar of Patent Rolls on 10 September 1470, a week before Francis's fourteenth birthday, the pardon for the FitzHugh household itself naturally including 'Henry FitzHugh of FitzHugh, knight, and Alice his wife' but also 'Francis Lovell son and heir of John Lovell, knight, and Anne Lovell his wife', as well as 'Richard Nevile son and heir of George Nevile, knight, Richard FitzHugh son of the said Henry FitzHugh, George FitzHugh, Edward FitzHugh, Thomas FitzHugh and John FitzHugh, sons of the same Henry, Elizabeth FitzHugh, daughter of the same Henry, Joan Lovell and Frideswide, sisters of the same Francis Lovell',[11] among a number of other, lower-born members of the household.[12]

The mention of Francis in the pardon does not have to mean that he was personally involved in the rebellion. He was still fairly young, perhaps too young to be considered responsible for his actions even if he had helped his father-in-law. Most likely, he was simply included in the pardon so that the taint of his father-in-law's treachery did not stick to him and so his presence in his household at the time could not be used against him at a later date. This was common practice and explains also why the ten-year-old Anne Lovell, as well as the six-year-old Frideswide and the young FitzHugh sons, of whom at least John and Thomas cannot have been much older, were included despite being far too young even to understand what was happening.

Even though it seems unlikely Francis was actively involved in the rebellion, he would have definitely had an opinion on events. It could very well be that he sided with his in-laws and wished to see Edward IV removed from the throne at this point. Though he had already made the acquaintance of Richard of Gloucester and therefore had a connection to the Yorkist side, there is no indication that their friendship was so strong that Francis would have wished his side to win solely on the strength of it, and in fact Francis and Richard may not have been more than acquaintances at this time. Almost all Francis's known close friends were either involved in rebellion against Edward IV or in the care of those who were, so it seems unlikely that they were particularly close.

If indeed Francis sided with his father-in-law, he would have been happy to hear of Warwick and Clarence returning from France only three days after Edward issued his pardon to those involved in the FitzHugh Rebellion.[13] Though Edward IV made arrangements to negate their influence, he appears to have underestimated the threat they posed. Less than a month after Warwick and Clarence had landed, Edward, together with his other brother Richard of Gloucester, his lord chamberlain William, Lord Hastings and his brother-in-law Anthony, Earl Rivers, had to flee into exile, having been overwhelmed in an attack by John Neville – the man Edward IV had deprived of the earldom of Northumberland when he gave it back to Henry Percy.[14]

The Lancastrian Readeption

With Edward IV now in exile, Henry VI was reinstated as king. Many of Edward's Lancastrian enemies, who had spent recent years in exile, returned to England. Warwick was said to be running the government, and Henry, incapacitated by bouts of mental illness, was rumoured to be little more than a puppet at this point.[15] Certainly Warwick appears to have enjoyed the fulfilment of all his aims. Under the terms of an agreement with Margaret of Anjou, now queen again, Warwick's younger daughter, Anne Neville, was married to Henry's heir, Edward of Lancaster, and was set to become queen when the young prince eventually became king. The parliament which sat that winter is also said to have passed an Act stating if Edward and Anne never had children, Clarence and his issue would inherit the throne after Edward's death. The earl did everything in his power to ensure one of his grandchildren would eventually inherit the throne.

It is most likely that Francis was not present at the centre of government when all this was decided, since his father-in-law Henry FitzHugh does not seem to have been. It is tempting to imagine Francis eagerly awaiting news from the capital, but even if he did, the changes in government and the transfer of royal power probably didn't affect his life. However, his uncle William Beaumont, who was one of the Lancastrian nobles who had returned from exile after Edward was ousted, probably now met with Francis for the first time in ten years. If they met during this time, it would have constituted the only profound change in Francis's life, which despite all the upheaval in the country must have gone on in a similar vein to the years before. At fourteen, he would have still received lessons and perhaps spent his free time trying to test the rules set for him – just like any teenager.

Whatever Francis thought and felt at the time, whether the political situation dominated his mind or whether other, more domestic issues did, it seems his father-in-law was worried about the future. During the time his brother-in-law Warwick led the English government, he was apparently already thinking of what might happen should Edward IV return and take back his throne. Since FitzHugh's actions in the north had been instrumental in providing the distraction that allowed Warwick and his brother to take Edward by surprise, costing him his throne, he might have feared the consequences if Edward returned, and he made arrangements for his family to escape to Scotland in such a case. His motivations can only be surmised, but he definitely tried to procure safe conducts for his family. Perhaps he had solid plans to head north, or maybe he was just securing the option should it become necessary to escape. Luckily for Henry FitzHugh, he never had to act on these fears.

We do not know when Henry applied for the safe conducts, but they were only issued on 19 June 1471,[16] by which time it was already too late. It is easy to imagine him worrying, waiting for news from Scotland as winter turned into spring and news came that the exiled Edward IV was making his way towards England, that he brought troops from his brother-in-law the Duke of Burgundy. Maybe such excitement also gripped Francis, or maybe he wished that he could do something himself, get involved in the strife. However, whatever his feelings, Francis did not get to fight when Edward IV and those who had fled with him returned from exile.

On 14 March 1471 Edward landed at Ravenspurn,[17] quite close to the FitzHughs' ancestral castle of Ravensworth, where Francis was most likely staying. Copying the actions of Henry VI's grandfather Henry IV, Edward claimed to want to take possession of his dukedom of York only,[18] went into Yorkshire, and then marched on. News would have reached Francis and his family quickly, and it is easy to imagine him reacting with shock, and perhaps resentment, to the news that Clarence had deserted Warwick to join his brothers,[19] that John Neville had failed to catch up with Edward's men[20] and that Edward had returned to London in triumph, taking custody of Henry VI, who supposedly surrendered himself into Edward's care without complaint, announcing that he knew the latter would not harm him.[21]

None of this would have pleased Francis if he hoped for the Lancastrian side to win, and worse news was to follow. Within days of regaining possession of London, Edward's men caught up with the forces of Warwick and other Lancastrians, including the Earl of Oxford and Francis's uncle William Beaumont, near Barnet. Because his forces were outnumbered, Edward's plan was to quickly catch up with the Lancastrians and attack before they thought his men were ready.[22] Only a month after landing in England, Edward's forces met with the Lancastrian ones, and in the early morning of 14 April the two sides engaged in battle.

Though the battle was said to have hung in the balance for a while, the Yorkist forces were helped by a battleground covered in mist, which spread confusion in the larger Lancastrian force. In the thick mist, the Earl of Oxford's badge was mistaken for Edward's badge due to a passing similarity, and in the belief he was attacking Yorkist men John Neville charged his ally Oxford, naturally leading to infighting between the Lancastrian forces. In this attack, John Neville was killed.[23]

This was not the sole cause of the eventual Yorkist victory, but it helped immensely. By mid-morning, Edward and his men were victorious. Both his brothers, Clarence and Gloucester, are supposed to have sustained minor injuries during the battle,[24] but the Yorkist side sustained fewer casualties than the Lancastrian side and, notably, lost none of their noble commanders. The same could not be said for the Lancastrians. Not only was John Neville killed, but so was Warwick. Seeing his brother fall and knowing the battle to be lost, Warwick had fled from the site, probably hoping to catch up with his family and regroup. However, Edward sent men after Warwick to capture him.

He supposedly wanted to his cousin to be brought to him alive, but this did not happen; Warwick was killed while fleeing.[25]

The news must have been a blow to the fourteen-year-old Francis, who had spent around four years in the earl's care and must have known him well. We don't know how he felt about Warwick, but even if he did not like the man he would have almost certainly felt for his mother-in-law Alice as she mourned her brother's death. He might also have worried about his uncle William Beaumont; he was said to have been fighting alongside Oxford. He would have been saddened by the possibility of never seeing him again should the Yorkists go on to defeat the remnants of the Lancastrians, having only recently seen his uncle return from exile.

It is sometimes speculated that Henry FitzHugh, sticking to his earlier plans, fled to Scotland with a safe conduct at this point, and died there in 1472. This cannot be proven.[26] While his death in 1472 is a fact, where he was at the time of death is unknown. That he left for Scotland is mainly suggested by the fact that he neither received a pardon nor a punishment for supporting the Lancastrian side once Edward IV had taken back the throne. This could mean that he was no longer within Edward's reach, but it could also mean that Edward considered him too insignificant in the events of winter and spring 1470–71 to single him out for pardon or punishment.

If Henry did leave for Scotland, however, he did not wait to take Francis with him, nor any of the others for whom he had sought safe conducts: 'Lady Alice, lady FitzHugh, Francis, Lord Lovell, Richard, Lord Latimer, and Richard FitzHugh son of Lord FitzHugh, and forty or less persons in their or any of their company'.[27] It is interesting to note that Lord Latimer, who was only three years old in 1471, was mentioned, but Henry's younger sons, his unmarried daughter Elizabeth and Francis's sisters Joan and Frideswide, who at that time still lived in the household, are missing. This does not indicate that they would have been left behind; they were probably simply too unimportant to mention, as they neither held any titles in their own name nor were heirs/heiresses apparent, though Joan and Frideswide were still Francis's heirs presumptive. Henry FitzHugh himself is not mentioned in the safe conduct, which could mean he had already secured one for himself at an earlier date, though no documentation survives to suggest this.

If Henry FitzHugh did leave, this would have had quite an impact on Francis. Not only would the patriarch be greatly missed, but with his departure Francis would have become the eldest male in the FitzHugh household, and therefore would have had to assume some of Henry's responsibilities. However, since Henry's whereabouts are unknown, whether or not this happened cannot be ascertained. Perhaps Henry remained at Ravensworth, waiting for the outcome of the struggle for the throne.

Whoever was with Francis at this moment, they did not have had to wait long for more news. Within two weeks of the Battle of Barnet, Edward's men had caught up with Margaret of Anjou's force at Tewkesbury. She had been heading for Wales, perhaps to flee to France again. In the ensuing battle, the Lancastrians were defeated, and Edward of Lancaster, Henry VI's heir, was killed.[28] Margaret of Anjou and Edward's widow, Anne Neville, were taken captive by the Yorkist forces, though Anne, perhaps due to her youth, was treated with respect by the newly reinstated Edward IV and soon released into the household of her sister Isabel and Isabel's husband Clarence.[29]

Whether this news meant a lot to Francis, crushing hopes he might have harboured of a Lancastrian victory, it would soon set him on a new path in his life. After Edward had retaken the crown, most surviving Lancastrian nobles – such as Francis's uncle William – had fled. Henry VI was dead, most likely killed on Edward's orders.[30] The king began asserting his control and shaping government to his liking. Quite naturally, this included rewards to those who had fought for him as much as punishments for those who had turned against him.

5

In the Duke and Duchess of Suffolk's Household

Among the measures Edward IV enacted soon after regaining his throne was the granting of Francis's wardship to his sister Elizabeth, Duchess of Suffolk, and her husband John, Duke of Suffolk. The grant was recorded on 11 July 1471, and interestingly was stated to have been due to the king's 'special gratitude' to the Suffolks. However, Edward added a condition to the wardship. Though the Suffolks were granted 'all lordships, manors, lands, rents, services and possessions with advowsons, kinghts' fees, franchises, liberties, warrens, courts leet and other commodities late of John Lovell, knight, deceased', in addition to 'the custody and marriage of Francis', as Warwick had been, the grant explicitly excluded any possessions Francis might still inherit while in the Suffolks' care, stating that the ducal couple were only to keep the wardship 'provided that this grant shall not extend to any possessions which may afterwards descend to the heir.'[1]

When adding this condition, Edward doubtlessly thought of Francis's wealthy grandmother Alice Deincourt, already sixty-seven years of age. Edward would have expected Alice to die in the six years before Francis came of age, and so he clearly intended to inherit her possessions himself.

Naturally, this was not the only limitation to Francis's wardship, as he was already married, which robbed the Suffolks of the chance to find him a bride and establish a fruitful connection between their young ward's family and their own. Despite this, though, Francis's wardship was doubtlessly valuable, and would have given both the Suffolks and the young ward a chance to build a lasting relationship, even if it was one which could not be cemented with a marriage.

It is not known when Francis arrived in the Suffolk household, though he was there by 11 July at the latest and may have been there before that. Though Edward did not punish the FitzHugh family in any other way, he would have wanted to remove forthwith the wealthy young baron and all his possessions from the care of those whose loyalty was somewhat in question. It is therefore possible that Francis arrived in the Suffolks' household, probably in their main manor at Ewelme,[2] as early as late May or early June 1471. It appears that his sisters Joan and Frideswide joined him in the Suffolk household, though this was not a decision made by the king. It could have been Francis, the FitzHughs or the Suffolks who made the decision. Certainly, the Suffolks would have seen potential in the Lovell heiresses.

Duke John's Influence on Francis

Little is known about the lives of Francis and his sisters in the Suffolk household, but Francis's time there surely must have had a considerable impact upon him. John de la Pole, Duke of Suffolk, was a quiet man. Present at court for important occasions but reluctant to draw attention to himself, he preferred to establish local ties rather than deliberate on the government of the kingdom.[3] Francis, in time, would grow into a similar kind of man. It is possible that Francis's own tendencies toward discretion were encouraged by John, or else that Francis consciously emulated the duke's behaviour. The similarities between the two are certainly worth noting.

It was not only the duke and his choice of a quiet life which likely influenced Francis's future while he stayed in the ducal household. While there, he would have made the acquaintance of the Suffolks' eldest son John, Earl of Lincoln, then around nine years old, close in age to Frideswide. The relationship between John and Francis would turn out to be a close and fruitful one, with massive significance for the throne of England in later years, but at the time of their first meeting they cannot have had a lot in common. Perhaps John regarded Francis as something of an older brother, and Francis enjoyed the admiration felt by a small boy for a teenager, but it's equally possible they hardly saw anything of one another.

Francis, though not having much in common with the younger boy at the time, probably saw getting to know John and building a good relationship even this early as an opportunity, an investment in the future. John, as the king's nephew, would surely become an influential man, and his friendship was therefore worth winning. The same thinking might have informed Francis's interactions with the duke and duchess themselves, while they in turn saw the benefits of cultivating a good relationship with a baron who stood to inherit wealth and lands.

Even if Francis's interactions with his guardians and their family were not informed by such astute considerations, by the time he arrived in the Suffolk household in mid-1471 the young ward would most likely have been aware of the importance of building connections, and may have attempted to build relationships that would sustain him in his life as a lord. It is possible that he an opportunity arose to do so when attending his stepfather William Stanley's wedding to Elizabeth Hopton.[4] It is tempting to speculate that this was a melancholy occasion for Francis, but this is perhaps overly romantic. Francis may not have remembered much of his mother, and thus felt little loyalty to her memory beyond what was expected. Whatever the case, it did not throw a shadow over his relationship with William Stanley. The two would apparently remain on good terms for many years yet.[5]

This may not have been the only chance for Francis to make important friends. The Suffolks may have introduced him to other significant figures, and encouraged networking. He would by now have learnt that even if he was not in the centre of things, intending instead to live his life quietly away from weighty matters of government, he needed good relationships to those in high standing to protect him from exploitation by those with greater power.

Though he almost certainly would have continued to receive formal lessons in the Suffolk household, covering mathematics, Latin, music and all the other skills expected of a nobleman, it may have been observing the duke's daily routines and networking techniques that proved the most important lessons for Francis. The formal tutelage he received would have differed little from his previous education, but it was Duke John's lifestyle that Francis would emulate most closely until 1483, not the Earl of Warwick's or Henry FitzHugh's.[6]

It can therefore be said with reasonable certainty that Francis's stay with the Suffolks proved the most formative time in his youth. It is nice to think that he enjoyed his time with the Suffolks, as he remained close to them and would work together with them repeatedly in the years to come. It would not be surprising if Francis retained fond memories, as Duke John and Duchess Elizabeth do not appear to have simply used his wardship for their own gain but worked for Francis's benefit. This can be seen clearly in the fact that they tried to establish his rights and theirs as his guardians, demanding possessions which technically belonged to Francis's inheritance from his father but which had not been passed to them with his wardship, being held by other men instead. At least two such demands were taken to court by the duke and duchess; one for lands and possessions in Yoxhale, Staffordshire, which were held by one William Averall,[7] and one for the manor of Denford in Berkshire, held by a man called William Bampton.[8] The documents of these court cases are still held in the National Archives. These were not the only cases of the Suffolks trying to consolidate Francis's possessions.

Naturally, in doing this, the Suffolks were not completely selfless; after all, the more lands they held, the more money fell to them. However, there is no indication that John and Elizabeth exploited Francis's possessions, nor do they seem to have spent lavishly from the proceeds of his lands; the same cannot be said of Edward IV, who would help himself to Francis's inheritance from his grandmother Alice Deincourt.[9]

Francis would have been old enough to appreciate the duke and duchess's efforts for his benefit, and their decent treatment of him and his possessions. At the very least, this would have engendered some trust between the ducal couple and the teenage baron, but perhaps it was more than that. Perhaps Francis came to genuinely like them. All that can be said with certainty is that their relationship remained close.

Whatever Francis's thoughts and opinions on the Suffolks, whatever he learnt at their hands, we know that his stay with them was a long one. On 5 February 1472, the king renewed the grant of wardship to his sister and brother-in-law,[10] and they continued to hold it until Francis came of age some five-and-a-half years later, though as time went on Edward assumed some of the benefits and possessions of the wardship for himself.

Presumably, for at least a few years after 1471, Francis lived with them in their household at Ewelme, as did his sisters. However, as he matured and outgrew the routine of daily lessons, he would have travelled increasingly often as he set about establishing himself as more than a mere teenager under the Suffolks' care.

First Steps into Independence

It is possible that Francis's first time leaving his guardians' household by himself and travelling on his own was in summer 1472. It was then that his father-in-law Henry died, either in England or Scotland, of causes unknown, and Francis's brother-in-law Richard became Lord FitzHugh at the age of thirteen. Edward IV assumed Richard's wardship at that time, but did not appoint anyone to take over his education, and Richard stayed with his mother Alice.

It may be that Francis, almost sixteen and just old enough to travel unsupervised, went to the FitzHugh household at that time to attend the funeral, if it took place there, or perhaps to offer support in their time of mourning; maybe he just went to comfort his youthful wife and her family for a while. If he did so, it would have hardly been a challenging duty, though doubtless a solemn one, which might very well have involved a feeling of personal loss as well as one of obligation.

The summer of 1472 marked something of a turning point in Francis's life. At nearly sixteen, he would have most likely been considered too old for formal education, now of an age sufficient to slowly take up more and more of his duties as a lord, perhaps with the support of the Suffolks and Alice FitzHugh. Among those duties would have been seeing to his possessions, their administration and organisation, listening to petitioners and trying to solve conflicts that arose. Naturally, his lessons would have prepared him for such duties, but it is very likely that he learned the practicalities with the help of his guardians who held the possessions for him. Since many of Francis's lands in the Midlands were close to the Suffolk household's main residence at Ewelme, it would have been easy for him and Duke John to visit them, where the duke could teach Francis in practice what he had so far only learnt in theory.[11]

It is likely that this is what kept Francis busy throughout most of 1472, though by winter of that year there may have been something else that required his attention: the planning of his sister Joan's wedding. We do not know the exact date of the ceremony, only that it appears to have been before the summer of 1473, perhaps shortly after her sixteenth birthday. It is possible that Francis was involved, or at least consulted, in the choice of his sister's bridegroom, Brian Stapleton, a knight from Carlton in Yorkshire and a member of the gentry, some four years Joan's senior.

Brian was the scion of a family which had come to prominence during the Hundred Years War. One of his ancestors, also named Brian, had been a man of some importance at the courts of Edward III and Richard II, distinguishing himself as a doughty fighter. He was involved in several diplomatic missions, most notably in the escort of Richard II's bride Anne of Bohemia, and had been rewarded by appointment as a Knight of the Garter. The Stapleton family subsequently suffered a decline in political influence, although they retained some wealth and connections. There can be no doubt that Brian was a good match for Joan, and there is no reason why Francis should not have approved of the union. However, it was likely not his decision to make. The Stapleton family had connections to the Suffolks, Brian's late uncle having been the husband of Duke John's cousin Katherine, so the match was presumably their suggestion.

We cannot know what Francis felt about seeing his sister married, nor what Joan was feeling on the day, but if either was unhappy about it they would have nonetheless seen it as an unavoidable duty, long expected. It is, however, also possible that Joan was happy to be married and Francis was pleased his sister had made a good match.

The wedding itself may have taken place in Yorkshire, in one of the groom's manors, or else at the Suffolk household in Ewelme.

There is no way of saying, but it is almost certain that not only Brian's family and Francis and his younger sister Frideswide would have attended the wedding, but also the Suffolks, or at least the ducal couple, as they were the ones who had arranged the match and were the guardians of the young bride. In fact, just as the Earl of Warwick had probably done for Francis at his wedding, the Duke of Suffolk likely acted in the place of Joan's late father when she married, taking over such duties as giving her away.

The wedding was not only an important occasion for Joan, however; it was probably an exciting time for Francis, not least because it gave him a rare opportunity to see his mother-in-law Alice and young wife Anne. Anne was by now approaching her thirteenth birthday. As she and her siblings had spent six years of their childhood growing up with Joan Lovell, they may well have been happy and eager to attend her wedding. The presence of Anne, as the bride's sister-in-law, would certainly have been expected, and at her young age it is unlikely she would have travelled without her mother.

Naturally, Anne was still too young to be anything but Francis's wife in name only, but from late 1472 she and Francis were to see more and more of one another, and perhaps they would have tried to get to know each other and find common ground so that their eventual living together would be as easy as possible for them. It is even possible that Anne and her mother stayed with the Suffolks for a while, although it cannot be proven. In any case, Francis saw them again either soon afterwards or just before, when the king's youngest brother Richard of Gloucester married Edward of Lancaster's widow Anne Neville, their wedding taking place in January or February 1473.

Though we do not know anything about the relationship between Francis and his erstwhile classmate Richard of Gloucester at this time, the fact that Francis's wife was closely related to the duke's bride[12] means that their presence would have been expected at the wedding, for networking purposes if nothing else. Moreover, Francis's guardians the Suffolks were almost definitely present at the wedding, as Duchess Elizabeth was the groom's sister, and it stands to reason that they would have taken their teenage ward with them.

It is possible that Francis and Richard reconnected at the wedding and began their friendship. They might have stayed in touch since their joint stay in the Earl of Warwick's household, or become close when Francis became the ward of Richard's sister and brother-in-law. Or the friendship could still be some way off. However, even if the two were not yet friends in 1473, they would soon see a lot more of one another as Francis began carving out his place as a lord and, perhaps still under the instructions of Duke John, accumulating influence through his possessions, some of which lay in the north of England, especially in Yorkshire, close to many of Richard's holdings.[13]

In June 1473, as he established himself in northern society, Francis, together with his wife and her family, joined a guild which was very influential in Yorkshire and in fact all of England – the Corpus Christi Guild of York. The guild, which had been founded in 1408, had several members of high standing: Cecily Neville, the king's mother; Lord Clifford, who has since gained historical notoriety as the killer of Edmund of Rutland; Lord Scrope, an influential Yorkist; as well as a number of bishops and archbishops.[14] On the feast day of Corpus Christi of the year 1473, which fell on 13 June, Francis, his wife Anne, her mother Alice and most of her siblings joined their ranks.

This move, taken without his guardians, was a step towards independence for Francis, and that he chose to join together with Anne and her family was doubtlessly a sign of his wish for a close and fruitful relationship with them. It would have also been a further occasion on which to establish a personal relationship with his wife, and for both of them, young as they were, to present themselves as future authorities in the north of the country.

Membership of the guild cost two shillings a year[15] and was open to anyone who could afford the fee, which meant that by joining Francis chose to establish himself in a place visible to all, not simply those of high birth. The ordinances of the guild stated that 'all candidates for admission to the guild [are] to be received by the six masters or keepers. No oath [is] to be required by them, but they shall charge their conscience to contribute, according to their means, to the support of the guild.'[16] This probably means that nobles were popular members, as they would have been able to give a lot if they so wished. We do not know how much Francis contributed, but since he was to become a very rich man,[17] it may have been a significant amount.

The guild was 'dedicated to the praise and honour of the most sacred body of our Lord Jesus Christ' and aimed to see to the proper observation of the holiday of Corpus Christi. While on the actual day of Corpus Christi the York Mystery Plays took place, the next day saw a parade, still in the essentials the same as Corpus Christi parades today, to the honour of the body of Christ. At least two of the guild's six 'keepers', clergymen in charge of the guild, would be leading the parade. Guild members joined it, together with officials of the city of York, following the clergymen who led the parade.[18]

In addition to Francis, Anne and most of her family, over a hundred others joined the guild in 1473. The register of the guild names them all, and states that Francis 'and his wife Anne' joined with 'Lady Alice FitzHugh' and 'Richard, Roger, Edward, Thomas and Elizabeth, children of the said Alice FitzHugh'.[19]

Curiously, this is the only reference to a FitzHugh child called Roger, and it is likely that it was a scribe's mistake, accidentally writing 'Roger' instead of 'George'. George FitzHugh, then around eleven years old, was still his brother Richard's heir at this time, and would most likely have been mentioned between him and their younger brother Edward.

Notably missing is the eldest FitzHugh child – Alice, who was by then married with children and lived in her own household – and the youngest, a boy named John. This could be due to John being too young to join, having perhaps not yet had his first communion, or equally he could have died between 1470, when he was mentioned in the pardon issued to his father, and summer 1473 when the family joined the guild. The fact that an Edward FitzHugh, son of Alice, Lady FitzHugh, and Henry, Lord FitzHugh, is recorded to have joined the guild some years later suggests the former.[20] Their son Edward had in fact joined with his siblings in 1473, so this later mention must have been a mistake, in fact referring to his younger brother John, who may have been around seven in 1473.

Francis himself was still several months shy of his seventeenth birthday when he joined the guild, while his wife Anne was around thirteen. It must have been an exciting event for both: a way of becoming a full member of society for Francis, and a chance to appear in public not merely as her parents' child but as a wife, given preference over her mother, for Anne.

If so, for Anne it was at first a singular occasion, a taste of what the future might hold. For Francis, it may have been more than just a gesture. At his age, he would certainly have been expected to begin assuming more and more of his rights and duties as lord by himself, rather than as the Duke of Suffolk's ward. Few traces survive to suggest this, but that does not mean he did not do anything, as even during his time at the very centre of the court during later years he left little trace of his actions. However, it is notable that even as late as 1473 and 1474, when Francis was in his late teens, the few times he is mentioned in the sources he appears to be little more than a chess piece pushed around here and there; his only truly independent actions seem to be personal ones, such as his joining the Corpus Christi Guild. He was still helpless when it came to money and power, these matters being managed by others. The Suffolks were still involved in court cases to get hold of some of Francis's estates, while the king assumed more and more of them himself. [21] Francis may have been involved by the Suffolks in their attempts to establish his rights, and their rights as his guardians, but if this is the case it went unrecorded.

Francis presumably still lived in the Suffolk household when his paternal grandmother, Alice Deincourt, died on 10 February 1474[22] at the age of around seventy, less than a year after her second husband Sir Ralph Butler, Lord Sudeley. She had been a very wealthy woman, and upon her death Francis not only inherited the Lovell lands she had held in dower for her lifetime but also the baronies of Deincourt and Grey of Rotherfield, and the vast lands attached to them. Francis immediately assumed the titles, but as he was still a minor he could not yet hold any of his grandmother's lands and corresponding possessions. As had been stipulated in the grant of wardship to the Suffolks, these lands did not fall to them but to the king, who soon started granting privileges attached to them to men of his choosing. Already on 20 February, only ten days after Alice's death, Edward had appointed a man called John Fitzbeau 'to the office of receiver of the castles, lordships, manors and lands late of Alesia, dame Lovell, Deyncourt and Gray, deceased, during the minority of Francis, lord Lovell, her kinsman and heir'.[23]

This was a perfectly common grant, followed by similar ones to other men, such as Ralph Hastings,[24] brother to Edward's lord chamberlain William, and Francis would have expected nothing else. However, a grant Edward made on 30 July to a wine merchant named Gerard Caniziani gives a rather interesting insight into Edward's fiscal policies. This grant was of 'all castles, lordships, manors, lands, rents, services and possessions late of Alice, lady of Lovell, deceased', with the explanation that Caniziani 'has spent divers sums of money amounting to 4000 marks for the king and has as yet had no payment'.[25] It is perhaps unlikely that Edward was waiting for Alice's death in order to pay his debts, but it is interesting to note that he clearly had not made any move towards settling them when he received her lands, which suggests that he was waiting for a chance to pay off his debts without using money from his own revenues.

If such actions made Francis angry, he never gave any public indication. Whatever he said in private, he would remain Edward's loyal subject throughout his reign. This ties in with what we know of Francis's character, which by this time would have been well formed: he was a calm man, not given to making enemies.

It would be interesting to know how Francis reacted to his grandmother's death; was it simply sad but distant news for him, or might he have been driven to sincere mourning by a closeness we know nothing about? No will from Alice Deincourt survives to shine any light on their relationship, so it is yet another aspect of Francis's life that remains shrouded in mystery.

Even if Francis was not close to his grandmother, he may well have been on at least cordial terms with her son, his uncle William Lovell, Lord Morley. Perhaps William took some interest in his late brother's children, but again we cannot say for certain. It is known, however, that for at least some time Francis was on friendly terms with William's son Henry Lovell. This may have been due to a good relationship with William Lovell, but it is also possible that when William died in 1474, followed soon after by his wife Eleanor,[26] Francis took the young Henry under his wing for some time, if only to offer some comfort and support. Not quite eighteen, and thus still only a minor himself, Francis would have been too young to offer a home to his cousin, but it is possible he took some interest in the boy, ensured that he and his older sister were treated well and tried to build a connection with them.

Though Henry Lovell and his sister Alice were very young when their parents died and therefore of no political use to Francis, his attempts to establish good relations with them early on might have been motivated by more than mere family feeling. Being on good terms with Henry could have prevented arguments about inheritance and later claims by Henry to some of the manors left to his father in their grandfather's will that were nonetheless set to fall to Francis.

Whether or not Francis approached the friendship with these more cynical designs in mind, it is hard to believe that these benefits never occurred to him. As he grew older, like most noblemen of the time, he began to show a distinct interest in the accumulation of wealth, and it is likely that he already pondered on his future as a rich nobleman and all its attendant privileges and difficulties.

It seems that Francis spent most of the year 1474 establishing connections and relationships, perhaps even independently – a first for him. Those are Francis's only accountable actions in 1474, anyway. For one, he continued his close association with his wife and her family. By now Anne was fourteen, and slowly approaching the age at which she and Francis could begin to live as man and wife. It would come as no surprise if this was a preoccupying thought for Francis and Anne when they attended the wedding of Anne's older sister Elizabeth together in the summer of that year.

Elizabeth, then eighteen years old, married the much older Sir William Parr, who was in his early forties in 1474. A knight with strong Yorkist connections, Sir William's loyalty to Edward IV had been amply rewarded. Just before his marriage he had become a member of the Order of the Garter, with the result that despite not holding any title he was wealthy and well connected enough to be a suitable match for Elizabeth. More than this, the match might have at least partly been made to strengthen the connections of the FitzHugh family to the Yorkist government.

Francis would have been aware of this. He would not only have seen the wedding as a mandatory social occasion, but quite possibly also as yet another opportunity to establish useful relationships. He appears to have been successful in this; as time went on, both he and his wife were on good terms with the Parrs. Whether their time at the wedding also brought Francis and Anne closer together is sadly not known, though having attended several ceremonies together in the preceding years it is likely that they knew each other quite well by this point. No longer children but teenagers, each would have begun to grasp the other's character and together they would have set about forming the tentative relationship on which they would base their future together.

In any case, at fourteen Anne was still deemed too young to live with Francis and run a household with him. This was not a common view at the time; while the consummation of a marriage was usually delayed until a girl was at least in her mid-teens, cohabitation often happened earlier, with bride or groom barely in their teens. Why the Lovells did not yet share a home is unclear, though Lady FitzHugh and the Suffolks may well have had something to do with it.

Perhaps one factor that played into the decision was the fact that Francis was still dependent on the king and his guardians, having little access to any of his possessions and little standing in society as yet. Francis, the Suffolks and Lady FitzHugh may have felt that it would be best if he first carved out a place for himself before meeting the challenge of living together with his wife.

Francis was clearly working on establishing himself as his own independent man in the early 1470s, and by late 1474 he finally appears to have had some success. On 5 November 1474, he affirmed a lease 'of the manor and lordship of Longendale, together with the town of Tyngetwisell'[27] to his stepfather Sir William Stanley. Though the manor, lordship and town were recorded 'by the minority of the said Francis' to be in the hands of Edward IV's four-year-old son and heir, Edward, Prince of Wales, and so really in the king's hands, Francis appears to have been allowed to make the decision on the lease for himself, as the record states that 'Francis, son of John Lord Lovell' was the one leasing the possessions to Sir William. This suggests that stepfather and stepson had made the arrangement between themselves; they must have been on cordial terms to do this.

If the king not only allowed Francis to make the decision of the lease and the choice of leaseholder but also to keep the income, or some of the income, from it, this would have given the young baron some of his own money, to be used as he saw fit. It would have been his first taste of financial freedom, and he could very well have used it to prepare for independent life. No matter how much Francis may have liked the Suffolks, this must have felt like a release from dependency and control.

It is possible that around this time, as he began making his own name, Francis might have also become more politically engaged. Edward IV seems to have been more concerned with the young man's possessions than his person or politics, however. It is hard to believe that Francis did not concern himself with any political activity at this juncture, but there is no evidence of his involvement in government, and given the lack of interest he would show in political developments even during his time at the centre of court from 1483 to 1485, perhaps he really didn't get involved.

In fact, despite Francis's new-found independence, he kept such a low profile that it is not even known whether he was present when Edward IV gathered troops to go to France in summer 1475. Nearly nineteen, Francis would definitely have been considered old enough to fight, and it stands to reason he would have wanted to be present, to show loyalty to the king and take part in what was happening. His status as a minor, a king's ward and, moreover, a baron of comparatively low standing, suggests he was not considered important enough to be mentioned by any chronicler.

This might also explain why he was not mentioned in the peace treaty negotiated between Louis and Edward. The Treaty of Picquigny circumvented any fighting by stipulating a marriage between Edward's oldest daughter Elizabeth and Louis's oldest son and heir, Charles. It also included large annuities to be paid to Edward and also to various other English nobles and bishops.[28] Being so politically insignificant, Francis's presence would have made no difference to the two kings and neither of them would have seen any necessity to include him in the treaty as one of the receivers of annuities.

If Francis was not present, this would have most likely been for everyday, practical reasons rather than representing some kind of political stand. Since Edward and men of his choosing still held most of his lands, it is possible that Francis did not have the funds to raise many men of his own to bring to the campaign, and could not throw any political weight in with them. It is also possible that Francis was simply ill, though we would expect to find surviving comment from later years criticising him for this; cynical commenters would have made much of him apparently ducking his military duties.

Whether or not Francis went with Edward, his actions do not seem to have made an impression, suggesting that he behaved conventionally and appropriately for a young baron in whatever he did. This means, then, that he did not vocally agree with the king's brother Richard of Gloucester, who disapproved of the contract with the French,[29] though it is possible he shared the duke's opinion privately but thought it prudent to keep this opinion to himself, or only share it with those closest to him.

It is often suggested that this aborted French campaign was one of the main reasons Richard of Gloucester became disillusioned with his brother Edward IV,[30] and it would be fascinating to know what Francis thought of it given his later allegiances. We have no indication of Francis's feelings about Edward and his politics, however, so this must remain a matter of speculation.

6

In His Own Household

It is quite possible that whatever his opinion on the French campaign, Francis did not, in fact, dwell on it long, for within the next year changes took place in his personal life which might very well have commanded his attention and taken his mind off more distant political matters. Shortly after the campaign, Francis appears to have left the Suffolk household to establish his own household in his ancestral manor of Minster Lovell Hall, presumably in preparation for his wife's imminent arrival. This appears to have kept him occupied during the winter of 1475 and early 1476. Anne must have been making her own preparations for the impending move and the independence it entailed. Naturally, she would have been taught how to run a household, much as Francis would have, but it is still reasonable to assume that it was an exciting and possibly somewhat frightening step for both to take.

Francis and Anne's first unsupervised action as man and wife may not have been moving in together, but visiting Anne's sister Elizabeth. Around this time, roughly two years after her wedding, Elizabeth gave birth to her first child, a daughter who was named Anne. She would go on to have three more children by William Parr, boys who were named after her husband, his father and his brother; given that there was no other Anne in either her or her husband William's closest family, it seems that their daughter was named after Francis's wife. It might be an attestation to the good relationship between the two sisters that Elizabeth chose her as namesake over her mother and older sister. It is likely that Anne, then around sixteen, was also the child's godmother, and possibly, if Elizabeth and William followed the tradition of having a married couple for godparents, Francis was her godfather.

It is tempting to imagine that it was after this happy occasion that Anne and Francis moved in together and began living as man and wife in his ancestral home of Minster Lovell Hall, though it is not entirely certain. Since we only know the year in which Anne Parr was born, not the day or even month, the baby's arrival could have occurred very late in the year and therefore most likely after her aunt and uncle had already set up their household.

Sadly, no accounts from the Lovell household survive to this day, so the details of how it was run are lost to history. It is not even known if Francis's unmarried younger sister, Frideswide, then around twelve years old, moved in with them. It is possible that she did, but it is also possible she stayed where she was, either with her sister Joan or with the Suffolks and their children.

Though there is no evidence as to how they ran their household, there is evidence that Francis and Anne wanted to make their own mark on their living arrangements. Though the manor was still comparatively recent, having been rebuilt by Francis's grandfather William in the 1430s, Francis chose to have several significant changes made to it, adding a tower, which has been described as:

[A] four-storeyed tower overlapping the south-west corner of the west wing and almost touching the edge of the river. It was a combined garderobe and lodging tower with prospect room, standing to roof level on the west side and partially so to the north and south. It was built in better quality stone than the adjoining west wing and was richly decorated with traceried windows and gargoyles at roof level and supporting the newel turret. The ground floor was divided into two garderobe closets served by a pit against the end wall, flushed by the river. An external stair rose to the first floor, retaining a single light and splay evidence of a south facing window. The two principal rooms above were reached from the first floor landing by the newel that terminates in an octagonal head above roof level. The second floor room was fairly low, with a drain and south-facing window, while the uppermost room retains part of a larger south-facing oriel with stopped hood.[1]

It is intriguing to speculate as to why Francis took on this project. Though he might have wanted to add some of his own touches to the manor, this was a massive change that would have cost him a lot of money. Historians Peter Hammond and Livia Visser-Fuchs have speculated that Francis employed for this work the architect William Orchard, one of the most popular architects of the time, among whose works was the Great Tower at Magdalen College in Oxford. Considering that Francis had connections to this college,[2] and that Oxford is relatively close to Minster Lovell Hall, it could very well be that Francis admired the work done by Orchard on the college and therefore chose him as architect for his manor. It could also be that Francis chose him for reasons of prestige.

It seems likely that when the work was done, Francis and Anne lived mainly in the new quarters, but it would have taken a while to complete the construction, over a year. During that time, the young couple presumably used the living quarters once used by Francis's parents and grandparents.

Naturally, making arrangements for new living quarters suited to their tastes and needs was not the only concern Francis and Anne had after they moved in together. Once the couple had settled in, Francis's mind appears to have turned to the future, and his upcoming twenty-first birthday. On 'the last day of February' 1477, a grant of special livery is recorded to him for Cheshire.[3] As Francis was still underage at the time, this grant gave him permission to enter his lands there earlier than usual and without having to prove his age, meaning he could claim his lands and possessions in Cheshire from their current holders much sooner than expected.

We can only speculate as to why Edward IV was prepared to grant Francis special livery when he had been helping himself to the lands and income meant for Francis's guardians for years. It might well be that Francis had by this time formed a close relationship with Richard of Gloucester; if so, a brother's word could have convinced the king. Alternatively, the king might have been persuaded by his sister Elizabeth, Duchess of Suffolk. Most likely, however, is that Francis simply paid a hefty fee for the grant, sweetening the king on the prospect of losing custody of his lands and possessions several months earlier than expected.

Clearly, Francis was eager to finally come into his rights, and the year 1477 was a busy one for him. Apart from doing all he could to smooth his imminent coming of age, with its attendant granting of rights, Francis had to become accustomed to living with his wife. He was doubtless trying to start a family with her, and they would also have begun to form friendly relationships with the neighbouring gentry as they tried to carve out their place as lord and lady.

Some evidence of these attempts and their success is found in a letter written by Elizabeth Stonor, wife of William Stonor, on 6 March 1477, informing him of recent events and some personal troubles. The Stonors lived in Oxfordshire, not far from Minster Lovell Hall, and Elizabeth's letter is the first surviving mention of Francis and his wife in connection to their neighbours. Here is the full text of the letter:

Right reverent and worshipful and entirely best beloved husband, I recommend me unto you in the most heartiest wise ever more desiring to hear of your good welfare, the which I pray God long to continue unto your heart's desire. Sir, I received a token from you by Tawbose, my lord Lovelly's servant. And Sir, I have sent my lord Lovell a token and my lady's, as you command me to do, such as shall please them. Sir, you shall understand that the bishop of Bath is brought into the Tower since you departed. Also Sir, you shall understand the the wool [?] has departed, as tomorrow is, for as I understand: I pray Jesus by their good speed: and Goodard departs also: and I pray you that you will send me some of your servants and mine to wait upon me, for now I am right bare off servants, and that you know well. Sir, I sent you half a [honder welkys?] by Gardenar, and I would have sent you some other [desys?], but truly I could not get none: but and I can get any tomorrow, Sir William shall bring it with him. Sir, I pray you that I may be recommended unto my mistress your mother, and unto all good friends. No more unto you at this time, but the blessed trinity have you in his keeping now and ever. Amen. At London the 6th day of March.

Cousin, I was crazed at the making of this letter, but I thank God I am right well amended, blessed be Jesus.

By your own wife Elizabeth Stonor.

To my right reverent and worshipful cousin, Sir William Stonor, knight.[4]

Though the Lovells are clearly not the main focus of the letter, they were obviously on Elizabeth's mind as the news connected to them is the first item Elizabeth mentions, and it is quite illuminating as to the relationship between the Lovells and the Stonors. That one of Francis's servants, a man called Tawbose, had been running an errand for William Stonor bringing something from him to his wife, suggests that a degree of friendliness had already been established between the two couples. This is also supported by the fact that Elizabeth had sent Francis and Anne some sort of gift by the time of the letter, though the fact that she had to be 'commanded' to do so could well mean that either she did not want to, or else, perhaps more likely, that it had not been her own idea but rather her husband's attempt to develop a connection. Sadly, Elizabeth does not specify the nature of this 'token [which] shall please them'.

It clearly seems that the Stonors and the Lovells shared an interest in maintaining and furthering their relationship, though it may well be that at this time their connection was not very personal. After all, while William Stonor apparently thought it important enough to send Francis and Anne a gift that he commanded his wife to do it, he was not secure enough in his friendship to them to wait until he had returned home; nor was he able to identify for his wife what kind of present would 'please' them.

It could be argued that Elizabeth knew Francis and Anne better than her husband, as she was apparently in a position to know what a suitable present for them would be. Additionally, as Elizabeth did not join her husband when he travelled away from home, she had more chance to get to know them. However, given that we know she was ordered to send the present, it could well be that she was not yet close with the Lovells either, and that the token was a conventional one. All in all, it seems that the relationship between the two couples, while cordial, was very formal at this time.

It is only natural that a relationship to the Stonors would have been relatively tenuous at this time; Francis and Anne had only moved to Minster Lovell Hall the previous year, and were only just beginning to establish themselves there. Francis was twenty years old at the time the letter was written, while Anne was sixteen, or perhaps just about seventeen. The young couple's recent arrival would explain why Stonor was eager at that time to be on friendly terms with them despite the fact Francis would not yet attain his majority for several months, and also explains why the relationship was still apparently formal.

It is interesting, too, that William Stonor explicitly wanted his wife to send a token not simply to Francis, but to Francis and 'my lady's', indicating that the Lovells, whatever their relationship was in private at that point, knew how to show themselves as united, a contented married couple. Given that the Stonors knew the couple a little, if not closely, and can probably be assumed to have heard talk about them from servants and other neighbours, it might well be that they had at least something of an insight; in this light, William's decision to make the present out to both Francis and Anne suggests he knew or believed that Anne mattered to her husband to such an extent that including her would please him, or even that she held some sway over Francis and her opinion mattered to him, making her friendship worth cultivating.

Francis's Character

There is, in fact, some indication that William Stonor was right about this, and that not only was Anne Lovell an intelligent woman whose opinions were valued by her husband, but that the couple were in fact close. Though very little survives about Anne, it is known that she was opinionated, popular and ready to risk a lot to do something she believed right, as she would show later on.[5] Her husband clearly trusted her, and, at least in later years, showed her affection in somewhat unusual ways, eventually making arrangements for her to inherit some of his manors in the event of his death and having the chance to pass them on to children she might have with another man.[6]

All this, of course, still was in the future in 1477, and whether or not their relationship was already so strong then cannot be known. Certainly, however, it would have been in their interest to build a good relationship, and William Stonor, at least, seemed to believe that they had succeeded.

While we have very little on which to build an understanding of Anne's character, for Francis we have at least slightly more, as more of his actions, and even some of his own words, survive to this day, giving an invaluable insight into his state of mind. Among those words are two letters, written by Francis to William Stonor in the years 1482 and 1483,[7] at which point they would have known each other for several years. Interestingly, it seems that the two men did not strike up a friendship during that time, as the tone of the letters remains distant, if friendly. In them, Francis does not share any more information than strictly necessary, and it appears that any expression of feelings is unintended.

The content of the letters is discussed in chapters 7 and 10, but for any analysis of Francis's character the letters and their tone are invaluable, giving a glimpse of a polite but reserved, almost slightly stiff man, someone not given to unctuousness and unnecessary flourishes. Francis was seemingly not the type to share much of his life, thoughts or motivation.

It could be argued that this taciturnity stemmed from a simple lack of friendship between Francis and William Stonor. However, that Francis was polite but reserved is supported by most of his actions. There is no indication, even in his later years as Richard III's best friend and one of his closest advisors, that he had any wish to be centre stage, instead preferring to stay in the background. His 1483 letter to William Stonor, asking him – unsuccessfully, as it would turn out – to come to the aid of King Richard III during the Buckingham Rebellion of 1483, also betrays some slight awkwardness, as if putting himself out in the open and asking for favours is something he would rather avoid. It can be said with reasonable certainty, therefore, that Francis was a polite but quiet man, unwilling to draw attention to himself.

Despite this discretion, however, he also appears to have had a tendency to be rather unconventional. This would manifest most famously in his actions in 1485, of which more later, but this would be rather weak as evidence for a character trait. The circumstances at that time were extreme, and would not necessarily have to reflect a pattern of behaviour he always showed. There are other actions, however, which confirm the idea that he was not the most conventional of men.

First and foremost would be his aforementioned refusal to give his father John a marker for his grave, or have prayers said for him, or to acknowledge him in any way. While he might have deeply disliked him, even hated him, it would have been normal and expected for him to still make the usual gestures, his emotions being considered irrelevant. Francis clearly did not care for what was expected in this case, and if this refusal to help his father's soul or preserve his memory ever caused comment, it does not seem to have bothered him. Certainly, nothing was said or done to make him change his decision.

On a more positive note, there is the aforementioned indenture[8] favouring his wife Anne, making arrangements for her in the event of his death, endowing her with some of the traditional Lovell possessions and giving her leave to do with them as she wished. This document shows that Francis was not particularly concerned with conventions. He clearly cared a lot for his wife, and expressing this and doing something to benefit her meant more to him than following the usual way of things.

Interestingly, in this same indenture he asked his wife to arrange for two priests to read his obituary. There is nothing very unusual in this, and in fact both his grandfathers included similar wishes in their wills. Francis, however, did not simply charge his wife with it but *asked* her to do it in return for the generosity he had shown her in leaving her so much – a rather strange addition to the request, and very uncommon. Since Francis and Anne were in no way estranged – in fact what little evidence there is about their relationship suggests the very opposite – it appears that rather than being based on a fear that Anne might not have his obituary read unless persuaded, this was due to a more nebulous insecurity. If this is true, it would seem that Francis's self-esteem was rather low, at least in his personal life.

All in all, it seems that the Francis who started carving out his place in Oxfordshire was calm, reserved, polite and possibly a little stiff, while at the same time quietly emotional, and possibly lacking in confidence. His wife Anne, an outspoken, popular woman who knew what she wanted, appears to have been supportive of him.

New Relationships

As the year 1477 went on Francis slowly appears to have become more secure in his position as a lord, and as his twenty-first birthday approached, on which date he would attain his majority, he also became rather interested in making his rights known.

Perhpas it was now that Francis also began cultivating the friendship with Richard of Gloucester for which he would chiefly be remembered. It has been suggested that the aforementioned renovations Francis undertook at Minster Lovell Hall might have been inspired by the renovations at nearby Sudeley Castle,[9] where Francis's grandmother Alice Deincourt had once lived and which in 1477 belonged to Richard of Gloucester; if so, the work could indicate the two men were friends by this time.

Certainly, from the time Francis began to live in his various manors, the two would have come into regular contact. Lots of their possessions were quite close to one another; not only Minster Lovell Hall and Sudeley Castle, but also Bedale, which Francis had inherited from his paternal grandmother, and Richard's favoured castle at Middleham.[10]

In fact, there is some evidence that it was mainly in the north that Francis began making his mark. Most of his known servants came from the north or at the very least had connections there,[11] and in the tumult of 1486 it was in the north that he would find support, and in the north that he would hide. Why this was so is unknown. It might be that Francis, having spent several years of his childhood and adolescence in the north, preferred it to the Midlands where he had been born and spent his earliest years. It is also possible that he preferred the north because his in-laws, the FitzHughs, had their main lands there, and Francis could profit from that connection while enjoying their company. If he was already a friend of Richard of Gloucester, he would also have benefitted from close proximity.

If indeed it was around 1477 that Francis and Richard started forming their famous friendship, the catalyst might have been Richard and his wife Anne Neville, Warwick's daughter and first cousin of Francis's wife, joining the Corpus Christi Guild, which already had Francis and Anne as members.[12] They could also have become familiar as Francis began looking into in his possessions in the north in preparation for his majority.

That Francis and Richard moved in similar circles is made clear by their mutual acquaintances. Francis is known to have been close to Geoffrey Franke,[13] who worked as receiver for Richard at Middleham. Geoffrey's brother Edward worked for Francis,[14] and by 1485 was one of his closest men. Francis and Richard also both appear to have been close to Richard Ratcliffe, who would later attain dubious fame alongside Lovell in the famous doggerel lambasting Richard III's reign. Some of the men Francis employed were also close to his in-laws, especially his mother-in-law Alice, which supports the idea Francis – and presumably Anne – appreciated the presence of the FitzHughs in the north.

As far as Francis is concerned, however, there was someone else living in the north with whom he would have pursued a close connection: his twin sister Joan, living with her husband Brian Stapleton. Though we do not know any details of the relationship, it seems that Francis and Anne were close with Joan and Brian; there is some evidence Francis turned to Brian for support during the difficulties of 1486,[15] and their second child, who went on to father sixteen children, named one of his offspring for Francis and one for Anne.

In 1477 Joan had given birth to her first child, a son named Brian after his father. It is quite possible that Francis went to see his first nephew that year and that Anne came along as well. The Stapleton family came from Carleton in Yorkshire and still lived there for the most part. Their home was quite close to some of Francis's own possessions, most notably Bedale, and therefore would not have been difficult for the Lovells to reach. It is very possible that Francis and Anne stayed there a while around the time of baby Brian's birth. It is even possible that they were young Brian's godparents; they certainly appear to have shown an interest in both of Joan's children.

The birth of Francis's nephew would have made him and Anne think of having children of their own. Sadly, this would never come to pass. They could not know this at the time, however, and surely expected to become parents sooner or later. Even though they had been living together for around a year by the time little Brian was born, they would not have worried yet; Joan was nearly twenty-one when she gave birth to her first son, and she had married and begun living with her husband at the same age Anne had moved in with Francis.

In fact, it was probably at least partly with future children in mind that Francis, on reaching his majority, began clamouring for his right to several manors and lands owed to him.

7

Francis, Lord Lovell

Francis turned twenty-one and thus of age on 17 September 1477. On 6 November of that year, the Calendar of Patent Rolls records the licence given to him:

> Francis Lovell, son and heir of John Lovell, knight, and Joan his wife, and kinsman and heir of Alesia late the wife of Ralph Botteler, knight, sometime the wife of William Lovell, knight, to enter freely into all castles, lordships, manors, lands, fee farms, annuities, reversions, farms, rents, services, hundreds, fees, views of frank-pledge, courts, leets, sherrifs' turns, liberties, franchises, fairs, markets, jurisdictions, stews, fisheries, warrens, knights' fees, advowsons and other possessions within the realm of which the said John, Joan and Alesia were seised and which should descend to him, saving to the king homage and fealty.[1]

This, of course, was the normal text used for a licence to someone who had just attained his or her majority to enter their lands. It is notable, however, that he received it less than two months after his twenty-first birthday – this was a particularly speedy acknowledgement. This may have been down to the influence of Richard of Gloucester, or Elizabeth, Duchess of Suffolk influencing their brother; alternatively, Francis may have simply paid to expedite proceedings. If so, it was money well spent.

Francis was clearly eager to receive his lands, and ready to fight for what he considered rightfully his. It seems he waited until he had attained his majority by turning twenty-one but did not hold on for official recognition of the fact. Almost immediately after his birthday, in October 1477, Francis brought a case against the king, arguing for his own right to hold some lands in Oxfordshire which he – correctly – claimed his grandfather William Lovell had purchased from the king's father Richard, Duke of York. In the Calendar of Close Rolls, it is recorded that the king appointed two arbiters to the case, Thomas Byllyng and Thomas Brown, who were both king's justices. On 14 October 1477, three people, among them Francis's mother-in-law Alice FitzHugh, entered into a bond of surety of £200, with the condition that Francis would accept Brown and Byllyng's decision.[2] Apparently this was seen as insufficient, however, and not quite two weeks later, on 26 October, another three men entered into a bond of £400 on the same condition.[3] Among them was William Stonor, which gives us the interesting insight that Stonor either trusted Francis, thought winning his favour was worth the possibility of losing money, or else had become so close to Francis that he did this out of sheer affection for him. This last possibility is not supported by any other evidence, though, and the most unlikely.

It was agreed that the bonds were to be voided by 25 July the next year if the conflict had been settled by that time and the arbiters allowed to come to an independent decision.[4] This outcome appears to have occurred, with Byllyng and Brown, perhaps unsurprisingly, deciding for the king against Francis. There is no indication that Francis protested against the decision in any way, though he was surely displeased.

This was not the only argument Francis pursued after attaining his majority. Over the next few years, he was intermittently involved in conflicts for lands and manors he claimed for himself, sometimes with solid reasoning and sometimes on rather more shaky grounds. Though, as discussed, Francis does not seem to have wished to draw attention to himself, this reticence did not slow him down when exposure could help him get what he considered rightfully his, nor did it stop him from making a case against several of those closest to the king, such as William Hastings or Edward's younger stepson Richard Grey.

In a petition made to Parliament in 1484, by which time he had obtained honours and a very high position in government, Francis stated he began the argument for some of his ancestral manors, namely Thorpe Waterville, Aldwincle, Achurch and Chelveston, immediately after he had come of age.[5] However, given that Richard Grey, their holder, was about a year younger than Francis and had therefore not attained his majority in 1477, it may well be that the parliamentary petition was either misdated or had been dated to give the impression that Francis had argued for his rights as soon as he was able to. It may, however, also be that Richard Grey, twenty years old, had nominal possession of the holdings at this time already, while in practice they were in his stepfather Edward IV's keeping.

There can be no doubt that these manors had once been held by Francis's grandfather, but clearly Grey also considered them rightfully his. The quarrel dragged on over several years, though unusually there is absolutely no violence recorded. Francis never tried to take any of these manors by force – violence was in fact quite normal during such conflicts – nor is there any record of Grey ever sending armed men to defend them or threatening Francis to prevent him from acting. It seems the argument was strictly a legal matter until Edward IV's last parliament in 1483, the first parliament Francis attended, granted the manors to Richard Grey in fee tail male (passed only to sons).[6] However, this was not the end of the matter, and Richard Grey would not get to enjoy the ruling for long.

It seems that Francis's time was largely occupied with arguments over his possessions for the two years following his twenty-first birthday. Even after he reached his majority, Edward IV did not seem inclined to involve him in any way in his government. Despite the fact that Francis's long minority was officially declared over on 6 November 1477, he does not appear to have received a summons to Parliament two weeks later; he did not attend, and if he had been summoned this absence would have prompted a written warning. Edward's only concession to Francis was an appointment in January 1478 to a commission of peace for Oxfordshire;[7] there is no indication that this was anything more than a nominal appointment or that Francis actually did any work for it.

At this time, Edward IV had more on his mind than seeing to the just treatment of a politically insignificant baron, albeit a very wealthy one. In early 1478, he and his court celebrated the marriage of his younger son Richard of Shrewsbury to the slightly older Anne Mowbray.[8] Only shortly afterwards, however, Parliament condemned Edward's brother George of Clarence to death. Having enjoyed relative peace during recent years, Clarence had fallen once more into rebellion after the death of his wife. After some of his retainers were rounded up and confessed to treasonous designs, Clarence was arrested. The death sentence was carried out on 18 February 1478.[9]

Clarence's execution was the cause for a lot of rumours, gossip and whispers against Edward IV. It was remarked upon at the time that Richard of Gloucester was both shaken by and furious at these events,[10] and as many as six years later he called Clarence's execution 'murder by the colour of law'[11] in a letter. It could well be that Francis saw the execution in a similar way, if only because he was influenced by Richard, but of course we do not know. Perhaps he also thought, as some others did – and as many if not most historians have thought since – that Clarence's own actions had condemned him and that he deserved it.[12]

However, Richard of Gloucester seems to have been the only link between Francis and Clarence. There is no way of saying if the two men ever met; if they did, history has not recorded the meeting, and it cannot have been very significant. Neither in life nor in death does he appear to have made any impact on Francis or his life.

The one consequence Francis may have felt after Clarence's execution was that Richard stayed mostly in his own lands from this point on, especially in the north of England, and Francis may have therefore seen more of him and they could have had a chance to deepen their friendship. However, Francis's whereabouts throughout 1478 are unrecorded. It is not until 1479 that he resurfaces in the historical sources. In May of that year he was appointed to another commission of peace in Oxfordshire,[13] though once again there is no evidence he ever acted as a commissioner there or saw the appointment as anything but nominal. In fact, it seems that his fight for property still took up most of his time and efforts, for on 14 August of that year – coincidentally his late grandfather John Beaumont's birthday – he appeared in York before the city council with a legal representative to argue for his right to have twenty cows and one bull on a pasture in Knavesmire, near York.[14] This, like so many of Francis's efforts, was unsuccessful; he would not get the right to it until Richard III ascended the throne.

Building and Using Connections

That so many of his efforts were in vain must have been disappointing and frustrating for Francis, but his stay in Yorkshire in 1479 held some positives. In that year, his twin sister Joan gave birth to her second child and son, who was named George.

Why she and Brian selected that name is lost to history. It is notable that she did not, as would have been traditional, name the boy John after her father. This may not have been a deliberate snub to him, however; George might have been named after the saint in thanksgiving. Another possibility is that he was named after George FitzHugh, with whom Joan, after all, had spent four long years of her childhood and early adolescence in his parents' household. Though it would be rather unconventional, the couple may even have simply chosen a name they liked.[15]

Since Francis was in Yorkshire in the summer of the year 1479, it is quite possible that he went to visit his sister and brother-in-law and see his new nephew. This happy occasion may have been the last time Francis and his sister saw each other, however; she appears to have died mysteriously between 1479 and 1481, in her mid-twenties.

Joan's death would have been a shock and a blow to Francis, but one that was hardly uncommon at the time. Though it must have been personally hard for him, life had to go on and it did. In fact, it seems that 1480 was a busy year for Francis, which might have taken his mind off his twin sister's death if it occurred around that time. This was the year that he first 'received an appointment that was somewhat more than routine when he became a commissioner of array for the North Riding of Yorkshire'[16] on 23 May. This appointment was also the first which gave him a task in the north of the country, and marked the first time he officially served together with Richard of Gloucester.

Another event that would have occupied Francis in 1480 would have been his youngest sister Frideswide's wedding. Aged around sixteen at that time, she was married to the fifteen-year-old Edward Norris. Edward was the oldest child and son of Sir William Norris of Yattendon and his first wife Joan de Vere. Through his mother, Edward was the nephew of the Lancastrian Earl of Oxford, who was a close friend of the Lancastrian Viscount Beaumont, Frideswide's maternal uncle. This cannot have been the cause of the connection, as neither Edward nor Frideswide could have seen their respective uncles since they were little more than toddlers, if at all, before 1485. Though Edward's father William would have naturally remembered his brother-in-law and might well have known William Beaumont, he would have known that with Frideswide's parents dead, her brother too young to have any connection to him and her guardians the sister and brother-in-law of the king, the marriage would not provide him or his son with any sort of valuable link to Viscount Beaumont.

Why the marriage was arranged, and if it was arranged by Francis, William Norris, the king, the Suffolks or even one of Francis's FitzHugh relations, we no longer know. Unlike the Stapletons, the Norrises do not appear to have had any previous ties to the Suffolks, nor to the Lovells before Frideswide's marriage, but they did have ties to the Neville family, and therefore to Francis's mother-in-law Alice, by politics and by marriage. Edward's father William had married as his second wife Isabel Ingoldisthorpe, the widow of Alice's brother John Neville, who had fallen at Barnet. Though Isabel died four years before Frideswide's marriage, it is well possible that Alice had kept in touch with her second husband.

Since there is no other obvious connection between Francis, his extended family and erstwhile guardians and the Norris family, it does seem likely that this link to Alice FitzHugh at least influenced the choice of Frideswide's husband. Another fact that must have played into the decision was the fact that the Norris lands, which Edward would one day inherit, were close to Francis's possessions in the north of England.

Francis, by then around twenty-four, must have been the one to lead the negotiations for the details of the match together with the groom's father. As with his twin Joan, however, we sadly have no indications of what was eventually agreed upon, only that they must have agreed on something and that the wedding was celebrated in 1480. As for the date of the wedding, it likely depended on when Frideswide's birthday was – given that her older sister Joan only married after her sixteenth birthday and her sister-in-law Anne only started living with Francis when she was sixteen, it seems very unlikely that Francis would have agreed to let Frideswide marry before she turned sixteen. Only her birth year is known, however, so this does not narrow down the possibilities. No details of the wedding are recorded, but with Francis an adult in all senses of the word in 1480, he was almost certainly the one who acted in the place of their father, giving away his sister.

Frideswide must have become pregnant within a year of her wedding, because at some point during 1481 she gave birth to her first child, a son called John. The child may have received the name in honour of Frideswide's father; she cannot have remembered him, and therefore likely did not share her siblings' disdain for him. Baby John may have also been named after his father Edward's grandfather or uncle, who were both named John as well, or after the Duke of Suffolk, who had been Frideswide's guardian for at least six years and perhaps until her marriage.

Francis surely would have wanted to have visit his new nephew, but it is possible he didn't get the chance as 1481, like 1477, proved to be a comparatively busy year for him, and one for which we have an uncommon wealth of evidence about Francis's activities.

As in the previous years, Francis spent the first part of 1481 struggling to receive possessions he considered his own, namely the manor of East Bridgeford, which was in the possession of William Wayneflete, Bishop of Winchester, who had purchased it from the heir of Francis's great-aunt, his paternal grandmother Alice Deincourt's sister.[17] Though it was not worth much, only around £11 per annum, it was clearly important to Francis to have it – so much so, in fact, that in June 1481 he sent an associate of his, one Sir Robert Markham, together with some men to take possession of it.[18]

They could make their entrance there without any difficulty or opposition. One of Wayneflete's men, Sir Gervais Clifton, who held the manor for the bishop, reported to Wayneflete that he did not wish to take action against Francis's men and make them leave, saying that 'considering he is a lorde, I may not soo deale.'[19]

It is perhaps telling that Sir Gervais had such reservations despite Francis's lack of importance in Edward's government at this point. It could point towards Francis having built personal relationships which would have made it difficult to go against him. Maybe the fact that he was now closely connected to Richard of Gloucester gave grounds for such a fear.

However, Sir Gervais clearly did not think that opposing Francis would be hopeless; he merely thought it would be unwise to do so directly, without an intermediary. He suggested Wayneflete take the matter to court and offered to build good connections to Edward IV's lord chamberlain, William, Lord Hastings, to ensure he would support them and influence Edward. It is interesting to note that Gervais feared Lord Hastings might support Francis instead of Wayneflete unless he cultivated connections, and points out that it would be best to seek the 'help of such others as ye shall easily have the good willes of, soo that my lord Chaumbreleyne take not the contrarie part'.[20] This suggests that Wayneflete, and by extension Sir Gervais, was not certain that the bishop's claim on the manor was definite or would appear so to others, though at least Sir Gervais seemed ready to fight for it.

Bishop Wayneflete wished to have the manor to annex it to Magdalen College at Oxford University,[21] but Francis's interest in the manor is unexplained. It must have been important to Francis, however, for he was unusually firm in his attempts to secure it. The dispute over East Bridgeford marked the only time he ever sent men to take possession of a manor after claiming it, with his usual preference being to deal with such matters through the courts.

There is no indication that Lord Hastings ever got involved, but the matter was to escalate further. Perhaps because he was angry at the resistance offered by Sir Gervais and Bishop Wayneflete, or perhaps because the bishop's other possessions had only been brought to his attention through this conflict, shortly after having sent men to take East Bridgeford Francis also laid claim to the manor of Doddington in Northampton,[22] which was worth slightly more than East Bridgeford, with an estimated annual income of £14.[23] This manor had belonged to his grandmother Alice Deincort, and Wayneflete claimed, probably correctly, that Alice had arranged for the manor to be assigned to Magdalen College after her death, in return for prayers to be said for her soul in a chantry at the college.[24] However, it appears that such an agreement was not put down in writing, making it easy for Francis to challenge it.

The matter would drag on for nearly two years after that, but it seems that no further action was taken, no more men sent or notable courtiers recruited. In the end, in early 1483, Francis and Wayneflete came to a peaceable compromise, apparently out of court and with no mediator mentioned.[25]

Perhaps the reason why Francis could not follow this argument further in the summer of 1481 was because he became involved, for the first time in his life, in armed conflict.

Francis at War

In the years before 1481, the always difficult and sometimes violent relations with England's northern neighbour worsened steadily, with each side raiding across the border, until Edward IV decided to solve matters by invading Scotland. Preparations were made by men of such high standing as his only remaining brother, Richard of Gloucester, and Lord Howard, later Duke of Norfolk. Edward himself intended to lead the invasion but eventually decided against it due to 'adverse turmoil',[26] instead leaving the campaigns to his brother Richard.

It speaks to Francis's standing that he was a part of the army when the campaign started in the summer of 1481, and probably brought some of his own men. As far as any later sources are concerned Francis still had a very low profile, but his presence indicates that he now held a certain significance, at least as a northern landholder. The campaign to invade Scotland was greeted with enthusiasm by the English population, and it is possible Francis shared in the feeling. However, in a letter written to William Stonor a year later, in which he mentions the continuation of the 1481 campaign, such enthusiasm is remarkably lacking.[27] Given his attitude in the letter, it is more likely that Francis saw his participation as a duty, not a privilege, from the first.

Whatever he felt about the campaign, it seems that he comported himself well during the actual fighting. Though the campaign of

1481 did not achieve much on either side, Francis was among those knighted by Richard of Gloucester towards the end of the year's military actions, on 22 August 1481.[28] Francis's brother-in-law Richard FitzHugh was also honoured,[29] but Francis was especially singled out for an honour, being granted permission to knight two fighters himself after receiving his knighthood. The men were William Hilton and Richard Ratcliffe,[30] and Francis would go on to work with them in Richard's government.

The reason for this special honour is not recorded. It could be that it was a reward for especially good fighting. It has been speculated that Francis may have saved Richard of Gloucester's life during the skirmishes, but none of these suggestions are contemporary. There is no indication from the time of any such thought, and even the rumour of such an act would probably have survived in the historical record. More likely, perhaps, is that Richard granted Francis the honour out of affection, a wish to single out his friend and give him something special. Whatever the cause, it is notable that we have no record of anybody disputing the honour or wishing Francis any ill will.

The 1481 campaign ended in autumn with little to show for it, and the unpleasant prospect of another year of fighting loomed. Francis, like many others, would have been expected to join again in the new year, and perhaps that thought hung over him when he returned home to his wife.

If so, it did not stop Francis from taking up his legal arguments again. In the winter of 1481, an argument he had with William Hastings over his grandfather John Beaumont's manors of Ashby-de-la-Zouche, Bagsworth, and Thornton, in Leicestershire, was decided against him; on 5 February 1482,[31] Francis quitclaimed (formally renounced) them to William Hastings, as well as some others. He clearly did not do this happily, and would carry a grudge about it for the next few years, which suggests that he was forced to do it, perhaps by the king's courts. Since there are no documents to suggest the matter was ever taken to court, however, it could also be that Francis was pressured or threatened, or forced into an unsatisfactory compromise.

Regardless of how he was compelled to quit his claims, Francis was powerless to do anything about the situation, and there is no indication he was vocal about his displeasure at the time. Nor is there any indication that this argument with one of the mightiest in the realm influenced his standing at court, or with Edward IV. Edward continued giving him small commissions, such as on 5 March 1482[32] when he was included in a commission of oyer and terminer in Yorkshire.

This appointment was probably more than nominal and Francis actually could have taken part, for he was in Yorkshire at that time and clearly had duties there. He was still there when summer came and the war with Scotland was about to begin again, as we know from a letter Francis wrote to William Stonor on 24 June 1482:

Cousin Stonor, I command me to you as heartily as I can, letting you have knowledge that I intended to have been with the King at the feast of Saint John Baptist now late passed, to have attended upon his good grace; but, cousin, it is said in this country the King purposes to send northwards my lord of Gloucester and my brother Parr and such other folk of worship as has any rule in the north parties, trusting we shall have war of the Scots, for cause whereof, and if I should now depart southwards it would be said I withdrew me for the said war. But, cousin, as hastily as I can make a convenient season I purpose to be in the country. And, cousin, I pray you that you will see that my game be well kept at Rotherfield. And our lord ever more have you in his keeping. From Tanfield, the 24th day of June.

Francis Lovell

To my cousin William Stonor, knight[33]

As dry as this letter is, it nonetheless reveals quite a lot about Francis, especially since it is the only declaration, in his own hand, of what he wished and intended to do. Though the language is rather distant and Francis does not explain to Stonor why he wishes to return to the south soon, it gives an insight into Francis's thoughts on the prospect of more war with Scotland. Francis's lack of delight when mentioning the campaign is notable. While he clearly knew it was his duty and had no intention of shirking it, he did not seem to look forward to it, instead mentioning his wish to return south as soon as possible, which seems to indicate that while Francis could and did fight when he had to, his focus lay on other things.

The letter also provides the only definite mention of any personal hobbies and enjoyments on Francis's part. While we can guess at other interests, this letter makes it very clear that hunting was something Francis enjoyed and which was on his mind even with war looming. Even at such a time, he thought of his game and went to the trouble of writing a letter to see to it that, in his own words, it was 'well kept'. In fact, while his words imply that there were other, more weighty reasons for him to want to return to his more southern possessions soon, this is the only concern he explicitly mentions, and quite possibly it is the reason he wrote the letter.

The letter is also interesting in that Francis makes it clear that he is ready to join the invasion of Scotland as he did the year before, yet makes no mention of the preparations made for the new campaign, despite the fact that his letter is dated twelve days after Richard of Gloucester was made Lieutenant-General of the North at Fotheringhay Castle and charged with leading the campaign against the Scottish,[34] and a good month after Richard first led an attack against the Scots.[35] This indicates that news was travelling slowly and Francis as yet had heard only rumours of the appointment, confirming that for some reason, despite his involvement in the previous year's campaign and full intention to join the one that was starting, Francis had not taken part in the first attack. Nor did he even seem to be informed of it, which is rather strange since he obviously anticipated the new campaign starting presently and expected to participate.

Why Francis was left in the dark is a mystery, but it is likely that his lack of knowledge is connected with his inability to travel south due to his fear of public opinion swinging against him. There are several reasons why he might have at that time been in the north of the country, but not all of them offer any explanation as to why he would miss such important news, significant both for him personally and for England, and why he could not travel to meet with the king, which he would surely not have delayed for trivial reasons.

Though, as mentioned above, Francis might have gone to the north in early 1482 to fulfil his duties on the commission of oyer and terminer, it does not seem likely this would have prevented him from meeting with the king. Even less likely is that such work would have in any way isolated him from all information and even gossip about what was happening in the rest of the country at that moment.

Equally, while Francis might have wanted to be in the north to await the birth of his sister Frideswide's second child, a son who was born at some point during the year 1482 and named Henry, perhaps after Frideswide's one-time guardian Henry FitzHugh, it seems unlikely that such an event would have so distracted him from all that was happening elsewhere that he would not have known of the campaign's commencement. Moreover, it would not have been unexpected and thus changed Francis's plans to see the king. While it is possible that his sister was at that time visiting his mother-in-law Alice FitzHugh and gave birth in her manor, it is not the obvious conclusion. That Francis wrote the letter to Stonor from his mother-in-law's manor of Tanfield suggests that he, and probably his wife Anne, had been visiting her when something happened that prevented Francis from hearing any news and stopped him from travelling as intended.

Most likely is that that Francis fell ill while staying with his mother-in-law. A serious illness would explain why Francis was unable to keep up with what was happening, and unable to travel to see the king. An illness might also be something which Francis was reluctant to tell Stonor about, which is why he only wrote that he could not attend the king on St John the Baptist's day;[36] he might have hoped in vain to be sufficiently recovered to make the journey before long.

If illness was the cause for Francis's prolonged stay in the north, he must have been on the road to recovery at that time for he soon became involved in the preparations for the planned invasion of Scotland. Given that the campaign started in early to mid-July, he most likely got involved within a week or two of his letter to Stonor. Perhaps Francis met Richard's army as it was marching north, joining them en route and bringing some men of his own.[37]

According to Wendy E. A. Moorhen in her article about this campaign, the army crossed the border in the middle of July. They laid siege to Berwick, which surrendered to the English army, though only partially – the citadel held out. Richard deputised Lord Stanley to remain at Berwick, marching on through Scotland mostly unopposed due to the infighting at the Scottish court. Not long after the English army crossed into Scotland, according to Moorhen, 'dissatisfied [Scottish] subjects had taken their king [James III] prisoner,'[38] which naturally put the advancing English army at a distinct advantage. James's captors, whose first concern was their own country and its dynastic troubles, agreed to come to terms with Richard, and Richard could take Edinburgh without a fight.

We do not know Francis's whereabouts during all this, but he originally joined the army as it marched towards Scotland and appears to have been present when Berwick was besieged. He was there with other men of high standing, such as Lord Howard, Henry Percy, Earl of Northumberland, and the queen's brother Edward Woodville, as well as some of slightly lesser standing – including, as Francis had anticipated in his letter to William Stonor, his wife's brother-in-law Sir William Parr.[39]

Apart from his presence in the very early part of the campaign, Francis is not mentioned in any relevant source, contemporary or otherwise. Naturally, it could be that he was not yet famous enough to warrant mention on presence alone, and his actions were not remarkable enough to attract comment. However, this is somewhat contradicted by Francis's expectation that his presence would be required and that failure to take part would reflect badly on him. If he was still so minor that his presence wasn't worth recording, such a fear would have been illogical.

In the light of this, it is more likely that Francis was no longer present after the siege of Berwick. Historian Joanna Williams has pointed out that on 10 August 1482 Francis was 'among the lessors of the manor of Remenham, Berkshire, to Thomas Lovell for twenty years, to the use of Edmund Mountfort, knight',[40] and that this might indicate Francis had returned south by this point.

This supposition would explain Francis's absence from sources about the 1482 campaign. Naturally, the details of such a business transaction would have been handled by lawyers and not the key men involved, and Francis's presence would have been neither required nor expected. However, it is almost certain that he would have been consulted about it before any decisions were made final, even if he had made his wishes known beforehand, which suggests that either the final agreement was made before Francis joined Richard's army bound for Scotland, and was then delayed for several weeks, or that Francis had already returned in time to give the go-ahead.

Since the paperwork for the transaction is, according to Williams, in the Westminster Abbey Muniments,[41] it was therefore in all likelihood completed somewhere in the south or middle of England; given that Francis implied in his letter to Stonor that he had been in the north of the country for a while before the campaign, Williams's speculation is most likely correct, and Francis was no longer with Richard and the rest of the army in Scotland. In fact, Francis's desire to finish this transaction, and possibly other similar ones we no longer know about, could have been the reason he wanted to come south in the first place.

If this is true, and Francis did leave the campaign so soon after the first proper engagement at the siege of Berwick, we must ask why he was allowed to go. He could not have simply left without good reason, and such a transaction would not have justified his departure. Since Francis had explicitly mentioned staying in the north to do his duty and fight, it is unlikely he would have seen a property transaction as reason enough to abandon the field. Nor is it likely that he would have been allowed to do so. Moreover, given that Francis had expressed a fear of being thought to 'withdraw [himself] from the war' if he left, even before he was aware the war had even properly begun, he would not have thought of leaving in the middle of the campaign for personal reasons that could easily be postponed.

Added to this is the fact that not half a year later Edward IV granted Francis the signal honour of elevation to a viscountcy, an honour he bestowed on just one other man during his reign. Although it is probable that Richard of Gloucester's influence on his brother had a lot to do with this, it is exceedingly unlikely that Edward would have obliged him in this if the man in question had chosen to place his own concerns over the king's martial ambitions. Equally, if a man had been so elevated after quitting the field for what would have been regarded as selfish reasons, the news would have spread and drawn negative comment; in fact, the honour appears to have been accepted without comment or even complaint in the capital, which at the time of Francis's elevation was still agog with news from Scotland.[42]

If Francis genuinely was back in the south by 10 August 1482, then, it is likely he left Richard's army and company because he was physically unable to stay any longer. One possibility is that he sustained a minor injury during the campaign, for example when first laying siege to Berwick, or in a smaller skirmish on the way there. This could have rendered him unable to fight for some time, for example if it was on his fighting arm or a leg, making him a liability for the ride through Scotland, but well enough to journey home. Another possibility is that Francis, likely having been ill before the campaign started, was actually still too unwell to handle the strain of sustained campaigning and had to leave for that reason.

Both these scenarios could explain Edward's decision to honour Francis in January 1483, as at the time the whole capital, and even Parliament, was singing Richard's praises for his successful campaign. Rewarding a friend of his who had been involved in the campaign and had moreover sustained an injury, or else fought despite fragile health, would have been a popular move, and gave Edward the chance to please his younger brother without having to make any kind of sacrifice.

8

'Visconte Lovell, sieur de Holland, de Burnell, Deygnecort et de Grey de Rotherfilde'

Whatever his exact actions during the Scottish campaigns, and whatever his motivations, it seems that the engagement marked Francis's arrival as a figure of some consequence in Edward IV's court. On 15 November 1482[1] Francis received his first summons to Parliament, which was to convene in January 1483. He was also invited to spend Christmas at court, apparently for the first time. Francis accepted the invitation, and it was at court, on 4 January 1483,[2] that he was elevated to a viscountcy.

As mentioned above, Francis was one of only two men so honoured in Edward IV's reign – the other being William, Lord Berkeley in 1481 – and so the appointment may have come as a surprise to many, perhaps even to Francis himself. This was especially so considering Francis had rarely been involved in politics up to this point, being given only the most innocuous tasks, and had also generally been disadvantaged by all decisions made by the king or the king's men about possessions he laid a claim to. Francis may well have been astonished by the sudden preferment.

While it is likely that Richard persuaded his brother by explaining Francis's merits, we do not know why he chose to do so. Given Francis's lack of involvement in politics and Richard's fondness for him, it may have been a personal matter. However, it is rather unlikely that Edward would have agreed to honour Francis simply because his brother liked him, and it is a safe assumption that

Richard had some arguments to persuade him beyond the man's involvement on campaign in Scotland.

After Richard's success in Scotland, and in light of his growing popularity, Edward would have most likely been happy to oblige his brother and elevate Francis, especially since a viscountcy did not come with any lands or privileges that Edward would have needed to give up. In fact, this might be why Edward created a new viscountcy for Francis rather than simply creating him Viscount Beaumont, a title which had been taken from Francis's maternal uncle William by attainder in 1471[3] – incidentally in the same parliament that passed an attainder against the fourteen-year-old Henry Tudor and stripped him of his earldom of Richmond.[4]

Though the Beaumont viscountcy had not been granted to anyone else since William's attainder had been passed, granting it to Francis might have caused some difficulties, as Francis could have used it to argue for his right to hold certain ancestral Beaumont lands which had fallen to the Crown together with the viscountcy. Such complications could have been avoided by putting conditions on any grant of the Beaumont viscountcy, but creating a new viscountcy was the easiest course of action, with the certainty that no pitfalls remained; a fresh start.

Francis must have been informed of the upcoming elevation beforehand in order to prepare. It was without doubt a special occasion for him, though the actual ceremony appears to have been relatively low-key. A good description of it is found in the Additional Manuscripts of the British Library and is summed up as follows by Williams:

> The ceremony began with his entering the King's great chamber, dressed in his parliament robes, led between his cousin, Lord Morley, and his brother-in-law, Richard, Lord FitzHugh [his sponsors]. His patent was read aloud by the King's secretary, and he proceeded to his chamber accompanied by the sound of trumpets. There he distributed fees to the 'officers of arms' and his titles were recited in the hall – 'puissant et noble visconte Lovell, sieur de Holland, de Burnell, Deygnecort et de Grey de Rotherfilde'.[5]

That his brother-in-law and his young cousin, then around fifteen years old, were present, and even acted as his sponsors, certainly speaks to the fact that Francis had a cordial relationship with them. They were clearly ready and willing to support him, and happy for him to receive such an honour. Especially in the case of Richard FitzHugh, this is significant, for he was closely related to Edward IV, being his first cousin once removed, and had been involved in the Scottish campaigns of the previous two years. It would have been understandable if FitzHugh had been angry that he was not the one to receive this distinction, but instead he supported his brother-in-law.

Though we do not know FitzHugh's private feelings, he was at least prepared to put on a public show of support for Francis. Perhaps this was done out of affection, or in the hope that Francis's sudden rise might profit him as well. Perhaps it was done out of affection not for Francis himself but for his wife Anne, Richard's younger sister, who naturally became a viscountess when her husband became a viscount.

How Francis himself reacted to the honour is unrecorded. In fact, contemporary sources only state the bare fact of his elevation, without even adding any speculations as to why it occurred. Once more, it is a matter of speculation as to whether he was expecting the recognition or rather was taken aback. There is also no indication what impression he made on others during the ceremony and his time at Edward's court over Christmas. Most likely, despite his elevation, he made no special impact on anyone there.

There is an obvious explanation for the lack of fanfare accompanying Francis's appointment. At any other time in Edward's reign there might have been comments on the sudden promotion, but in late 1482 there were more weighty matters of state for chroniclers and courtiers alike to consider. On Christmas Eve of that year that Edward IV learnt that Louis XI had gone against the Treaty of Picquigny, which they had negotiated in 1475, and had chosen to ally his kingdom with Burgundy.[6] This was a devastating blow for English foreign policy, as it meant that Princess Elizabeth would not marry the French Dauphin and thereby create an alliance between the two countries as had been planned for seven years. It was also a blow for Edward himself and all those nobles who had received an annuity from France since 1475.

It is hardly surprising that this development occupied everyone's thoughts during Christmas 1482, leaving little room for anything else; there was certainly no chance of any detailed discussion on a politically insignificant baron's elevation to a viscountcy. What is surprising, however, is that even in later years, with the benefit of hindsight, still nobody attached any significance to this move. This was the start of Francis Lovell's rise.

Francis perhaps regarded this elevation as a stepping stone towards more importance, and also more grants from the king. Following the Christmas festivities and his elevation, Francis attended Parliament for the first time, and on 20 January 1483[7] was appointed a trier of petitions for England, which might have been understood as an attempt, at long last, to involve Francis, now twenty-six, in the affairs of the country.

However, elevation and inclusion in at least a small part of government work did not mean that Francis was in any way singled out by Edward IV for favour at that point. Indeed, less than a month after he made Francis a viscount, Edward saw to it that Parliament granted to Richard Grey the manors he had feuded over with Francis,[8] though it was Richard's older brother Thomas who took possession of several of them, most notably Thorpe Waterville[9] in Northamptonshire (now under the jursidiction of the impressively entitled parish council of Lilford-cum-Wigsthorpe and Thorpe Achurch).

Despite Edward's actions showing that Francis was still no unimpeachable favourite, and that at least where possessions were concerned the tide had not turned, Bishop William Wayneflete appeared to fear that Francis might gain yet more favour, accumulating greater influence at court. He now determined to solve the conflict over East Bridgeford and Doddington in which the pair had been embroiled for the last two years.

Francis was either uncertain of his privilege or felt it only put him on an even footing with Wayneflete. That, or he was open to compromise. Whatever the case, in February 1483, he and Wayneflete solved their long-standing conflict in a way that was satisfactory for both parties. Wayneflete was to keep East

Bridgeford for Magdalen College while conveying to Francis the manor of Doddington.[10] Though this meant that Francis got a slight fiscal advantage, as Doddington was worth a few pounds more per year, this was likely balanced out by the terms of the agreement, which required Francis to convey a chantry at Wansborough to Wayneflete and the college.[11]

This solution pleased everybody. The men were probably glad to have solved an argument in a satisfactory way for all involved. No hard feelings appear to have persisted between them, and they would do business together in the future. Francis also appears to have taken an interest in the college through the conflict with the bishop, as he also agreed to sponsor a scholar at the college.[12] This does not appear to have been a part of the deal struck in the property dispute, and did not profit either of them, meaning it was Francis's own choice, made out of genuine interest in the college or a desire to support scholarship. There is no indication Francis had held such an interest before his conflict with Bishop Wayneflete started, but it was not a passing fancy. Later in his career there are indications he continued to take an interest in universities, suggesting the unpleasant quarrel had some happy consequences.

It is possible that Francis would have quietly followed this new interest in the years to come, perhaps using his newly elevated status to support learning. On a less pleasant note, it is almost certain, given his dogged efforts to recoup his properties thus far, that he would have tried to use his newfound influence to solve several other such conflicts in his favour as well. However, before he could act on these considerations, such petty matters were thrown into disarray. The king, Edward IV, died suddenly at the age of forty.

9

'Our entierly beloved cousin'

Edward IV's death on 9 April 1483 appears to have come abruptly, with no more than a week's warning. Just what killed him is still not agreed upon by historians, but it seems that he became sick after a fishing trip on the River Thames and did not recover, dying after about a week of illness.[1]

Physicians of the time could not diagnose his illness, which naturally caused many rumours. Though most seemed to agree that he died as a result of a lifestyle too rich in food and drink,[2] there were other theories. In France it was rumoured that sorrow about the recent revocation of the Treaty of Picquigny had given him a heart attack,[3] while in England rumours of poison circulated.[4]

Whatever caused it, Edward's death left England's ruling elite in turmoil. Edward's second reign had seen the establishment of different factions at court, all opposed to each other and all dependent on Edward. It has been suggested that, like his great-granddaughter Elizabeth I after him, Edward encouraged this adversarial atmosphere at court, wanting his courtiers to know that they could depend only on him.[5]

Whether or not this was true, it seems that just before his death Edward expressed regret over the state of the government. According to tradition, this is why his choice for Lord Protector was his brother Richard, who had not spent much time at his court in recent years and was therefore not involved with either faction.[6] He is also alleged to have asked the leaders of the two most prominent factions, his lord chamberlain Lord William Hastings and his stepson Thomas Grey, to shake hands and promise to let bygones be bygones.[7] Even if this happened, the enforced goodwill did not long survive Edward.

There are many differing accounts of what happened next, though it appears that queen dowager Elizabeth Woodville's family took over the government immediately after Edward's death.[8] It also seems that the queen dowager herself neglected to inform Richard of Gloucester of his brother's death,[9] and this act, whether oversight or deliberate slight, was in part responsible for setting in motion what would happen next. William Hastings, who did not agree with the Woodville family's actions, was the one who informed Richard that his brother was dead and that he had been named Lord Protector in his brother's will.[10] In response to this, Richard made preparations to go to London, together with a retinue of some three hundred men, and to meet up on his way there with the new young king, Edward V, who was coming to London from Ludlow, where he and his household had been based since he was nearly three years old.[11] Also meeting them was Harry, Duke of Buckingham, grandson of the duke who had fought and died alongside John Beaumont, a man who despite his royal blood had not played a major role in Edward's government.

Francis does not seem to have been involved in any of these preparations, either in London or in the north of England. Though he had been in or near London attending Parliament until 20 February 1483, he does not seem to have stayed in his townhouse in the city afterwards, nor in any of his possessions near the capital. Perhaps he returned to his ancestral manor of Minster Lovell Hall, or went to visit a relative. Since he was not noted to have attended Edward's funeral on 19 April,[12] it is most likely he was not in the south; if he was, he would have had time to make it to the funeral.

Francis was not the only one to miss Edward's funeral, of course; Edward's brother Richard of Gloucester had not yet arrived in London, nor his son and heir Edward, and it does not seem as if events were delayed to await their arrival.[13] It is sometimes assumed that Francis arrived in London with them, having joined Richard on his progress south,[14] but there is no evidence of this. He was not mentioned in any of the sources detailing what happened between Richard and the Woodville faction, and no one appears to have thought he had any role in events. In a time rife with gossip and suspicion, this suggests that he did not.

We do not know when Francis learnt of Edward IV's death or when he arrived in London, save to say that he must have reached the capital after Edward's funeral. Perhaps he was already in London when reports reached the capital that Richard, having met up with his nephew Edward V's retinue, had ordered the arrests of his maternal uncle Anthony Woodville, Earl Rivers, the king's half-brother Richard Grey and his chamberlain Thomas Vaughan.[15]

In the writings of Dominic Mancini we have a decent impression of the rumours circulating in he capital. Though he only finished his report in December 1483 after having left England, and though he depended on the translations of others, the rumours he records sound like plausible, and are partly corroborated by other sources such as the *Great Chronicle of London*.

According to Mancini, Richard of Gloucester and Harry, Duke of Buckingham, met in Northampton, where they had arranged to meet the young king as well. Upon arriving there, however, they were only met by Earl Rivers, who informed them that the young king and the rest of his retinue had ridden ahead to Stony Stratford, some 16 miles closer to London, owing to lack of accommodation in Northampton.[16] Having ostensibly accepted this news, Richard and Harry nonetheless grew suspicious the following night. They had Rivers put under arrest in his guesthouse, then rode to Stony Stratford at dawn. Arriving there, they met the young king Edward V and his retinue, together with two thousand armed men, in the process of leaving towards London. Richard put a stop to this by informing the young king of the arrest of his maternal uncle and then arresting Thomas Vaughan and Richard Grey as well, before dismissing the two thousand men.[17] Mancini adds some extra details and flourishes to this story, mentioning a speech Edward V is supposed to have given in defence of his men, which makes for a good story but cannot possibly be confirmed.

If Francis was already in London when these stories started to spread, he would have had an opinion on them. Being close to Richard, he probably would have questioned the truth of the rumours, which made it look like Richard and Harry acted without much provocation. Sadly, Mancini does not give us any alternative takes on what happened, but certainly they would have existed, and Francis would likely have been inclined to more favourable interpretations. He, and others, might well have asked why not only King Edward V but all his retinue claimed that Northampton was too small to accommodate his army. This was a town big enough to have held both St George's Festival and a parliament at the same time in 1380, a town which had seen big events such as the trial of Thomas Becket in the twelfth century and where many nobles, including Francis himself, had townhouses. Francis might have also wondered why Edward V and his men were already leaving *at dawn* when Richard and Harry arrived, apparently without having tried waiting for them, if their only concern had been the matter of accommodation.

Moreover, Francis and the others might have felt it was important to know why Edward V was accompanied by an army two thousand strong. William Hastings certainly appeared to consider this an urgent issue, and is said to have insisted earlier that the retinue be no larger, supposedly thwarting a plan by the queen to bring five thousand men by threatening to oppose such a cause and to go to Calais with his men if it occurred.[18]

Perhaps, however, there was not much time for contemplation of such rumours, in light of events unfolding in the capital. Upon the news that Earl Rivers, Richard Grey and Thomas Vaughan had been arrested and sent to different manors in the north, the dowager queen fled to sanctuary at Westminster with her oldest son, Thomas Grey, her youngest son, Richard of Shrewsbury, and her five daughters Elizabeth, Cecily, Anne, Katherine and Bridget. Mancini, whose report is as hostile to the Woodville faction as it is to Richard of Gloucester,[19] claims that she took as much finery, jewellery and money with her as she could. There is no way to verify this, but it has been repeated over the centuries by various writers with differing biases, and was notably dramatised by Thomas More, who rather implausibly claimed that a wall had to be knocked down in order to transport all her possessions to the abbey.[20]

Having had some unpleasant interactions with the dowager queen's sons Thomas and Richard Grey over the possession of some manors, Francis might have been more willing to believe such rumours about the Woodvilles, and to endorse any views which cast them as the villains rather than Richard. Edward Woodville, who had fought alongside Richard and Francis on the Scottish border less than a year ago, was soon made captain of the fleet of England and left London to command the fleet in the English Channel around this time, and Francis likely found it easy to believe the story that the Woodville man took large parts of the treasury with him when he left.[21]

Francis was almost certainly present in the capital when Edward V and his uncle arrived in London. He must have been there – albeit beneath the notice of chroniclers – when the regency council led by Richard as Lord Protector took up its work afterwards.[22] Most likely he personally witnessed the new king's arrival. The retinue arrived to bells tolling all over the town, riding through London before being greeted by the city aldermen together with William Hastings. Though everything was done to make this a joyous occasion, two circumstances would have doubtlessly blighted proceedings. The first of these was the fact that the king's mother was still in sanctuary with his siblings and could not greet him, a glaring absence even to a casual observer; understandably, the young king is said to have been upset about this.[23] The second dampener on festivities was the presence behind the king's retinue of two carts of weapons bearing the Woodville coat of arms, accompanied by several men tasked with showing them off to the citizens of London and announcing that they had been confiscated from Earl Rivers, Richard Grey and Thomas Vaughan and had been intended for use against Richard and Harry.[24]

Francis might have believed this was true. Alternatively, he might not have cared whether it was or not, merely being happy to see the Woodvilles defeated. In the latter case, he would not have been alone; William Hastings is recorded to have been content about how things had turned out, 'with only so much bloodshed in the affair as might have come from a cut finger.'[25]

Some thought otherwise. Mancini reported claims – which he clearly believed – that the weapons on display had been stockpiled near London for use against the Scots in the coming campaign.[26] While, as Annette Carson points out, it seems somewhat unlikely that weapons for such a purpose would be stockpiled so far from Scotland – a fact that Mancini, not well acquainted with England's geography, might have missed – this dissenting notion must have been popular if it reached Mancini's ears.[27]

Favours from the Lord Protector

If Dominic Mancini is to be believed, the regency council began work shortly after the king's arrival in London and Richard's confirmation as Lord Protector. He reports rumours that Richard wished to have Rivers, Grey and Vaughan executed for treason when he arrested them at Northampton but was overruled because he did not hold the position of Lord Protector at that point.[28] Mancini was not present at the council meetings, so there can be no telling if his account is accurate. Nonetheless, it is interesting to note that in the version he reports, the version that must have been rumoured in London at the time, the council did not overrule Richard because of the three men's innocence but rather on a mere technicality.

Whatever disagreements took place, the regency council appears to have been set up in a reasonably untroubled manner. There is no comprehensive list of members but we do know of some definite inclusions: William Hastings; Harry, Duke of Buckingham; John Morton, Bishop of Ely; John, Lord Howard; and Thomas Stanley.[29] Francis may have been a member too, but on balance it seems rather unlikely. He had not been important enough, politically or personally, to merit a place on the council in Edward's reign, and he had not recommended himself by his actions after Edward's death as Harry of Buckingham had. He does not appear in any of the contemporary or quasi-contemporary sources about the council's actions and decisions.

Even so, Francis soon profited from Richard's rise to power. As Joanna Williams points out, the regency council appointed Francis to several commissions of peace despite him having only served on such a commission once before. His first new commissions were for the East Riding of Yorkshire and for Northamptonshire, and date as far back as 14 May,[30] just ten days after Richard and the young king arrived in the capital. Much like his few appointments under Edward IV, these placements appear to have been nominal, and he could not possibly have actively worked for both of them. The fact that over May and June he was appointed to nine commissions of peace – twice for Northamptonshire, East Riding and Bedfordshire and once in Oxfordshire, Berkshire and Essex – reinforces the idea that these appointments were symbolic rather than practical.[31]

Francis's increasing prominence under Richard's regency council was not only reflected in this sudden flood of appointments. As early as 19 May he was given the imprisoned Anthony Woodville's job as chief butler,[32] and two days later he was given the 'Rule & Keping' of the manor of Thorpe Waterville and 'alle the Landes & tenements belonging to the same',[33] which in Edward IV's last parliament had been granted to Richard Grey, and about which Francis had been in conflict with Grey for the last few years.

Both these grants were due to Richard's influence. In fact, the grant passed for Thorpe Waterville was in the names of both Richard and the king, rather than being signed by Richard in the name of the king. As was standard for such grants, Francis is called Richard's 'entierly beloved cousin', and the displeasure of both the duke and the king is threatened should anyone not recognise Francis as the owner and lord of the property.[34] This suggests that Richard took a personal interest in the matter, though it was unlikely to have been motivated by personal affection alone. Presumably this action was rooted as much in a desire to weaken the Woodville faction as in a desire to see Francis regain a manor he considered rightfully his.

Putting aside Richard's personal influence, however, the very fact that young Edward V signed this grant, and was formally responsible for choosing Francis as his uncle Anthony's replacement as chief butler, means these decisions would have been discussed by the council. While young Edward presumably had little say in what was decided, the regency council would not have simply agreed to everything Richard wanted. They would have definitely protested against inordinate favour shown to somebody relatively unknown to the members of the council, suggesting that Francis was introduced.

Richard may have trusted Francis implicitly, but it is unlikely most of the council would have agreed to bestow a government role and a grant of land on a new viscount who had previously made little, if any, impact on Edward IV's reign, especially if he didn't come to the capital to make himself known. On the other hand, the grants to Francis also reinforce the idea that he was not a member of the council, and uninvolved in the quarrels among the developing factions at court: it would have surely caused trouble if somebody considered a partisan member of Richard's entourage had received such large grants while relative opponents were not so favoured.

In the light of these grants, though, Francis's complete absence from any report of what went on in London during May and June is fascinating. There is no indication he was in any way involved in anything controversial, which sets him apart from almost everybody else of standing who was present at the time. Even if Francis's relative obscurity at the time allowed him to escape scrutiny, hostile sources from later years could easily have re-examined his importance in Richard's reign and called him to account.

In fact, this is what happened to both Sir Richard Ratcliffe and William Catesby, who were of far lesser standing than Francis and became important in Richard's ascendancy. These two men are later recorded in the Croyland Chronicle as fearing retribution for their actions against the Woodvilles. Meanwhile, no source, whether sympathetic contemporary record or deeply hostile later account, ever mentioned Francis as involved in any of the plotting and counterplotting that was rife in London in the summer of 1483. There is no mention of him in connection with the quarrels of the different factions that started to form as time went on, despite the evident benefits he accrued through the Woodvilles' downfall and Richard's rise.

A letter from Richard to the City of York dating from 5 June 1483 gives the impression that the regency council's government is running smoothly after initial difficulties. This is supported by the setting of a date for Edward V's coronation[35] and the fact that all the vacancies caused by the arrest of Anthony Woodville had been filled. There were still issues to be addressed; most notably, the dowager queen was still in sanctuary together with the king's siblings, having refused to come out even if an oath was sworn to her and her children's safety. Nevertheless, the most immediate concerns had been addressed.

Richard himself was feeling confident at this time. Not only did he show no sign of apprehension in his letter to the City of York, but he also sent for his wife, Anne Neville, to join him in London, probably in anticipation of his nephew's upcoming coronation. She arrived on 8 June.[36] Perhaps Francis also sent for his wife around this time. It has been claimed that her mother Alice FitzHugh was present and supported Richard during the crisis that would unfold soon after Anne Neville's arrival in the capital, which might mean that Anne Lovell was present as well. Since she appears to have been close to her mother, it is reasonable to suggest that she would have arrived in the capital with Alice FitzHugh if she hadn't already joined Francis by that time.

It was surely intended that Anne Neville only arrive in the capital after things had settled down and the regency council had bedded in, but a new crisis was looming. Whether or not Richard engineered it has been a matter of dispute for historians down through the centuries. If it was Richard's doing, Francis would have certainly been complicit, though once again he has no mention in the sources, spared one even by those hostile to Richard. Even if Richard was blameless, however, Francis would still have been close to the centre of the controversy, in a position to observe Richard and possibly even advise him.

It is a great shame that no personal letters or documents belonging to Francis survive from that time, as his close friendship with Richard would have given him a unique perspective on events, and anything he wrote about the coming crisis would be illuminating about both him and Richard. As it is, we are once more forced to deduce his actions, or lack thereof, from objective – but indirect and impersonal – evidence.

The Invisible Courtier

The succession crisis of 1483 has been covered by a multitude of sources, histories, chronicles and assessments. Despite this, there is no consensus on what exactly occurred, how it came about and who was involved. Only some facts can be definitely ascertained.

What is a fact is that on 9 June 1483 something unusual appears to have happened in the regency council. A letter from one Simon Stallworth to William Stonor dated to that day suggests as much:

'My lord protector [Richard], my lord of Bukyngham with all othyr lordys, as well temporale as spirituale were at Westm [Westminster] in the councel chambre from x to ii, but there wass none that spake with the Qwene.' Rather intriguingly, he added that '[t]here is gret besyness ageyns the coronacion, wyche schalbe this day fortnyght as we say.'[37]

It has often been assumed that what caused tempers to flare was Richard's claim that the late king had signed a marriage precontract with one Eleanor Butler before his marriage to Elizabeth Woodville, and that this rendered his marriage illegitimate, disinheriting her issue and thus making young Edward ineligible for the throne. This conundrum was supposedly put before *all* the lords spiritual and temporal present in London, not just the council. It is clear that Stallworth considered it notable that lords from *outside* the council were present to discuss the matter for four hours. That Stallworth immediately follows this observation with a reference to 'great business against the coronation', and moreover thinks it worth stating that 'none […] spake with the queen',[38] supports the notion that the precontract was discussed not only by the council but all lords spiritual and temporal in London.

Francis must have been present at this meeting, and it would be interesting to note what he thought of the revelations. It is certainly possible he was already aware of the news, having been informed by Richard when the precontract was either discovered or invented. If Francis did support Richard in his claim, working or even speaking in his favour at this meeting, no traces have survived to prove it. In fact, except Stallworth's words that 'all other lordes' were present, there is no indication Francis was even present. As Williams points out, it is quite possible that Francis acted for Richard 'behind the scenes'.[39] If so, he did a very good job of avoiding exposure. As we already know that he was more generally inclined to discretion, this is not hard to believe.

Of course, one could just as easily make the argument that Francis was not a man to involve himself in politics, that even in his time as Richard's closest friend he showed little interest in the intricacies of state affairs. Perhaps he stayed out of it entirely, simply observing events. The idea that he was involved and worked for Richard rests solely on the fact that Richard had already shown, and would go on to show, complete trust in Francis. Given this trust it would make sense for him to want Francis, who was also a political lightweight with very few enemies, to argue his case for him.

On the other hand, his very insignificance and inexperience could easily have worked against him, as his word might not have counted for much against men like William Hastings and John Howard, who were veterans not only of high politics but of battles in which they had fought for Edward IV. Moreover, the last month's grants and appointments would have made it clear to everyone that Francis was Richard's man, so he might not have seemed as unbiased as this argument presupposes.

All in all, it is most likely that Francis, while present, did nothing to draw the attention of chroniclers or later historians. His later actions make it clear that he supported Richard, but there is no evidence that he did so openly at this point. Nonetheless, Richard would continue to favour him after these difficulties passed.

Naturally, the revelation of the precontract, whether or not it occurred during the meeting on 9 June, caused quite a stir. It is safe to assume that the meeting following the announcement was not entirely friendly. Whatever was said, Richard was clearly alarmed. On 10 June, he wrote a rather hectic letter to York, addressed to 'the mayor, aldermen and commons' and asking them to send men, 'as many as ye can defensibly arrayed'.[40] He states that they are to 'aid and assist us against the Queen, her blood adherents and affinity, which have intended, and daily doth intend, to murder and utterly destroy us and our cousin the duke of Buckingham, and the old royal blood of this realm, and as it is now openly known, by their subtle and damnable ways forecasted the same'.[41]

Richard does not state how the queen 'and her adherents' are going about their designs, nor does he explain who else is meant by 'the old royal blood of the realm'. After some more generic accusations – the queen intends to destroy the lives and livelihoods of all honest men – he then writes that he entrusts the details of these accusations to the messenger, and entreats the receivers to believe him and 'haste you to us hither.'

Whatever one thinks of Richard, and the revelation of the precontract, it is hard to deny that this letter conveys some real fear. This impression is strengthened by the fact that a day later, on 11 June, Richard wrote an even more frantic letter to Lord Neville, asking him to come to his help, 'defensibly arrayed'. In this letter he includes no explanation, instead asking Neville to believe Sir Richard Ratcliffe, 'this bearer'.[42]

Even if one is sceptical about Richard and his claim that he was in danger, the idea that the situation had suddenly become fraught and dangerous is corroborated in sources hostile to Richard. The *Great Chronicle of London* hints at plotting among the members of the council,[43] and even Thomas More suggests that several men, including Thomas Stanley and William Hastings, were meeting to discuss how they intended to move against Richard of Gloucester.[44]

Francis, once more, appears to have stayed out of the drama, more a spectator than an active participant. He does not seem to have sent for any troops of his own to come to London to aid Richard in the sudden crisis, nor does he seem to have had any men with him. Unlike John Howard,[45] Francis could offer no armed assistance to Richard, nor did he ever show a talent for military matters. It may well be that this was the reason he kept a low profile – he would not have wanted to become involved in any trouble he was ill-equipped to meet.

He was almost certainly absent when the situation in the capital escalated on 13 June at a meeting of the regency council in the Tower of London. Myths about this meeting began to develop practically from the day it happened, and the truth is very hard to ascertain. Town criers instructed by the Lord Protector stated that several of the council, chief among them William Hastings and John Morton, Bishop of Ely, had plotted against Richard and Buckingham and intended to kill them. For that purpose they are supposed to have smuggled weapons into the meeting. However, Richard had been warned of their intentions and confronted the conspirators about the plot during the council meeting, accusing Hastings of having been in contact with the dowager queen in sanctuary and having plotted with her via his mistress Elizabeth Shore. William Hastings was said to have lunged at Richard upon hearing this but was prevented and subsequently arrested by troops lent to Richard by John Howard. While some of the supposed plotters were soon released, notably the Bishop of Ely, Hastings was immediately sentenced to death and executed.[46]

The summary execution of Hastings has, perhaps naturally, overshadowed the events preceding it, monopolising all discussions about the meeting at the Tower. Often it is assumed that the very fact Hastings was so quickly executed means that the charges against him were fabricated.[47] However, not all historians share this opinion,[48] and nor did all contemporary observers. Mancini, in his report, states that news of the execution caused much worry and turmoil in the city before town criers were sent to explain the matter and reassure the people. Though Mancini then adds that 'the truth was on the lips of many,'[49] he does not justify his position, instead seeming to simply assume that all explanations offered by the Lord Protector were excuses. It is clear that many agreed with Mancini, but not everyone did. Moreover, it is notable that he admits the explanation effectively dispelled the panic in the city.

It has been argued in Richard's favour that the execution was prefaced by a short trial over which he presided. This argument is presented in Annette Carson's book *Richard Duke of Gloucester as Lord Protector and Hugh Constable*, in which it is claimed that the latter post gave Richard the right to have individuals tried immediately before a court of peers – which the regency council were – and, if a death sentence was passed, to execute any guilty party immediately.[50]

As the author Matthew Lewis notes in his biography on Richard, this does not in any way argue for the *morality* of this action, nor prove the truth of the accusations against Hastings, but it does show that the execution, for centuries decried as unlawful, was not in fact so.[51] This is supported by Mancini stating that evidence was shown to the city fathers.

The involvement of the regency council in the execution suggests that many, if not most, agreed with Richard's actions, or at least were prepared to support him. John and Thomas Howard, being heavily involved in the arrests of the alleged rebels, are mentioned in sources, but Francis is absent once more. Not only does he seem to have missed the infamous meeting itself, and with it Hastings' short trial, he also appears to have steered clear of the fallout, such as the trials and executions of the Earl Rivers, Richard Grey and Thomas Vaughan.[52] No source, not even dry and unbiased lists of expenses, so much as mentions Francis until 28 June 1483.

With Hastings' execution and the removal of those hostile to Richard from the regency council, Richard's way to the throne was clear. Depending on how one reads the evidence, Richard either removed men trying to stop him from wrongfully taking the throne from his young nephew or ousted plotters trying to stop him from taking his rightful place as king. Even now there is no consensus, and there was definitely no consensus at the time.

Francis firmly supported Richard, and given their closeness it seems likely he knew whether or not the precontract was real. Whatever the case, Francis clearly did not waver in his decision to support his friend. It is quite likely that he was present when Richard, in the following days, showed himself to the Londoners in increasingly regal attire, which Mancini interpreted as an attempt to prepare the Londoners for his eventual bid for the throne.[53]

Maybe Francis was also present when, on 23 June, Dr Ralph Shaa preached a sermon in London on the subject that 'Bastard slips shall take no root,'[54] informing passers-by of the precontract that rendered Edward V illegitimate and therefore made his uncle Richard the rightful king. If Francis was present he was likely there to gauge the mood, not to hear what the man had to say, as he would have already known what the preacher told the crowds. Perhaps he was also one of the men whom Richard, with the help of Harry of Buckingham, supposedly planted among the crowd to cheer for him. The latter story is not contemporary, however, and sounds like a later invention to ridicule Richard's claim to the throne.[55]

While Francis clearly kept a low profile during the succession crisis, with only his grants and appointments to tell us he was even present in London at the time, it is hard to believe he would have missed the events which set Richard on the path to the throne – events like Shaa's sermon and, later, the official delegation arriving at Crosby Place to formally ask Richard to accept the crown. Though Harry of Buckingham is the only named attendant in most reports,[56] Francis would have been among the many unnamed supporters who were said to have been present. If he genuinely was not present then, nor at any other important meetings during the succession crisis, it begs the question as to why no chronicler so much as expressed surprise at Francis's sudden rise once Richard became king. An explanation as to Francis's whereabouts is unlikely ever to be found. However, the fact that he was so well rewarded while remaining so uncontroversial in the historical record certainly reveals a lot about the man who was about to rise to unexpected heights in the summer of 1483.

The Question of Francis's Health

Even in 1483, when presented with opportunities to take a hand in shaping the future of the kingdom, Francis was not a man eager to make an impact. On the contrary, he seems to have been so wary of publicity that he opted for obscurity instead; or, alternatively, he was in some other way hindered.

Perhaps the latter is more likely, as throughout his life Francis, though shy and evasive, didn't let his reserved nature prevent him from doing what he considered right or acting for his own gain, as later events would show. Nor was he a man to be cautious about committing to one side or the other, and therefore likely to have kept his head down. His apparent inaction during the succession crisis is therefore more likely to have been enforced, not voluntary. It is quite possible that he was simply ill during most of May and June 1483 and, while showing a willingness to work in the regency council, explaining why they readily agreed to the appointments and grants made to him, he was physically incapable.

Naturally, for Francis to suffer an illness for the duration of the succession crisis and to resurface the moment it is resolved may seem too big of a coincidence to be believable. However, it might not be so implausible, for Francis does, on the whole, seem to have suffered from relatively poor health. Since none of his paperwork, such as account books, survives to this day, this is an assumption based on circumstantial evidence, but it is notable that the succession crisis was not the first time Francis had been inexplicably absent, nor would it be the last. Two instances mentioned previously are the Scottish campaign of 1482 and the parliament of 1478. In fact, it seems that Francis avoided travelling whenever possible, choosing to stay put whenever possible.

As mentioned above, even during his early years up to 1483, Francis did not build power bases everywhere he had possessions. This is unusual; he had the resources to do so, and most others in similar positions did so. While he did try to establish himself somewhat in Oxfordshire by building connections to neighbours such as William Stonor, and there is no suggestion he was disliked there, equally there is no indication he tried to garner special loyalty there.[57] His attempts to win hearts and minds were apparently restricted to his northern lands, where he succeeded in inspiring loyalty. This suggests that most of his time was spent in the north, though the letter to William Stonor discussed above would imply that this was not entirely voluntary and might have been enforced by an inability to travel a lot.

This is a pattern that would continue as Francis gained prominence at court. Unlike other courtiers, he did not seem ever to leave court to look after his own possessions. In fact, Rosemary Horrox has pointed out that it is remarkable and somewhat unusual that Francis made no attempt to establish himself as a local power in the Midlands even after he was granted yet more lands there.[58] Horrox notes that his lack of personal involvement there was unusual, and there is no indication that he ever even went to see some of his new possessions. Since he had already amply demonstrated an interest in lands and possessions to rival that of any other noble, it is unlikely that this was down to a lack of interest. Once more, it is tempting to think that Francis was simply unable to travel a great deal.

There is some indication that Francis's lack of mobility was well known at the time. Though we do not have any direct reference to this in a letter or account book, Richard's later actions speak to it. There can be absolutely no doubt that Richard favoured Francis beyond all other courtiers, and gave him tasks and importance at court, including the post of lord chamberlain. However, none of these appointments required him to leave court. His eventual roles of lord chamberlain, chief butler and privy counsellor demanded no travel, no action away from court, which again suggests that Francis did not want to travel, or found himself unable to; Richard, who knew Francis well, appears to have been entirely accommodating about this.

Though Francis's known movements (or lack thereof) attest to this, we cannot conclusively identify the problem that prevented Francis from travelling, or at the very least made him hesitant to do so. It is probable that it was a chronic condition, which either regularly flared up, making it impossible for him to travel, or was aggravated by travel, leading Francis to stay put whenever he could.

Since Francis was not an invalid, and even strenuous actions did not appear to make him ill – he was, for example, able to fight at the Scottish border in 1481, and later to travel with Richard's court on royal progress – the latter possibility is more likely, which of course makes it even more difficult to guess at his possible condition.

Having been born to such a young mother, and having been born a twin, perhaps Francis was born slightly prematurely, resulting in complications throughout his life. Even today premature babies can have health problems in their later lives, especially pulmonary diseases. In fact, a chronic condition like asthma could very well explain Francis's behaviour and his fear of triggering illness through travelling. Given that such illnesses are also often exacerbated by stress, this could explain his absence during the succession crisis. It would also account for the fact that no source expressed incredulity at his sudden rise to power and prominence despite his obscurity.

As this is the only explanation which answers all the questions raised by Francis's inactivity and the lack of historical comment on it, a chronic physical condition seems likely to have been the cause of his failure to become involved until Richard had taken, or been offered, the throne. It is at this point that Francis Lovell emerges as more than a mere recipient of favours.

10

The King's Kinsman and Chamberlain

The steady flow of grants and appointments made to Francis culminated when the new, as yet uncrowned, king made him his lord chamberlain on 28 June 1483, two days after his accession. It must have been a dazzling rise to power for a recent viscount who had been of no importance in the previous reign, and the appointment speaks of Richard's trust in and affection for Francis. As Charles Ross points out, the post was usually held by the monarch's closest friend, as it was a job neccessitating close personal contact with the king on a daily basis.[1] The lord chamberlain not only presided over all appointments in the king's household, from cleaners to physicians, but also controlled access to the king for everyone but his closest family. As has been pointed out by Rosemary Horrox, this offered the chance for manifold abuses of office,[2] though Francis was never accused of that. Even in such a high position, Francis kept a low profile and stayed out of quarrels except when he had to stick up for Richard.

Francis's first task as lord chamberlain must have been to help prepare Richard's coronation, which had been set for 6 July 1483, with celebrations beginning two days beforehand. This left little time between Richard's accession and the coronation, and must have required gargantuan efforts to arrange everything in time. While preparations for the coronation of a new king had been going on ever since the regency council took power, and there is even a famous reference to a cloak being ordered for Edward V, Richard unexpectedly becoming king changed the requirements.

Since he, unlike his young nephew, was married, the coronation to be prepared became a double coronation with accession, and items had to be purchased for the queen's use.

It is in connection with this matter that we find the first mention of any task performed by Francis in his capacity as lord chamberlain. It is in the Little Device, in a note next to the description of the queen's coronation, quoted by Sutton and Hammond:

> The Cardinall after that shall blesse a rich rynge saynge this orison, Creator, castinge holy water apon itt and putte the same rynge on the iiijth fynger of the Quenys right hand, saynge in this wise Accipe anulum, that endyd he shall say Dominus vobiscum with this collecte, Deus cuius.[3]

Next to this, in the margin, is written: 'Remembre A Ryng that Lovell shall ordeyne for.' As Anne Sutton and Peter Hammond point out, this note 'must have been written for Richard III's coronation, the reference to plain "Lovell" is suggestive of a note by the King himself.'[4]

It is interesting that Richard found it necessary to write this reminder, though there is no indication as to why he chose to explicitly mention that the item would be purchased by Francis. It may be because this was part of Francis's recent appointment as lord chamberlain, or because unlike most other details of the coronation it was not organised by Harry of Buckingham in his position as Great Chamberlain of England.

It is not known which explanation is the correct one, but it is known that Francis rose to the occasion and purchased a fitting ring for Queen Anne, with a sapphire and pearls. As Sutton and Hammond point out, while there is no way to know whether the ring was chosen by Richard, Francis or the queen herself, and the Little Device itself does not give any specifics as to what it should look like, it appears that a sapphire was traditional from the time of Queen Matilda, consort to William the Conqueror.[5]

Along with jewellery, the new queen also needed proper clothing for the ceremonies. Purchases of valuable materials such as cloth of gold are recorded for Anne, as they are for Richard, as well as purchases of clothes for the noble lords and ladies in the king's and queen's trains. Among these nobles were Francis's wife Anne, his sister-in-law Elizabeth Parr and their mother Alice FitzHugh. Like all other ladies taking part in the processions during the coronation, such as Elizabeth of Suffolk and Margaret Beaufort, each woman was given 'a gown of blue velvet with crimson satin and another of crimson velvet and white damask',[6] the former to be worn on the procession the day before the actual coronation, the second during the coronation ceremony and following festivities.

The attendant lords were each given six ells of red cloth from which to have clothes made,[7] but strangely, Francis is not listed among the lords who received this gift. Since he played a prominent part in the coronation, this is unlikely to have been an oversight, and even more unlikely to have been a deliberate snub. That there is no record of a purchase made of cloth or clothing for Francis in the official expenses presumably means that he received his attire for the coronation not from the office of the monarch but from the person of the king himself, a personal gift rather than a standard grant. Sadly, since the accounts of Richard's personal spending no longer exist, this cannot be proven. This means we cannot know what Francis wore and how his attire differed to that worn by the rest of the lords.

It could well be that these accounts of personal expenses would also shine a light on other preparations for the coronation dealt with by Francis, since what we have suggests that purchasing a ring for the coronation of the queen was all he did. As in Francis's next two years as lord chamberlain, it is likely that he assisted Richard quietly and unobtrusively, without drawing much attention.

For his part, Richard certainly wished to honour Francis, making sure that Francis was in his train during the coronation itself with the task of carrying the third sword of state. This is notable because that position was not the one he was originally meant to have had. As Williams notes, he should have borne the gold sceptre with a dove before the Queen,[8] while the Earl of Huntingdon, an associate of Richard who would go on to marry his illegitimate daughter, was to bear the third sword of state. That their roles were reversed represents a high honour for Francis, and was no small gesture on the part of the king.

That this was a personal decision which held significance for the new king is also supported by the fact that Francis was the only person included in Richard's train at his coronation for solely personal reasons.

Sutton and Hammond point out the political reasons for the inclusions of men like John Howard, Duke of Norfolk, his son the Earl of Surrey, Thomas Stanley, Earl of Derby, and many others, but note that Francis is the only one who was of no political significance at that point and therefore the only one who was given his role for solely personal reasons.[9] Many others with places in the train were also friendly with Richard, men like Norfolk and Lincoln, but Francis was the only one for whom no other reason but friendship could explain the appointment. He was the only member of the train whose exclusion would not have risked discontent at court.

Francis's wife Anne, however, was not as favoured by the queen as Francis was by the king – quite the contrary. Though she, like her sister Elizabeth and mother Alice, joined the queen's procession on 4 July,[10] she was not among the seven ladies given special favour, though her mother and sister were. Nor was she made a lady-in-waiting like them. Indeed, she appears to have never served the queen. She was nonetheless present during all the coronation festivities, though she is explicitly mentioned only in the procession of 4 July. Presumably she joined the wives of other lords, whose presence was noted but not dwelt upon.

Francis, on the other hand, continued playing a significant part even during the banquet following the coronation ceremony. The Little Device notes that 'my lorde Lovell stode before the King all the diner tyme'[11] during the banquet following the coronation ceremony. It is usually assumed that Francis served the king's meals along with Sir Robert Percy, Richard's lord comptroller and also a close friend whom Francis would have known from his time in the Earl of Warwick's household.[12]

Serving the king in this way would have been traditional, but neither the Little Device nor any other source makes any mention of Francis performing such a task. In fact, the statement quoted above actually contradicts this assumption, specifying that Francis did not leave the king's presence, and a separate statement detailing who served the royal couple makes no mention of Francis. So the traditional assumption is incorrect.

There is no explanation offered as to why Francis stood before the king. It seems to be implied that it was a high honour as it put him in close proximity to the king, but at the same time it does not seem to have been an official, traditional task. In fact, there is no mention of anyone doing this during the coronation of Edward IV, nor that of Henry VII. Presumably it was another honour for Francis, albeit obscure, which has been shorn of its significance over the centuries.

It is certainly notable that even Francis's significant and honoured position in Richard's coronation reflects the personal nature of his relationship to the new king – a certain informal, non-traditional element, performed discreetly, attracting little comment. This would prove an apt comparison as Richard began his reign and Francis continued rising in favour.

The King's Closest Friend

After the coronation, the newly crowned king and his queen retired to Westminster for two weeks. While there, Richard made several grants to his supporters, and did what could perhaps best be described as wrapping up the loose ends of the succession crisis, as well as making arrangements for his first royal progress, which he began on 19 July.[13]

Francis was at Richard's side all throughout the progress, unobstrusively fulfilling his duties as lord chamberlain. In fact, he was one of the few important men at court who did not leave the progress at any point. Harry of Buckingham did not join the progress at all, only coming to see the king briefly at Gloucester.[14] John Howard, newly made Duke of Norfolk, had to leave for London after two weeks to see to his duties. Even the queen spent ten days on her own at Windsor for reasons unknown while the king toured the country.[15] Thomas Stanley's whereabouts during large parts of the progress are unknown, though it seems that Richard's oldest nephew John de la Pole, Earl of Lincoln, much like Francis, stayed at the king's side the whole time.

The sources about the early part of this progress are not very illuminating, at least not as to the situation at court and between the courtiers. They suggest that Richard made a good impression on the populace, stressing that he wished to win goodwill and famously refused presents of money with the explanation he would prefer to have his subjects' love. Thomas Langton, Bishop-elect of St Davids in 1483, famously stated in a private letter that Richard 'contents the people wher he goys best that ever did prince', explaining this high praise with the statement that 'many a poor man that hath suffred wrong many days have be relevyd and helpyd by hym and his commands in his progresse.'[16] This probably means that Francis, controlling access to the king, had his hands full during the progress, granting most requests for an audience with Richard, even – perhaps especially – from those with no standing to recommend them, while at the same time having to keep a close eye out for timewasters and potential threats.

For any historian wishing to illuminate Francis's part in Richard's government, he frustratingly appears to have acquitted himself discreetly enough to avoid comment yet again. This reflects well on him; as Rosemary Horrox pointed out, there were manifold ways to abuse the position of lord chamberlain, to demand favours in return for access to the king, to allow the privilege only arbitrarily. There is no accusation of this sort against Francis.

This does not mean that Francis could not be greedy, however, or that he had forgotten the property quarrels he had been involved in before Edward IV's sudden death forced such matters to be put aside. Even while on progress with Richard, Francis laid claim to the manors of Ashby-de-la-Zouche and Bagworth, which he had been quarrelling about with William Hastings for at least a year, and which he had quitclaimed against his will in February 1482. He also claimed several of the Beaumont properties which had been granted to William Hastings by Edward IV, but which Francis argued should have been exempt from his uncle's attainder.[17]

Presumably, Francis was aware that with William Hastings' power and influence gone and his own standing massively increased, his chances of getting these manors from Hastings' family were much better than they had ever been before. In the first and only contemporary comment on any sort of enmity between Francis and anyone other than Henry Tudor, one source records that this claim caused 'variaunce and grudge'[18] between him and Katherine Hastings, though as with almost all disputes Francis had pursued until this point, it did not descend into violence. Francis did not send men to take possession of the manors and lands, nor did he pressure either the Hastings family or a judge to quickly decide in his favour. In fact, the conflict simmered for nearly two years, after which the matter was decided by the 'mediation of frendes'.[19]

Though hungry for possessions, Francis now had the patience to wait. He had presumably learnt this patience during his earlier conflicts, but equally he would have been less single-minded now that he had so much else to do. There was a lot to distract him. It does not seem that he spent a lot of time dwelling on quarrels after having made this claim, and most of the time Richard indulged him with whatever he wanted anyway.

In fact, even in the planning of his progress Richard saw to it that Francis was honoured. In a gesture that did not come as a surprise to anybody, Richard chose to honour Francis above all other courtiers by visiting Francis's ancestral home of Minster Lovell Hall. It was the only private home of a courtier he chose to visit.

Richard appears to have mixed pleasure and duty in this first progress. His first stops were probably more about duty – on 19 July he and the queen moved to Windsor, a palace which was never favoured by the royal couple. The queen chose to stay at Windsor while Richard, after a stay of two days, went to Reading.[20] Naturally, her ladies stayed with her, among them Elizabeth Parr and Alice FitzHugh. Anne Lovell's whereabouts, however, are not known. She does not appear to ever have been in the queen's household, except for the procession on the day before the coronation.

Why Anne did not join her mother and sister in becoming a lady-in-waiting is a mystery. While it is possible that she and the queen simply did not like each other, this would not have precluded such an appointment. While favour was naturally bestowed by the queen on those she liked, the actual appointment of her ladies-in-waiting was a political issue, and as the wife of one of the most important men in Richard's government, Anne Lovell would have been entitled to the position.

It is therefore more likely that Anne herself chose not to be a lady-in-waiting. Perhaps this was because she felt she was at a different point in life to her mother and sister. In 1483, Anne's mother Alice had been widowed for more than a decade and all her children were grown up, so that she had no cause to reject active involvement in the queen's household. Anne's sister Elizabeth, though married and the mother of four young children, does not appear to have spent a lot of time with her much older husband William Parr, who had not attended Richard's coronation. There is no certainty as to why he did not go; while he claimed to be too ill to attend and he died some months later, many historians believe that this was an excuse and in fact he did not support Richard's accession. This could have caused a rift between husband and wife, and Elizabeth might have been keen to show that she herself supported the new king. Others have opined that William was indeed too ill to attend the coronation and so wanted his wife to show support to the new regime on his behalf – what better way than in service?

Anne Lovell, however, was in a very different position to both her relatives. Being married to a man who was hugely favoured by the new king, she had no need to show her own loyalty by serving the queen like Elizabeth. Nor was she so free of other obligations that she could comfortably serve if she so wished, as in her mother's case. In fact, it may have been Anne's wish to stay with her husband that drove her decision. The two royal households were often apart, by necessity and by choice. The royal progress in 1483, when the queen decided to remain at Windsor for ten days, is just one example. In his capacity as the king's lord chamberlain and closest friend, Francis was always at court unless dire necessity forced him to leave. It is therefore very likely that Anne Lovell, when having to choose, decided to stay with her husband rather than in the queen's household as her lady-in-waiting.

This does not mean that Francis and Anne were constantly together, and it is in fact quite likely that when they both left Windsor Anne rode to Minster Lovell Hall to make all the preparations for the royal visit while Francis went with Richard to Reading, where the court stayed for two nights.

From Reading the court rode on to Oxford, a city apparently chosen by Richard for his own pleasure, so he could visit the university. Upon arriving there, he and his courtiers were received in the university by Bishop Wayneflete. The visit was recorded by the university, the record stating that 'the illustrious lord King Richard the Third was respectfully received at first out[side] the university by the chancellor of the university and by counsilors and non-counsilors' and that they spent the two days of the royal visit 'with many spiritual and temporal lords and other nobles, as befitted them'.[21] Those lords spiritual and temporal are named as 'the lord bishop of Durham, the lord bishop of Worcester, the lord bishop of St Asaph and master Thomas Langton, bishop-elect of St David's, his lordship the earl of Lincoln, the lord steward the earl of Surrey, the lord chamberlain, lord of Lovell, lord Stanley, lord Audeley, lord Becham, lord Richard Radclyff knight' together with 'several other nobles' who 'stayed the night in the college, and our lord founder received them with honour'.[22]

It would be interesting to know if Bishop Wayneflete and Francis had the opportunity to speak during the visit any more than the official ceremony demanded. Since the conclusion of their conflict earlier in the year they appear to have been on friendly terms, and they would do business together again the next year. Perhaps they discussed this future transaction when Francis came to the university with Richard, or Wayneflete informed Francis of the progress of the scholar Francis was sponsoring. It is also possible that Francis spoke to this scholar himself. Maybe this was what he did during the next day when, 'commanded and desired by the lord king, there were made in the great hall of the college two disputations.'[23] Though Richard's presence during these events and his pleasure at them is recorded, there is no mention of any of the nobles being present.

After two days in Oxford, the court moved on to Woodstock. Of that visit little is reported, except that the king chose to ride back to Oxford after having been greeted in Woodstock. This appears to have been a spontaneous action and did not involve moving the entire court, just Richard and some courtiers. Francis, as Richard's chamberlain, presumably went with him. In the evening, Richard and Francis and all the others who had accompanied the king on this detour returned to Woodstock, and Richard attended festivities given for him there.[24] The court stayed in the town for another day and night, before then riding on to Francis's ancestral manor of Minster Lovell Hall, where Richard stayed for four days – longer than he had spent in any other city or manor on his progress since leaving Westminster.

It is hard to explain this choice of accommodation. Minster Lovell Hall is not located very close to any big cities, and it offered no chance for meeting many subjects. It therefore seems likely that this was a choice based on personal pleasure; Richard likely wanted to relax in his close friend's manor, where he might well have stayed before.

It would have been a great honour for Francis to entertain the king and court at his ancestral manor, and it is certain that festivities were prepared. As mentioned above, it is most likely that Anne Lovell rode ahead to make the proper arrangements, and Richard's choice to stay there for so long must mean he enjoyed whatever festivities, banquets and entertainments she had prepared.

However, it is not because of the gesture of friendship from Richard, nor the entertainments offered, that this visit has gone down in history. While residing at Minster Lovell Hall, Richard penned a mysterious letter to the Bishop of Lincoln on 29 July, the day he arrived there:

To the Right Reverend fader in god, our right trusti and welbiloved the Bishop of Lincoln, our Chauncellr of England.

By the King RR [Ricardus Rex]

Right Reverend fader in god right trusti and welbiloved. We grete you wele. And where as we undrestand that certaine personnes (of such as of late had taken upon thaym the fact of an enterprise, as we doubte nat ye have herd) bee attached and in warde, we desir and wok you that ye doo make our letters of commission to such personnes as by you and our counsaill shalbee advised forto sitte upon thaym, and to procede to the due execucion of our lawes in that behalve. Faille ye not hereof as our perfect trust is in you.

Yeven undre our signet at this Mainor of Mynster lovel the xxixth day Juyll.

Herbert. [One of Richard's secretaries][25]

This letter has been variously interpreted. Most historians believe that it refers to a plot to remove the Princes in the Tower, Richard's famous nephews, from the Tower of London, or to a similar plot to remove their sisters from sanctuary and bring them abroad so that they might become a focal point for rebellion among those dissatisfied with Richard.

In fact, the Croyland Chronicle explicitly points out that there were such plans at the time, making the letter's meaning clear.[26] According to Croyland, Richard not only instructed his chancellor to appoint suitable persons for the trial of those caught engaging in one such plot, but also sent one of his trusted servants, a northerner called John Nesfield, with some men to guard the sanctuary of Westminster against further plots.[27] He also had some of his nephews' attendants dismissed and replaced with others whom he must have regarded as more loyal to him.[28]

Traditional retellings of the events of 1483 often postulate that this was when Richard decided to have his nephews killed. However, he was yet to show any outward sign that he had formed such a plan, instead simply taking precautions that the Princes in the Tower could not be removed from the palace in which they were staying. These precautions could not have been undertaken by Richard himself, though; they would have been discussed with his courtiers, Francis among them. Sadly, since most chronicles covering this event were written after Richard's death, and are at best heavily tinged by hindsight and at worst actively hostile, more concerned with telling a story to suit the new Tudor dynasty than reporting the truth, we do not know who was involved in helping Richard make these decisions.

It is hardly a leap to assume that Francis was one of the men Richard turned to when he wanted to discuss how he should react to the plots supposedly afoot. He would have heeded Francis's counsel, for by this time it had become clear that Francis was one of the men closest to Richard, perhaps the closest of all. Though no one ever commented on this closeness in the chronicles, it is made clear by their own actions and by the behaviour of those around them. By now recognised as the man who could most likely influence the king, Francis began to receive gifts from many different people. These offerings ranged from twelve oxen[29] to the keys to the City of Salisbury,[30] and Francis received far more than anybody else in Richard's court. In fact, it seems that his influence on the king was thought to surpass that of the queen, who received far fewer gifts.

The full extent of Francis's influence is impossible to gauge as it was very personal and thus hard to define from the outside. Nonetheless, it is clear that however much or little Richard listened to Francis's personal advice and opinions, he clearly wished to reward his friend for his service, and continued sending grants and appointments his way. These ranged from the commonplace and unremarkable, such as several commissions of peace, to special honours, such as his summer 1483 elevation to the Order of the Garter and Richard's decision to make him a privy councillor.[31]

In light of all this, it is strange that Francis was only confirmed as Chief Butler on 14 August, affirming the appointment made in the short, abortive reign of Edward V.[32] On the same day, he was given 'the offices of constable of Walyngford and the king's castle of Walyngford and steward of the king's honour of Walyngford'[33] for life. This was a rather remarkable grant, as the constableship of Wallingford had previously belonged to Francis's former guardian, John, Duke of Suffolk, who was the king's brother-in-law and had given Richard no reason to take away the title. Nor does this appear to have caused any hard feelings; Francis and Duke John continued to be on good terms.[34] It is entirely possible that there was some sort of arrangement between the two men to explain the grant.

It is also possible that Francis, aware that the constableship of Wallingford had once belonged to his grandfather William Lovell,[35] had petitioned Richard to grant it to him for this reason. Duke John would not have approved of this, but given his own struggles for grants and possessions as a young man he would have definitely understood.[36] In fact, this is perhaps the most likely theory, for while Francis would have been busy working for Richard and fulfilling all tasks given to him to the king's satisfaction, he most definitely did not forget about his own interests.

He was surely busy ensuring that some of his long-running conflicts were being solved in his favour. Under Richard's influence, implicitly or explicitly, the City of York granted him the right to have his cows and one bull on a field on 15 September 1483.[37] The court was in York at the time and this concession to Francis was another gesture of goodwill by the city to the new king, who was very popular in the north of the country.

Francis might also have taken full advantage of this unprecedented opportunity to exercise his privileges, seeing to it that those who had served him and been close to him in the preceding years were suitably rewarded. Using his new influence and impressive position, Francis insisted that one Henry Walton was made a member of the rectory of Lynton, though the Register of Thomas Rotherham reports that this was a very unpopular choice.[38] In the months after he first came to power in Richard's government, Francis also saw to it that loyal servants like Geoffrey Franke were recognised with appointments that would both elevate their own status and help him with his work. On 18 December 1483, Geoffrey was appointed to be Francis's deputy as chief butler 'in the port of Newcastle on Tyne and the ports and places pertaining to it'.[39]

The fact that Geoffrey was receiver of Middleham,[40] worked for Richard and was trusted by Francis once more shows the closeness between Francis and Richard. They had been in close proximity ever since Richard became king, starting with the progress on which Francis shadowed the king every step of the way, and this clearly strengthened their friendship.

The appointments made by Francis show more than his closeness to Richard, though. Another man appointed to act as his deputy as chief butler, Richard Rugge, was associated with his mother-in-law Alice[41], suggesting that Francis also took care to cultivate this connection, perhaps under the influence of his wife. It is not hard to imagine that as early as summer 1483, during Richard's first royal progress, Francis not only used his newfound power to indulge himself and those who had so far served him well, but also sought to form new relationships which might be of help to him in the future.

After the stay in Minster Lovell Hall, the court, and Francis with it, moved on through Gloucester and Tewkesbury, where Richard paid his respects to the tombs of his brother George of Clarence and Clarence's wife Isabel, and settled some debts in his deceased brother's name.[42] From there they passed through Worcester and finally reached Warwick. It was there that the queen joined the royal progress again, arriving from Windsor with a Spanish ambassador.[43]

The chronicler John Rous later recorded this meeting, naming all those who were present. Interestingly, despite the fact he chronicled the history of the Beauchamps, the queen's maternal family, Rous does not speak at length about the queen. Nor did he claim to be present himself, suggesting he was going by what he had heard.

According to Rous, 'there were then at Warwick with the king the prelates of Worcester, Coventry, Lichfield, Durham, and the bishop of St Asaph, the Duke of Albany, brother of the Scottish king, Edward Earl of Warwick, Thomas Earl of Surrey, seneschal of the lord king, the Earl of Huntingdon, John Earl of Lincoln, and the lords Stanley, Dudley, Morley, Scrope, and Francis Lord Lovell, chamberlain of the king, and William Hussy, main justiciar of England, and many other lords.'[44]

Rous does not give any details of what any of these men did during the meeting with the ambassador, simply stating that the ambassador discussed the marriage of one of the Spanish monarchs' daughters with Richard's son. The implication is, of course, that the lords and prelates present would have been consulted, but this is not stated outright. What is most notable about this list of lords and bishops is that like most other sources which mention Francis during Richard's reign, it simply includes him in a list of those present without assigning special political importance to him.

Chronologically, the next mention of Francis in a contemporary source is very similar in nature, referring to Richard's visit to York and the extensive festivities given there after the court came to the city, having travelled from Warwick to Coventry, then to Leicester, from there to Nottingham Castle, and then via Pontefract Castle to York. Richard had been to York many times given he had been Lord of the North since 1471, and over the years he had built a special relationship with the city, something that was much commented upon at the time and is still a well-known fact today.[45] Indeed, when Richard took the crown it was feared by many that he would favour York and the north over the south. This concern was soon to cause major problems.

At the time of Richard's arrival in York, though, there appears to have been no sign of the trouble to come. His entry into the city was said to be a very joyous occasion for everyone. There are records of the king, together with Queen Anne and the newly arrived Prince Edward, entering the city to much delight. The York Civic Records describe the procession in detail, stating that a delegation of the city's aldermen met them immediately outside the city, and then processed into York, where they were greeted by 'persons of every occupation'[46] dressed finely as they went through the streets to reach the archbishop's palace, where they were to stay during their visit. Along the way, three pageants were staged for them, and the king and queen were presented with generous gifts of money and plate. Those present are said to have been, apart from the king himself, 'the Queen and the Prince, and many other magnates, both spiritual and temporal, including five bishops, those of Durham, Worcester, St Asaph, Carlisle and St David's, the Earls of Northumberland, Surrey and Lincoln, Lords Lovell, FitzHugh, Stanley, Strange, Lisle and Greystoke and many others'.[47]

This shows that once more Francis was present among others of high standing, a fact noted but not commented upon. A clear pattern emerges, from which we can infer that Richard's reliance upon Francis was noted and accepted. Unusually, there appear to have been no voices lamenting this mere viscount's rise to power, no accusations of flattery, of holding a position wrongfully gained. Anybody close to a reigning monarch could expect to be the subject of hostility in the fifteenth century as much as at any other time. The extent to which jealousy and gossip were able to poison the atmosphere at a royal court had been clearly shown during Edward IV's reign in the enmity faced by the Woodvilles, who were met from the first with accusations of all kinds.[48] Such accusations were in fact so commonplace that they cannot be reliably used to make a judgment on those maligned. That there were no such accusations about Francis says more about him than any accusations would have. Even after he began using his power to decide conflicts in his own favour and to reward his entourage, he was markedly uncontroversial. No one appeared to resent his position close to Richard, nor fear his mounting influence.

The ceremonies at York must have felt as much a triumph for the well-liked, newly powerful Francis as they were for Richard. Surrounded by those who meant most to him – his wife, his brother-in-law Richard, his mother-in-law Alice and, of course, King Richard himself – Francis must have felt on top of the world. Perhaps even his sister Frideswide was present during the festivities, for according to Paul Murray Kendall, she received a 'reward' of £50 from the king around this time.[49] As mentioned above, it was also during his stay in York that Francis finally got to settle a long-standing quarrel with the city for some of his rights in his favour. Clearly, Francis and his family were on the up, and the festivities in York showed it well. There is another pattern recognisable there: whenever King Richard was happy, he wanted to share it with those closest to him, and whenever he wanted to share, Francis was one of the first to receive his favour.

Francis was rarely the sole recipient of the king's favour, of course, and this holds true for the festivities in York. Many others were rewarded. However, as with the coronation, the perks and honours given to Francis's family are the only ones offered for solely personal reasons, with the exception of a knighthood conferred on Richard's illegitimate son John, who was then in his teens.[50]

Francis, who is not recorded to have ever showed any sign of jealousy, probably enjoyed all the festivities that followed the successful procession into York, which were recorded by the York Civic Records. They included the official investment of King Richard's son Edward as Prince of Wales, which happened on '[o]n the feast of the Nativity of the Blessed Virgin Mary', meaning 8 September. At first, 'the King and the Queen both crowned, went in procession to the aforesaid church [...], the prince and all the other Lords, both spiritual and temporal, being in attendance'.[51] After a service until six in the evening, 'they all returned to the Palace, and there before dinner, he was created Prince by the Lord King, in the presence of all'.[52]

Very little is known about the boy, but presumably he knew his father's closest friend, if only in passing, and it must have been a great moment not only for him but for all those close to him to see him elevated to such a high office. The York Civic Records, quoted above, even reflect the delight of the citizens during the royal couple's procession into the city, and there is no reason why the appointment of the king's son as Prince of Wales should not have caused similar delight or why Francis, who knew the child, should not have shared it.

King Richard, together with his wife and son, chose to remain in York after the ceremonies were done, and Francis, naturally, stayed as well. Ignorant of the discontent brewing in the south of the country, Richard and his court appear to have enjoyed their stay in York, and the citizens seemed happy to entertain them. Francis was still there with Richard on his twenty-seventh birthday on 17 September when the king, in Francis's presence, granted the City of York a remission of taxes.[53]

Four days later, on 21 September, the royal couple, their son and the court left York. Queen Anne and Prince Edward, doubtlessly accompanied by the queen's household including Alice FitzHugh, went to Middleham Castle. Francis's sister-in-law Elizabeth Parr may not have been present, instead going to see her sick husband, whose condition was at that time becoming worse, and who died within two months. If Sir William's ill health in any way affected Francis, we do not know. He returned with Richard and several of his courtiers, and probably his wife, to Pontefract, where they stayed for around two weeks. On 8 October, they rode on to Lincoln.

The Rebellion of 1483

It must have been when Richard and his court were in Lincoln, perhaps on the day they arrived and definitely no more than a day later, that they learnt of the budding rebellion that would go down in history as the 'Buckingham Rebellion', though in recent years several voices have disputed this title as Buckingham, while the most notable of the rebels, was not one of the instigators.[54]

News of Buckingham's betrayal hit Richard hard. Never one to hide his feelings, the king expressed his fury and hurt in a letter to his chancellor, famously calling the duke the 'most untrue creature living'.[55] He no doubt vented his spleen to those around him as well. Francis would have been privy to this, likely discussing the betrayal with Richard. It is most likely that if Richard addressed the causes of the rebellion in a conversation with anyone, it would have been Francis. He would have known the truth about Richard's path to the throne, whatever it was, and would therefore have been in a position to judge the rebels' claims that Richard's disinherited nephew Edward V was the rightful king. Perhaps more importantly, Francis would have had intimate knowledge about another issue that arose when the rebellion broke out: the fate of the Princes in the Tower, Edward V and Richard of Shrewsbury.

Though the rebellion initially started with the apparent aim of reinstating Edward V on the throne, the Croyland Chronicle reports that, shortly after its beginning, 'a rumour was spread that the sons of king Edward before-named had died a violent death, but it was uncertain how.'[56] The rumour that the princes had been murdered was used by the rebels to stir up outrage against Richard, though what truly happened to the boys remains a mystery today. Several chroniclers claimed different versions of the boys' fate as fact, but there can be no doubt that Francis was one of the few who knew the truth. As the man responsible for granting audiences to Richard, Francis would have been in the best position to know. There are many books that point out the logical fallacies of 'traditional' accounts of Richard's supposed plot to murder the Princes in the Tower, but few point out the fact that the ever-present Francis appears in none of them. In fact, some of the most famous accounts are based on premises which could only be possible if Francis was absent. Thomas More's is one such account.

In More's account, Sir Richard Ratcliffe, associate of both Richard and Francis, and William Catesby, Richard's lawyer, are said to be Richard's closest men. In fact, they are even described as guarding their position jealously and not wanting to share it with anyone else. At one point in the account, they directly prevent James Tyrell, More's eventual choice for murderer, from gaining Richard's favour and stopping his advancement for the reason of 'longing for no more partners of the Prince's favour' and to have 'kept him [Tyrell] by secret plans out of all secret trust'.[57]

The obvious historical error in this is that William Catesby and Richard Ratcliffe, whatever their real reasons for serving Richard, were hardly Richard's only close confidants. Not only was Francis Lovell at least as high in Richard's favour as Richard Ratcliffe and William Catesby, as evidenced by his position as Richard's lord chamberlain, but the very position also gave him the power to decide who gained access to the king. The plan laid by Ratcliffe and Catesby as described by More would therefore have been impossible to realise without Francis's consent. Despite this, he is never mentioned, neither as a rival to Catesby and Ratcliffe's rise in Richard's favour nor as a co-conspirator, perhaps because Thomas More had no information about him. More's account is not the only one which suggests a fate for the Princes which is incompatible with the available facts and denies Francis's presence, but it is perhaps the most famous one, and is considered by many as the truest account.

What really happened to Edward V and his younger brother is still a matter of debate. Even five-and-a-half centuries on, we do not have an answer; perhaps we never will. But whatever it was that happened, Francis knew, and he stood by Richard entirely, showing love and loyalty. It might be argued that Francis, himself most likely an abused child, would not have retained such dedication to someone who harmed children, but of course this is speculation.

Perhaps when the rebellion broke Francis did not care to examine the rebels' motives, preferring to prioritise an immediate response. Already in the postscript to the letter to his chancellor mentioned above, written on 12 October, Richard mentioned that '[h]ere, loved be God, is all well and truly determined, and for to resist the malice of him that had best cause to be true, the Duke of Buckingham.'[58] The arrangements he made support his words. He gave orders for the protection of London, among others, to John Howard, Duke of Norfolk, and also saw to it that the coasts of his kingdom, especially in Wales, were protected.

Even before that, Richard must have instructed his lord chamberlain what he wanted him to do. On 11 October, Francis wrote a letter to William Stonor, which is worth quoting in full, as it illustrates several important points about him and his relationship to the king:

Cousin Stonor, I command me to you as heartily as I can: for as much as it pleases the King's grace to have warned you and all other to attend upon his grace, and your company that you would come in my cognisance and my company to come with you: and I am sure that shall please his grace best, and cause me to think that you love my honour, and I trust shall be to your surety. I pray you remember this, as I shall remember you in time to come, by the grace of Jesu, who ever preserve you. Written at Lincoln the 11th day of October.

Your heartily loving cousin Francis Lovell.

Also cousin, the king hath commanded me to send you word to make you ready, and all your company, in all haste to be with his grace at Leicester the Monday the 20th day of October, for I have sent for all my men to meet me at Banbury, the Saturday the 18th day of October.

To my cousin [Sir] William Stonor.[59]

That Francis states he is 'sure' – rather than that he 'knows' – the meeting he proposes would 'please his grace best' makes it obvious Richard had not given him precise orders on gathering his own men and what to tell Stonor before he met him. He appears to have left the details up to Francis. In the light of the fact that Richard had just been betrayed by the Duke of Buckingham, whom he trusted greatly, this complete trust is significant, especially considering Francis was not an experienced military man with applicable knowledge on leading troops.

It is also worth noting that Francis did not appear to be very comfortable in his role of both supplicant and commander. The letter is somewhat stilted and awkward, different from other letters written in similar situations, such as the one by John Howard to John Paston, written a day before Francis's letter.[60] There is also no recognisable trace of the slight familiarity found in Francis's previous letter to Stonor. While Francis couches the letter in some conventional assurances of affection, there is an undertone of suspicion. It is easy to read this letter with hindsight, of course, but all the same there is no mistaking Francis's repetition of the orders from the king, nor the assurance that this would be for the best and would not only please the king but also earn Francis's gratitude. Indeed, Francis seems to appeal to Stonor to do this not only for the king but also for him, and offers assurances that if Stonor does as asked he will not find Francis ungrateful.

In fact, while Francis naturally emphasises the king's wishes from the first, in the addendum after his signature he goes into detail about the king's orders and even directly mentions that it is because of them that he is writing. The impression given is one of Francis somewhat awkwardly trying to appeal to Stonor to follow the king's orders by reminding him of their previously friendly relationship rather than by invoking his duty to and love for the king.

The letter did not have its intended effect. Sir William Stonor instead chose to join the rebels. As Williams points out, Stonor chose the interests he shared with Thomas Grey over those he shared with Francis.[61] This failure must have hit Francis hard, even if he had suspected Stonor of sympathising with the rebels, or realised that Stonor's interests would be protected best by joining them. Though the two men do not appear to have been friends, as mentioned above, their relationship had previously been a fruitful and cordial one, so that Stonor's betrayal would have felt like a personal slight as well as a political failure.

Shortly after writing the letter, Francis left court to meet with his men at Banbury and to join forces with Stonor. It is not hard to imagine him waiting to see Sir William, first with impatience, then with mounting worry. Finally, when Sir William had not showed up on 19 October, he no doubt felt a pang of resignation.

Sticking to the plan, Francis would have returned to court with his own men to meet with Richard on 20 October, reporting his failure to bring Stonor and his men with him. Always emotional, yet reserved and hesitant to show it, Francis may have only allowed himself to give in to his horror and disappointment when seeing his royal friend, away from the eyes of his men. It may have been a scene full of pathos: the shame-faced viscount, tears in his eyes, falling to his knees in front of the king, bowing his head and quietly confessing to having failed in what he had been sent to do; the king listening, worried, helping his friend up, embracing him and assuring him that the failure would not be held against him.

While such a scene might be dismissed as sentimental fiction, something like it must have occurred as Richard did not hold the failure against Francis. On the contrary, shortly afterwards, on 23 October, Francis was granted a general commission of array 'for the resistance of the rebel Henry, Duke of Buckingham' in thirteen counties.[62]

We do not know how many men Francis raised during these commissions, and how many more Stonor would have brought. A letter from 1483 reports that Thomas Stanley had raised ten thousand men,[63] but it is unlikely that Francis had even a fraction of that number, as Stanley was seen as somebody who could influence – perhaps even decide – the outcome of the entire rebellion. Nobody ever made such an assumption about Francis, and in fact his efforts to help the king once more go unrecorded in the contemporary chronicles.

Most likely, those men Francis raised would have joined the king's army. Francis would have prepared himself to fight, but it did not come to that. For a variety of reasons, not least the bad weather, Buckingham's unpopularity in his own lands and what the Croyland Chronicler called a failure to win people's hearts,[64] the rebellion never really took off. Only ten days after Francis's planned meeting with Stonor, the danger had largely passed and the Duke of Buckingham was captured and executed. Francis might not have had to act at all.

Naturally, the death of the Duke of Buckingham on 2 November 1483 did not entirely close the book on Buckingham's Rebellion. Fleeing rebels still needed to be captured and sympathisers exposed, not to mention the task of ascertaining the true aim of the rebellion. The Croyland Chronicle, written with hindsight in 1486, claimed that Henry VI's nephew Henry Tudor was proposed as king after the rumours of the deaths of the Princes in the Tower. The plan was supposedly to depose Richard and marry Henry Tudor to Elizabeth of York, oldest sister of the Princes in the Tower.[65] Some have doubted this, and some have maintained that the Duke of Buckingham hoped to become king himself, having a better claim to the throne than Henry Tudor.[66]

While this would have been fully investigated at the time, for Francis it took a backseat to problems which required immediate action. He was appointed on 18 November to lead a commission 'to arrest and imprison all rebels in the counties of Oxford and Berks[hire], to take their castles, lordships, manors, lands, chattels and possessions into the king's hands and to enquire into the value and receive the issue of the same, and to certify thereon to the king and council'.[67] This commission also included Francis's close associate and servant Edward Franke, as well as William Catesby and one Richard Harcourt. Since William Stonor fled after the rebellion failed, he was not among those arrested by the commission.[68]

Even if the commission was otherwise successful, Stonor's escape, in addition to his betrayal, must have left a bitter residue for Francis. More bad news was still to come when Francis discovered that William Norris, Fridewide's father-in-law, had supported the rebellion.[69] It is unlikely Francis only found out in November, when Norris fled to the Continent, as he had been named as one of the rebels in October already, though perhaps Francis hoped it was untrue. In the light of all this, it is not hard to imagine that Francis returned to court an unhappy man at the beginning of December 1483. A lot was expected of him; he would have hoped to forget his troubles through hard work.

On Top of the World

Richard's first parliament had originally been planned for late 1483 but the rebellion prevented it from taking place.[70] With the fallout from the rebellion requiring the court's full attention, proper preparations could only be made from early December 1483 onwards. Along with other men, mostly of higher standing, Francis was appointed to proclaim Parliament. This appointment nicely illustrates his rise to power. Only a year before, he had received his first summons to Parliament at the age of twenty-six. He had attended Parliament for the first time just ten months before, as a politically insignificant viscount.

In those ten months, Francis had become the new monarch's closest man, a Knight of the Garter, a Privy Councillor, Lord Chamberlain of the King's Household, Chief Butler and a Speaker of Parliament. Now he was proclaiming Parliament himself. The list of grants, honours and appointments is impressive, and it would only grow. Richard, having granted Francis many of the lands and manors he had tried in vain tried to obtain in his early years, also granted his good friend many lands and manors newly confiscated from rebels.

Though some of these new possessions held a personal connection for Francis, such as the manor of Yattendon in Yorkshire that had belonged to William Norris, most of them were apparently not granted for personal reasons as Francis had no personal connection nor previous claim to them. In fact, most of Francis's new possessions were located in the Midlands, near his ancestral manor of Minster Lovell Hall, and were perhaps granted to him for their mere proximity.[71] Notable among the many lands Francis received were several of Sir William Stonor's former possessions, which may have been something of a comfort for him after his betrayal, letting him feel a modicum of revenge.

Much has been said about Richard's tendency to give lands and honours to men from the north of the country, alienating the southerners whom Edward IV, and most kings before him, had favoured and empowered. This criticism is not without merit, but Richard's behaviour is understandable.[72] While the extent of his bias has been exaggerated, the majority of those Richard rewarded with lands and honours did indeed come from the north. This should not be a surprise; Richard had spent the last twelve years in the north building up his alliances, and the north was home to most of his faithful followers.

Several of Francis's associates profited from this geographic shift. Most notable was Sir Edward Franke, who was made sheriff of Cornwall.[73] Franke's connection to Francis went back to an association with the FitzHugh family in 1470, and he was also connected with Richard's trusted receiver Geoffrey Franke. We don't know which connection brought him his role in Cornwall, but it is clear that Francis's friends were on the rise just as he was. Franke's preferment may not perhaps be sufficient evidence for this, but he was not the only one; another of Francis's associates, Sir Thomas Broughton, a man from the Midlands, was made sheriff of Berkshire and Oxfordshire.[74] Unlike Franke, Broughton did not have any ties to Richard independent of Francis and probably owed this appointment to his association with Francis. Clearly, by late 1483 Francis's friendship was worth cultivating.

As Rosemary Horrox has pointed out, the generous grants of land to Francis, especially near his ancestral lands in Oxfordshire, may indicate that Richard intended for his friend to capitalise on this and become a regional power in the Midlands.[75] If so, it would once more shown the impressive trust Richard placed in Francis, not entirely explained by his previous record. Though Francis's loyalty to Richard is undoubted, he had not shown an interest in building up power bases, nor had he shown an aptitude for it. In fact, Sir William Stonor's defection displayed a shocking lack of control or leverage in the Midlands on Francis's part. Clearly this did not influence Richard in his decision to give those lands to his lord chamberlain.

In fact, the idea that Richard was building Francis up as a Midlands power may well be incorrect. Assuming it really was Richard's intention, the plan was a failure, mainly due to Francis's 'own inclination',[76] meaning he did not even try to establish himself as a regional power there. As pointed out above, Francis did not even travel to see his new lands, let alone try to carve out a place for himself there as a local powerbroker. It seems unlikely that he would have shown such nonchalance had Richard truly wanted him to become a power in the Midlands, perhaps a similar figure to Richard himself and the Earl of Warwick before him, in the north of the country.

Knowing Francis closely, Richard understood Francis's unsuitability for such a task, how his reserved nature would make him a poor candidate for such a job. Given that the many tasks Francis had been given so far reflect an understanding of this, indicating that Richard clearly respected Francis's reluctance to travel more than necessary, it is unlikely that the king really expected Francis to build a significant power base in the Midlands. Presumably, the reason for the grants is more prosaic: Richard wished for these lands to be held by a loyal follower, and perhaps he also wanted to favour his friend some more. The relationship between Richard and Francis was still very close, making the latter motivation plausible.

Once Francis had returned to court from his commission to arrest rebels, he did not leave Richard's side for several months. During this time, he must have played a large part in the king's first Christmas festivities. Though the Christmas festivities of 1483 are not as notorious as those of 1484, they were very lavish. King Richard and his queen, who had arrived at court in December, ran up debts of over £1,000 for clothing worn at the festivities.[77] Richard also purchased jewels to be worn during the festivities; on 9 December, he gave a safe-conduct to a jeweller on the condition that he was allowed to choose first from the man's merchandise.[78] It may well be that, in addition to making purchases for himself, Richard also bought presents for those closest to him. Francis, for his part, would have bought the king a New Year's gift.

It was at this time that Richard, for the first and only time in the surviving records, denied Francis something that he wanted. On 9 December 1483, the same day that he gave the safe-conduct to the jeweller, he decreed that a dispute about 'the issues of the manor and lordship of Claydon', in which Francis had opposed his cousin Lord Morley, was to be decided against both Francis and Lord Morley, and that neither of them should receive Claydon.[79] No more is known about this conflict between the cousins, although some historians have speculated further. David Baldwin, for example, suggests that Richard's intervention was necessary to stop Francis from resorting to violence.[80] This is possible, but no evidence exists to back up the notion. Francis had previously shown little inclination to violence; in all his many quarrels for possessions, he had only once resorted to force. Nor is there any evidence that Francis was the instigator of this argument with his cousin.

There is also no hint of impending violence in the decree, and it is possible that they themselves had agreed to put the matter before the king. If so, Francis probably hoped that his closeness to Richard would work in his favour. It speaks to Richard's sense of justice that he did not simply decide for his closest friend, and it is telling that Francis apparently accepted the decree with no effect on his relationship with the king.

The Christmas festivities of 1483 mark the beginning of a short but very triumphal period for King Richard III and his government. Having just defused a rebellion, he and his court must have felt they had something to celebrate, though perhaps not with the exuberance of the festivities at York three months earlier. It was a happy occasion, and perhaps for a time Francis forgot the bitterness of Sir William's betrayal as he basked in the king's favour.

Presumably, Francis's role in arranging the festivities was not dissimilar to his role in arranging those in 1484, described disapprovingly in the Croyland Chronicle as giving too much attention to dance and frivolities. Among these frivolities may have been the 'vain changes of apparell',[81] which, due to Elizabeth of York's participation, caused a lot of rumours the next year, supported by the massive bills for clothing run up by the court.

Francis was certainly rich enough to follow even the most extravagant fashions. His annual income at this time, with all the new lands already granted to him by Richard, has been conservatively estimated at around £2,000,[82] which made him the fifteenth-century equivalent of a multi-millionaire. If he wanted to flaunt this wealth, the court festivities would have been the perfect opportunity to do so (although there is no indication he did). Perhaps, as so often, he simply tried to blend in, wearing fine clothing that befitted the occasion without being ostentatious.

The same may have held true for the presents he chose to give his wife and other loved ones. There is an indication of a gift he made to Richard, possibly for that occasion or for his birthday three months earlier. Rather famously, the king owned a Book of Hours in which his date and place of birth are jotted down. The fact that the note identifies him as 'King Richard III', rather than 'Richard Gloucestre' makes it clear that he received this Book of Hours only after his accession to the throne.[83] The handwritten note is usually assumed to have been made by the king himself, but a handwriting comparison suggests the note was written by Francis, not Richard.[84] Perhaps, then, the Book of Hours was an extravagant gift made by Francis, rather than a purchase by the king for himself; if so, the gift further reinforces their closeness – not because of the choice of such an item but because whoever acquired it for Richard had clear knowledge of his favoured saints, having chosen a Book of Hours with special devotions to St George and St Christopher among others.[85]

While St George is a fairly obvious saint to favour for a man whose brother had been named thus and who was, moreover, very proud of his English ancestry, the choice of St Christopher is rather more obscure and Richard's devotion to him is less widely known or easily guessed. In fact, if the Book of Hours was indeed a gift from Francis, the choice of St Christopher may reflect his own preferences as well as Richard's, as St Christopher was traditionally worshipped by the Lovell family; Francis's grandfather William had founded a fraternity for St Christopher's worship.[86] This could even mean that the Book of Hours was a family heirloom, passed to Richard in a particularly moving gesture of friendship. This cannot be proven, but it is true that Richard was not the first owner of this Book of Hours and that William Lovell was not only a rich man but also an extremely pious one,[87] and might very well have owned a Book of Hours beautiful enough to be seen as a suitable gift for a king.

Soon after Christmas was over, Richard's first parliament began. Over the years, this parliament has been praised even by observers overtly biased against the king, and Victorian historian James Gairdner, an ardent believer that Richard was an evil man, notes his great laws and remarkable administration pertaining to this time.[88] Another Victorian commenter, Lord Campbell, stated that Richard's parliament was 'the most meritorious national assembly for protecting the liberty of the subject and putting down abuses in the administration of justice that had sat in England since the reign of Henry II', who had reigned three hundred years earlier.[89]

This is perhaps no surprise. As Matthew Lewis notes, whatever else Richard did, there can be no doubt that his laws broke new ground. In some ways they still influence law today.[90] Among the measures he enacted was a reform of the right to bail[91] and a protection of the rights of those who bought lands, making it illegal to sell anything with cloud on title (outside claims potentially preventing the legal ownership of land).[92] One measure brought by Richard's parliament that was less pleasant, and in fact rather shockingly xenophobic to a modern audience. It imposed heavy restrictions on foreign merchants,[93] with the exception of those selling books; this measure was greeted as a welcome boon to English merchants.

Nothing survives in the historical record to indicate whether Francis agreed, disagreed or even cared about these measures. None of his actions give even the slightest hint as to his political opinions beyond complete loyalty to Richard, and he does not appear to have said or done anything to make any chroniclers speculate on his opinion as to the laws enacted by the king. In that, Francis was notably different to the men who held the position of lord chamberlain before and after him, not to mention most others of note at court.

Perhaps because his time in a position of power and influence was comparatively short, Francis was one of those who did not voice political opinions or arouse suspicion regarding their ambitions. Both his predecessor and his successor are known to have held political views and to have involved themselves in legislation when they saw fit. An example of this is William Hastings' choice to offer military support to Margaret of York in Burgundy in 1481, even though Edward IV chose not to.[94] There are no rumours of Francis even contemplating something like this, and by neglecting to build an independent power base he deprived himself of the ability to do so anyway. His contemporaries recognised his lack of independent power, and on the frequent instances his favour was sought, it was to make him use his influence on Richard, not to get him personally involved. As Horrox points out, Francis's influence was based on personal affection between him and Richard, and is therefore hard to analyse in political terms.[95] In fact, for someone as powerful as Richard allowed him to become, Francis was singularly apolitical.

This apolitical stance might even explain Francis's lack of involvement in the government before Richard came to the throne. It might not have been that Edward IV kept him away from court, but rather that Francis had no interest in being involved. His rise to power under Richard was not due to any influence he could bring to the table, and during his time as lord chamberlain he showed no interest in or aptitude for the cut-and-thrust of government politics. This is, of course, reflected by the absence in the sources of any mention of Francis's actions, especially in technically political positions such as Speaker of Parliament.

The only thing that might have drawn attention to Francis as Parliament sat was the passing of a series of acts affirming his possession of all the lands Richard had given him in the last year.[96] Even that was not seen as important enough for any chronicler to mention, however, and the result is that we have no indication as to what contemporaries thought about these generous grants. We know of them only through dry accounts of parliamentary proceedings.

The Year 1484

Once Parliament had closed, Francis, perhaps inspired by this massive addition to his wealth and possessions being ratified, turned once more to personal concerns. In February 1484, a year after Francis and Bishop Wayneflete had reached their compromise, Francis sold Wayneflete the hospital of Saints John and James, located in Brackley in Northamptonshire, for 200 marks. This transaction was said to be done 'on the ground of the neglect there of hospitality and alms-giving'.[97]

This explanation has caused some historians to speculate about the true strength of Francis's piety. G. V. Belenger has argued that the description of the hospital means that Francis showed no interest in it before selling it to Wayneflete, and that even if he found himself unable to support the hospital properly before he came to power in Richard's government, a truly pious man would have given the hospital as a gift rather than selling it.[98]

This argument, while worth addressing, fails to take into account Francis's long minority, during which he would have had no chance to address any of the problems with the hospital. By the time Francis came of age the hospital would have suffered more than a decade of neglect, by which time he might have felt that Wayneflete was better qualified to deal with the issues that had accumulated. Though a certain avarice is undeniable in this transaction, the fact that Francis chose to address the situation by selling up, and the fact that its sorry condition was explicitly mentioned, argues that he was not indifferent. The conditions attached to Wayneflete's purchase also imply Francis was motivated by more than money: Wayneflete promised to have perpetual prayers said there for Francis and his wife Anne every year on 17 September.[99] Curiously, as mentioned earlier, Francis neglected to have prayers said for his ancestors, as would have been the norm.

Francis was involved in another religious transaction later that same month, once more arguing that he was at the very least conventionally pious. On the last day of the 1484 parliament, 20 February 1484, Francis, together with his former guardian John, Duke of Suffolk, and John Russell, Bishop of Lincoln, was granted licence for the foundation of a 'fraternity or gild', which was to renew an older foundation and was to be called the 'Fraternity of the Holy Cross of Abendon'. It was arranged to have 'twelve masters, secular persons or others of either sex', and was to have as its primary purpose 'the repair of the highway leading from Abendon to Dorcastre [Dorchester] co[unty] Oxford', to finance which it was given a 'licence to aquire in mortaim lands, annuities and other possessions, not held in chief, to the value of 100*l* yearly'.[100]

Apart from this secular task, the foundation was to have 'thirteen poor men and women and two chaplains to celebrate divine service daily', not only for 'the good estate of the king and his consort Anne, queen of England and his first-born son Edward, prince of Wales', but also for the good estate of 'the said founders and the brethren and sisters of the gild and for their souls after death and the souls of the king's father Richard, late duke of York, William, late duke of Suffolk, and William Lovell late of Lovell, knight'.[101] As mentioned above, it is highly unusual that Francis chose not to have any prayers said for his own father, John Lovell, instead opting to have them said for his grandfather. In both of the religious transactions of February 1484, Francis would have had the chance to have prayers read for his father John; in fact, it would have been expected. In both transactions, Francis deliberately chose not to do so.

Whatever it was John Lovell had done, Francis was clearly not prepared to forgive him, even nearly twenty years after his death. According to the belief system then prevalent, Francis's refusal to have prayers said for his father meant he deliberately chose to let his father suffer in purgatory without offering any help to shorten his time there.

Notably, even this transgression failed to draw any negative comment about Francis. Nobody cast doubt on his piety or his religious beliefs, and nobody accused him of filial disloyalty. That no chroniclers noted it is understandable; they would not have known of Francis's prayer requests. However, none of the clergymen who would have known about his requests, including two bishops, ever seem to have held anything against Francis. His decision didn't even attract disparaging comment in later years, when the men of Richard's court were so maligned. This is best explained by the theory that Francis was open about why he wanted no prayers said for his father, and that his reasoning was accepted as theologically sound. Given Francis's calm, unobtrusive nature, all we can say is that he must have had very strong feelings to break with tradition so blatantly, in a way that could well have drawn the attention he so often avoided.

Naturally, not only the bishops and men included in the licence would have known, but also the king himself, having given the permission for the foundation of the fraternity and its intended uses. If anyone knew all the details of Francis's troubled childhood, however, it would have been Richard. Francis's decision would not have surprised the king.

Whatever it was that Francis found so unforgivable, the ability revenge himself for it in this way might have given him a feeling of satisfaction. As he had spent much of the last year settling conflicts in his favour and rewarding those loyal to him to the best of his abilities, he might have also taken some pleasure in using what power he had to obtain justice for himself against his father, unearthly justice though it may have been. It might have been a triumph for him, a fitting way to end a parliament in which he had received everything he had wanted.

After the parliament was over, another triumph for Richard and his government occurred when the erstwhile dowager queen, Elizabeth Woodville, chose to come out of sanctuary with her children, on the condition that Richard swear to the safety of her and her daughters.

This is often presented as Elizabeth putting pressure on Richard and telling him her terms, which he had no choice but to fulfil,[102] but as Annette Carson points out, Elizabeth was fairly powerless at that moment and Richard was entirely in control of the situation.[103] It was politically convenient for the king to have Elizabeth and her children leave sanctuary, as it did look bad for him to have them in hiding. However, it was not a pressing matter for Richard. He could have chosen to wait her out; as far as anybody knew, Richard might remain king for decades. A rebellion to put Elizabeth's son on the throne or install her daughter as Henry Tudor's queen consort had only just failed and a repetition cannot have seemed very likely to succeed in early 1484. Without hindsight, Richard had time on his side, knowing that sooner or later Elizabeth would be forced to leave sanctuary if she did not want to stay there with her children for years, or forever.

That Richard instead chose to agree to Elizabeth's demands and guarantee her safety and that of her daughters is indeed remarkable, and may indicate a desire for reconciliation on his part. The oath he swore had already been proposed and read out in May 1483 as an unsuccessful attempt to convince Elizabeth to leave sanctuary,[104] but presumably it was altered to fit the situation now that Richard was king, including what dowry he would give his nieces if and when they married. Perhaps remarkably, this oath was sworn openly, in front of many lords spiritual and temporal. Richard wore royal regalia, doubtlessly intent on showing himself as a kind and forgiving king, and received oaths of fealty from Elizabeth and his nieces in a great spectacle.

Richard may have discussed the idea of this grand gesture with his closest men, Francis included. It was certainly viewed as a peaceful overture at the time, though in later years it was seen as both a sign of Richard's weakness and an admission of his guilt in various matters,[105] most notably the disappearance of his nephews. Though Francis was not a forgiving man and might not have thought Elizabeth deserved to be treated so well and have an oath sworn to her by the king, he would have been canny enough to know Richard was practising good public relations. He would surely have been present when the oath was sworn, though as usual he stayed below the radar and his presence is not recorded.

After this ceremony, which took place on 1 March 1484,[106] the court began to travel again, perhaps in a similar route to the progress of the year before. It can be assumed that Francis was in attendance, as the lord chamberlain's presence would have been required and there is no record of a substitute being appointed. However, there is some confusion on this point due to the dating of some documents. Several documents involving the king are dated to 10 March 1484, some said to have been signed and sealed in Westminster, others in Cambridge.[107] Obviously, Richard can't have been in both places at once, so it seems likely that he travelled from one to the other in a short time and that at least some of the documents were backdated by secretaries unsure of his exact whereabouts on 10 March.

In itself this says nothing about Francis's whereabouts, but to make matters more confusing, at around this time Francis drew up an enfeoffment (an exchange of land for service) dated to 10 March 1484 and with the location given as Minster Lovell.[108] As in the former case, this does not necessarily mean that Francis was there on that exact day or that the document was really drawn up on that day, but it does suggest that he was there around that time. It is therefore possible that he was not at court at this time, having perhaps departed to see to his own personal affairs, including this enfeoffment, but equally it could mean that the court travelled a similar course to the year before, with some additional stops such as Canterbury, starting in Westminster, then through Cambridge rather than Oxford, then Minster Lovell Hall and eventually Nottingham, where the court resided in April.

In fact, a year later, when Francis drew up an indenture to make arrangements for his wife in the event of his death, he stated in it that the 'charter [of enfeoffment]' was done 'while at Northampton',[109] meaning Francis himself was there when this charter was made in his name, and presumably tasked a lawyer with its completion, contradicting the statements made in the charter itself. If he was with the royal court, however, this is an easily explicable error, for the court went to Northampton on 17 March 1484 and it was there that the news of the Prince of Wales broke, which likely would have overshadowed most other memories of that time.

Regardless of his exact location, the enfeoffment shows that Francis clearly continued to concern himself with personal matters alongside his tasks for the king. In the enfeoffment he conveyed several manors, namely Thorpe Waterville, Halse, Duston, Titchmarsh and Brackley, to a number of men close to him, including most notably his brother-in-law George FitzHugh and his loyal associate Edward Franke, as well as Edward's brother Geoffrey, Richard Ratcliffe and William Catesby, the northerner Lord Scrope of Upsale, and two more northerners, James Walton and Thomas Metcalfe.[110] This list of men is interesting in that it shows once more that Francis's connections were mainly northern, and also that they overlapped with Richard's. It also indicates a close or at least functional and trusting relationship with one of his in-laws.

We do not know why Francis made the enfeoffment, but it could well be that he wished to pass on the troublesome task of being lord of the manors in question while at the same time rewarding those who had been close to him. Only thirteen days later he further endowed Edward Franke and Thomas Paleser, a clergyman, granting them outright the manors of Thorpe Waterville and corresponding lands in Higham Ferrers, Achurch, Chelveston, Ridlington, Aldwincle and Calcote. This was probably a pragmatic move; Francis had long been in conflict with Richard Grey over the manors, and his lordship may have been unpopular with the locals. It might have seemed wise to delegate the task of building trust and affection there to somebody who was untainted by the conflict with Grey, and free of preoccupying responsibilities.

Francis was probably glad to be rid of the lands, and he had every reason to be in high spirits in the spring of 1484. However, his good cheer was not to last. Around a month after Francis made the grant to Edward Franke, in late April, the king and queen, and apparently Francis as well, were staying at Nottingham Castle when they received the news that the seven-year-old Prince Edward had died.

The Croyland Chronicle, the only near-contemporary source to report the event (it was written two years later), states that the child 'was seized with an illness of but short duration, and died at Middleham Castle', and that upon hearing the news the king and queen were 'in a state almost bordering on madness, by reason of their sudden grief'.[111] We have no record of how the rest of the court reacted, but surely most would have felt for the grief-stricken parents, and sadly many would have been able to empathise from personal experience.

Since Prince Edward was the king and queen's only child, there would naturally have been concern about the succession. It appears that Richard soon decided to make his oldest nephew, John de la Pole, Earl of Lincoln, his heir presumptive.[112] Though he never issued any statement to this effect, Lincoln was the obvious choice, being Richard's next male relative not barred from the throne. Four months after his son's death, Richard endowed Lincoln with the lieutenancy of Ireland, a title usually held by the heir to the throne and previously held by the late price. Even so, appointing Lincoln would only have solved the issue of the succession temporarily. It would have been considered vital that Richard father an heir of his body, especially given what had happened the last time a king had died without a son to succeed him.

Francis would have been personally affected by the death of Prince Edward, having known the child and being close to his grieving father. Presumably he would also have shared concerns about the political ramifications of the prince's death, but there would have been no time for him to dwell on these feelings. As lord chamberlain, it was his sad duty to make arrangements for the prince's funeral. He would have been following the orders of the distraught parents, but those orders have been lost to history. How and where the short-lived prince was buried remains a mystery.

It has been pointed out that the prince dying 'at Easter time' must have made the arrangements for his funeral rather more difficult, especially if he died during Holy Week. Though the exact date of his death is unknown, as Annette Carson points out, it must have happened on a holy day when travel was restricted, as his parents were unable to leave Nottingham Castle at first.[113] This suggests he may have died on Maundy Thursday or Good Friday, with Good Friday being somewhat less likely as this surely would have been mentioned by John Rous, who was a clergyman.[114] What this meant for Francis was that he would have had to co-ordinate and organise the details of the prince's grave and funeral from a distance – no small task, but one to which he apparently rose. The fact that there was never any comment made on the prince's funeral attests to this; had there been any trouble, it would have surely been seized upon as an evil omen, just as the prince's death itself had been interpreted by the Croyland Chronicle and other sources.

The day after Easter, the court moved to York. It is possible that the prince was buried there, and that the king first went to visit his grave, but there were other duties Richard had to fulfil; his first recorded engagement after arriving in York was to attend the Garter festivities at York Minster.[115] Francis, as usual, was accompanying Richard at the time, while Queen Anne appears to have left his presence, possibly too overcome by grief to tolerate the prying eyes of the court. We have some knowledge of the royal movements and actions at that time in the form of the report made by the Silesian Imperial ambassador Nicholas von Popplau, who visited Richard's court only a fortnight after the prince's death and described the king and his court in detail, notably making no mention of the queen nor any of her ladies, suggesting she was not in attendance.[116]

Popplau was very impressed with Richard, to the extent that, sadly, he showed little interest in the personalities of his courtiers. His report is mostly concerned with the person of Richard himself and the displays he offered at court, which means we do not learn much of Francis from this report. He is only mentioned once, without being named, as one of 'two princes the king's blood-friends',[117] by which Popplau appears to have meant blood relatives of high standing who were also Richard's personal friends.

The first of these was almost certainly Richard's nephew, his new heir presumptive, the Earl of Lincoln, who was obviously a close blood relative of the king and enjoyed a warm and friendly relationship with him. Francis, naturally, was not related by blood to Richard, so whether he was the other lord, or 'prince', referred to by Popplau is not certain, but it seems that the ambassador, who communicated with Richard through interpreters, misunderstood the word 'kinsman', which Richard unfailingly used for Francis due to their close marital ties, as meaning 'blood relation'. In any case, when Popplau visited there were not two men at court who were blood related to Richard and close personal friends at the same time.

These two 'princes' were described by Popplau as 'sit[ting] very far away from the king though, almost at the end of the table', a position that was apparently one of honour, as Richard suggested '[Popplau] sit at the table also with his two blood-friends the abovenamed princes'.[118] So if Popplau was indeed describing Francis in that instance, it confirms once more he was in a place of high honour at Richard's court, allowed to sit next to the king's nephew and heir presumptive, and chosen to entertain ambassadors with him. Since this is a contemporary first-hand account from a man who had no reason to be biased, it might be the best description of Richard we have. Others have analysed the report in depth, but for a study of Francis it is interesting to note that the Richard described by Popplau is very different to the man Francis appears to have been. Talkative, extrovert, ostentatious and easily excited, Richard is described to have been in many ways the complete opposite of the calm, reserved, unobtrusive Francis.[119] The account throws an interesting light on their friendship, so strong despite these fundamental differences.

This personal bond must have made Francis an important person for the king to lean on as he mourned for his son, but even without their personal closeness Francis would have been invaluable at court during the spring and summer 1484, fulfilling his various duties as lord chamberlain. Soon after Popplau's departure, it would have fallen to Francis to organise proceedings when Richard's illegitimate daughter Katherine married in May 1484, an occasion for which Richard had already in March ordered rich materials for clothing, including crimson and blue cloth of gold, as well as velvet, damask and silk of various colours. These were not only for Katherine and her future husband, the Earl of Huntingdon, but also for his niece and nephew Edward, Earl of Warwick and Margaret Plantagenet.[120] This would suggest that his intention was to hold a lavish celebration for the wedding, though perhaps Prince Edward's death made it a more sombre affair than originally envisaged.

Naturally, Francis would not have had anything to do with orders for clothing, but the organisation of the celebration itself – who was allowed where, for instance – would have fallen to him. Once more, it appears he fulfilled his task to the complete satisfaction of the king, provoking no complaint in the historical record.

As ever, Richard appears to have been happy with Francis's work, and shortly afterwards he wrote a letter to his mother which attests to his belief in his friend's capabilities. This letter, dating from 3 June, is about a replacement for William Collyngbourne, one of his mother's estate managers for her properties in Wiltshire:[121]

Madam – I recommend me to you as heartily as is to me possible. Beseeching you in my most humble and affectuous wise of your daily blessing to my singular comfort and defence in my need. And madam, I heartily beseech you that I may often hear from you to my comfort. And such news as be here my servant, Thomas Bryan, this bearer, shall show you, to whom, please it you, to give credence unto. And, madam, I beseech you to be good and gracious, lady, to my lord my chamberlain to be your officer in Wiltshire in such as Collingbourne had. I trust he shall therein do you good service. And that it please you, that by this bearer I may understand your pleasure in this behalf. And I pray God to send you the accomplishment of your noble desires. Written at Pomfret [Pontefract] the 3rd day of June, 1484, with the hand of your most humble son, Ricardus Rex.[122]

The reason for Richard having to suggest a replacement as estate manager was that Collyngbourne had been discovered to have had ties with the rebels of 1483 and was removed from his position because of this. Though Richard courteously asks his mother to convey him 'her pleasure' about this suggestion, he clearly expects her to agree to it, assuring her that Francis would fulfil all expectations.

Interestingly, it sounds as if Cecily was not well acquainted with Francis. Presumably the two would have met before this date, but it is possible they only had a brief introduction. She would without a doubt have had some knowledge of him, his position and capabilities – not solely because he was her son's closest friend and an important if mysterious figure in his government, but also because he was her great-nephew by marriage twice over, being her great-niece Anne FitzHugh's husband and her sister Katherine's step-grandson. This does not mean that they had ever had more than a passing acquaintance, of course, and it is perfectly possible that Cecily only truly paid attention to him when her son suggested him as her estate manager.

Even so, probably to please Richard, Cecily accepted the suggestion and Francis received the position. It would be interesting to know if Cecily insisted on meeting Francis beforehand, and it is possible that it was such a wish that Richard anticipated when stating he wanted to hear her 'pleasure' about the suggestion, rather than any prevarication. In any case, Francis would have held the post only nominally, leaving the actual work to others, and it was probably these people who met with Cecily when necessary to discuss any issues that arose. Francis's work would have been choosing those men who would do the actual work. There is no evidence to indicate whether Francis (or his delegates) did a good job, as Richard so confidently expected, but it can be assumed. As with most of his positions, no frictions or anomalies are recorded, suggesting that Francis did good work.

The appointment as Cecily Neville's estate manager had unexpected and presumably unpleasant consequences for Francis. William Collyngbourne, already dissatisfied with Richard's kingship, did not take kindly to being replaced. Within less than two months of Richard's letter to his mother, on 18 July 1484, Collyngbourne had composed and distributed a scathing little couplet that would become famous over the centuries, lambasting Richard and those he favoured:

The Catte, the Ratte, and Lovell Our Dogge,
Rule All England Under The Hogge.[123]

Though not a challenge to the recently printed Chaucer, this doggerel makes its point loud and clear: Richard, dismissively referred to as 'the hogge', a play on his personal badge of a white boar, is claimed to allow 'the Catte' (his lawyer William Catesby), 'the Ratte' (Sir Richard Ratcliffe), and Francis, like Richard dismissively connected with his badge, to rule the country in his stead.

This couplet is the only negative mention of Francis from his lifetime. It is often taken as indicative of a widespread negative opinion of him, but nothing else survives to suggest Francis was seen as overreaching himself, allowed by Richard to act in a way unsuitable for his standing, more or less ruling the country. There is, however, evidence for the same being believed about William Catesby and Sir Richard Ratcliffe by more people. An example of this is found in the Croyland Chronicle, in which, as mentioned above, the two men are said to have been largely responsible for the executions of Anthony Woodville, Earl Rivers, Richard Grey and presumably Thomas Vaughan, though the latter is not mentioned in that context.

In fact, the text of the chronicle places more of the blame on Ratcliffe and Catesby than on the king, stating, rather strangely, that the two strongly counselled Richard against a marriage with his niece Elizabeth, fearing she would exact revenge against them for having counselled to the king to the execution of her maternal uncle and half-brother.[124] The fact that the chronicle does not include any indication of rumours Elizabeth was opposed to marrying her uncle for having *ordered* those executions creates an impression of her knowing that it was Catesby and Ratcliffe who bore most of the responsibility. This suggests a picture of Richard's government not unlike that invoked by Collyngbourne's couplet: two comparatively low-born advisors manipulating the king, making decisions in his stead. This impression is strengthened by the narrative also placing them at the centre of the supposed discussions about a match between the king and his niece.

Francis is not mentioned at all in Croyland's narrative, the anonymous chronicler clearly not connecting him with the other two or with any of the supposed nefarious goings-on at Richard's court. This suggests that William Catesby and Richard Ratcliffe had not simply become known as an interfering pair due to Collyngbourne's rhyme by the time the Croyland Chronicle was written. If this had been the case, Francis would surely have been lumped in with Ratcliffe and Catesby. More likely, the two had acquired a bad reputation as manipulative and sinister by 1484, or possibly even earlier, and this was why Collyngbourne, who appeared never to have had anything to do with either and cannot have had a personal problem with them, chose them for his couplet. Francis's inclusion was almost certainly the result of a personal grudge, though; coming so soon after he replaced Collyngbourne as Cecily Neville's estate manager, it was an angry reaction by the poetaster to his usurpation. Interestingly, this is a reflection of Francis's position in government – not political but personal.

The fact that the Croyland Chronicle does not include Francis in its complaints about Richard and his court is telling. Though he was undoubtedly very close to the monarch, Francis's work was unremarkable. Apart from Collyngbourne's couplet, there was no accusation of manipulation against him, no complaint he was abusing his position for his own gain. For most chroniclers, he was not interesting enough to excite any comment at all. He is rarely mentioned even by later chroniclers, writing for the dynasty that had replaced Richard on the throne and running a successful smear campaign against him. Nobody includes him in any of Richard's supposed nefarious crimes. In most of these chronicles he is not mentioned at all, perhaps because there was not much to use against him and because other figures at Richard's court made for more compelling scapegoats.

Even so, it is notable that no one ever claimed Francis was motivated by greed in his support of Richard, for the trickle of grants and favours to him continued. Only shortly after Richard secured Francis the position as his mother's estate manager in Wiltshire, he gave Francis a rather important position in the newly reformed Council of the North, a part of the royal council obviously especially concerned with matters pertaining to the north of the country, previously led by Richard in his brother Edward IV's reign and probably intended by him to continue the work he had started there as Lord of the North.[125] As Peter Hammond points out, while this council was only formally begun in late June 1484 and the founding documents were dated 24 June 1484,[126] it must have been planned before that, perhaps with young Prince Edward intended as its nominal head. With his death it was the new heir presumptive, Lincoln, who was put in charge.

It was because of his newfound significance that Lincoln received this honour, as he himself was not a northerner and apparently had few connections to the north. The men working under him in this council, however, were largely northerners, or strongly connected to the north. Francis would have been one of the latter, and his connections to the north would come to stand him in good stead, which once more suggests that what work he did for this council he did well.

In the ordinances drawn up for the Council of the North, Francis's young cousin Henry, Lord Morley, was mentioned prominently. With both sitting on the council and being of some importance, it is possible that the two worked together and possibly even grew close. Equally, despite both being members of the council, they might not have seen too much of one another; together with Lincoln, Lord Morley was apparently required to be present in the north as often as was possible, and was involved in the care of the 'children',[127] which presumably meant Richard's young nephew Edward, Earl of Warwick as well as Edward IV's younger daughters. This would suggest that Lord Morley often stayed at Sheriff Hutton, where at least Edward, Earl of Warwick's household is known to have been.

It is possible that Francis was present there in the summer of 1484, especially given that together with Sandal Castle it was the headquarters for the council, but if so he does not appear to have been there for very long. Francis had to be at court most of the time attending to his duties as lord chamberlain, organising Richard's day-to-day life and being richly rewarded for it. In August 1484, he received a grant of annuities, dated back to Michaelmas (29 September) 1483, 'from the issues of the lordships of Cokeham and Bray, county Berkshire' of '10*l* [pounds] for seven years, 40*l* during the life of Margaret Harcourt, widow, late the wife of Robert Harcourt, knight, and 24*l* during the life of Anne, sometime the wife of John Stonor, esquire'.[128] These lordships had been forfeited during the 1483 rebellion, and there is nothing particularly notable in this grant in itself; it is one of a number of similar grants Francis received from December 1483 onward. What is notable, however, is that the grant was made on the same day as one to his sister Frideswide of a very generous annuity of one hundred marks 'from the issues of the honour of lordship of Walingford', a castle of which Francis was constable, for unspecified services to the king.[129]

These grants may have been given to Francis at a time of great stress for him, as during the summer of 1484 he had a lot to organise in his position as lord chamberlain, seeing to it that all of the king's endeavours ran smoothly. This would not only have included all that has been mentioned above – the funeral of Prince Edward, the wedding of Richard's daughter Katherine, the establishment of the Council of the North – but also a very important piece of foreign policy.

Richard, eager to secure peace after his son's death, spent a lot of the summer of 1484 in Nottingham Castle, directing men against Scottish pirates intent on making war on England.[130] Scotland, defeated by Richard when he led Edward IV's army only two years before, was soon ready to negotiate with the English king. Richard, feeling conciliatory, agreed to receive the party sent by the Scottish king James III, a rather impressive group including the Bishop of Aberdeen, the Chancellor of Scotland and lords Oliphant and Lyle. This party arrived in Nottingham on 11 September 1484, and was received by Richard a day later. This reception is described by Paul Murray Kendall as having been attended by '[t]he greatest powers of his kingdom', specifically 'Norfolk, Northumberland, and Stanley, Chancellor Russell, the Earls of Shrewsbury and Nottingham, the Bishops of St Asaph's and Worcester, Sir Robert Percy, Comptroller of his Household, his councillors William Catesby and Sir Richard Ratcliffe, and the Chief Justices Bryan and Husee. Beyond them in ranks stood the Knights and Esquires of the King's Body and the royal henchmen, captained by Sir James Tyrell.'[131] The meeting was a success; a peace treaty was agreed upon and a marriage arranged between the crown prince of Scotland, another James, and Richard's niece Anne de la Pole, younger sister of Richard's heir presumptive.[132]

Naturally, such a meeting had to be perfectly planned. Not only would it have required all of Francis's attention, but also that of many other men of high standing. A lot of the organisational work would have fallen to Francis, passing on orders from the king and seeing to it that everything went well, selecting the workers and merchants involved and seeing to it that they were remunerated.

Despite his role, as we can see in Kendall's description, Francis is not noted to have been present. He might have been one of the unnamed lords in the report, but this would be unusual considering he had been named in the accounts for most festivities during 1483. This suggests that Francis was not present at the meeting, though his absence from such an important event is difficult to explain. Most likely he had no choice in the matter, either owing to some emergency or because he fell ill. If, as postulated above, Francis was easily susceptible to stress, his absence would hardly be a surprise; he would have been reeling by now after the difficulty of organising such a meeting hot on the heels of the prince's death and funeral, the wedding of the king's daughter, Collyngbourne's public attack and his new role reporting to the king's mother.

If Francis was suffering from stress, he had the early part of September as well as October and most of November to recover before he was first noted to be involved in government actions again, after the court had moved back to Westminster. On 29 November, he had the unpleasant duty of sitting on a jury, together with other influential men such as John Howard, Duke of Norfolk, to decide in the trial of William Collyngbourne, the man who had earlier in the year written the lampoon insulting Richard and Francis as well as William Catesby and Sir Richard Ratcliffe.[133] Despite this poem being Collyngbourne's biggest claim to fame, it was not what he had to stand trial for. Rather, it had been discovered that he was colluding with rebels, having written seditious letters to Henry Tudor in Brittany to ask him to invade and kill the king.[134]

This was treason, and Collyngbourne's gruesome punishment cannot have been in much doubt even before the trial began. The couplet he had written was mentioned in the condemnation, though not as the main charge. It was simply mentioned as a further act against the king he had committed. Unsurprisingly, the jury decided that Collyngbourne's seditious letters warranted the death sentence. Since Collyngbourne was a commoner, this meant he received the traditional punishment for traitors, being hanged, drawn and quartered, on Tower Hill in London.[135]

Things were going quite well for Richard. Rebels were being ferreted out and dealt with, the Scottish issue had been settled for the time being, and there were no troubles save the threat of Henry Tudor, which didn't worry Richard overmuch. Despite this, court would have been an unhappy place that autumn. Not only would the king and queen still have been mourning their son, but Queen Anne had not yet shown any signs of pregnancy, and this was being discussed, sotto voce, with concern.[136]

Francis would have known what measures, if any, were taken by the king and queen to address this problem – perhaps they saw physicians, drank special concoctions or had prayers said. Having no children himself, Francis may very well have sympathised with the desperate attempts to conceive,; the indenture he made in 1485 arranging for his wife in the event of his death strongly indicates he had given up any hope of having children. Richard and Anne did not have the luxury of such resignation. Under constant watch, their childlessness would have been a political issue – not just a personal failure but a national one.

Later rumours, chronicled by the anonymous author at Croyland and also by more hostile, Tudor-sponsored sources, indicate that the blame for this failure to conceive was fully assigned to Queen Anne.[137] This would have squared with the standard of the time whereby women were blamed for any difficulties with conception, pregnancy and birth. In this case it would have seemed only logical, given that King Richard had at least two healthy illegitimate children, while Queen Anne had only one child.

This pressure on Queen Anne might have already had an effect on her health, though she was famously said to have become ill only after the Christmas festivities of that year.[138] It can hardly be doubted that the expectations on her to conceive, as well as grief for her child, would have been detrimental. Again, Francis might have sympathised, knowing first-hand the personal strain of not being able to have children, but if he had such feelings of sympathy for her they remained private and none of his actions in any way reflect them. It is even possible that he did not particularly care; neither he nor his wife had ever shown any sign of affection for Queen Anne. In fact, Anne Lovell's decision not to serve the queen might argue that she, at least, was not close to Richard's wife, and Francis appeared to support his wife in this, arguing that he felt the same.

Francis's loyalty was always to Richard, and so it was in this case. His personal feelings can only be guessed at, but it would hardly be surprising if he also blamed Queen Anne for her failure to conceive and even resented her for it. Later chroniclers, such as Polydore Vergil, would claim that Richard blamed her too,[139] but of course this served a narrative and is impossible to ascertain. In more contemporary sources, such as the Croyland Chronicle, there is no hint of Richard showing such feelings, though this chronicle references rumours of Richard wanting a divorce.[140]

This has been strenuously denied by most historians sympathetic to Richard, but it is not a claim that can be so easily dismissed. It is known that in December 1484 the king sent an envoy on a mysterious mission to the Vatican,[141] and a month later, in January 1485, he made contact with the Portuguese royal family to arrange a new marriage for himself.[142] It is quite possible, though by no means certain, that having sought the approval of the Vatican, Richard wished to annul his marriage to Queen Anne and arrange a new match for himself.

This is important for any study of Francis and his life because he was completely supportive of whatever Richard planned to do. His loyalty was not to the royal family but to Richard alone, which is notable as it is an accepted myth that the northern lords gave their loyalty to Richard only because of Anne Neville, and that the rumours of divorce upset them and threatened their loyalty to him, forcing the king to change his plans. There is no actual indication in the actions of any of those lords that this is true, and in fact it is easy to see where the rumour first started, and how it grew.

The first such claim is found in the Croyland Chronicle, written less than two years after Richard's marital troubles. This chronicle presents the north's loyalty to Anne Neville as one of several arguments made by William Catesby and Sir Richard Ratcliffe to dissuade Richard from pursuing a marriage with his niece Elizabeth, eldest daughter of Edward IV. According to this account they then convinced Richard to deny he had ever intended such a course of action, a denial that the Croyland Chronicler held to be untrue, prompted by the fact that 'it was supposed by many, that these men, together with others like them, threw so many impediments in the way.'[143] One of these impediments was supposedly that 'all the people of the north, in whom he placed the greatest reliance, would rise in rebellion against him, and impute to him the death of the queen, the daughter and one of the heirs of the earl of Warwick, through whom he had first gained his present high position.'[144]

It was from this that Polydore Vergil spun his story that the north of the country was in fact loyal to Queen Anne, not King Richard, but evidence appears to contradict this. The north was steadfastly loyal to Richard, and showed no special allegiance to the queen. In fact, Francis himself was a lord of some importance in the north, as was his brother-in-law Richard FitzHugh.[145] Both of them, best placed to have information about both Richard's plans and Anne's state of health, showed no sign of disagreement with Richard. Francis may have been emotional, letting his affection for Richard rule over him, but this was probably not the case for Richard FitzHugh, who was nowhere near as close to the king. Presumably, he and the other lords would have felt sorry for Queen Anne but recognised the necessity of the king having an heir of his body, and that if she was not able to give him one then she had failed in her most important duty as queen.

Such contemplations, however, would not have been easy for anyone, and Francis, once more right in the middle of all planning that might have been going on, would have been stressed. It is unlikely that he, or anyone else at court, looked forward to the approaching Christmas festivities with the same happy anticipation and relief that characterised the celebrations the year before. However, this Christmas at court was a famously lavish affair, celebrated with 'remarkable splendour',[146] as the Croyland Chronicle put it, and one that would cause a scandal. The reason for this scandal was the arrival of the king's niece. Elizabeth, together with her younger sister Cecily, was entering her aunt Queen Anne's household as a lady-in-waiting.[147]

Richard famously appears to have liked his niece, which caused the rumour that he meant to marry her. There is no indication that he ever really intended to, and by the time of Christmas 1484 he must have already been making plans for a match with the Portuguese princess Joana of Aviz, whose brother Joao II he would contact with a proposal a month later.[148] However, there can be no doubt that Elizabeth was favoured during the Christmas festivities. Though these celebrations are so shrouded in myth that it is hard to say what happened when, it seems that Elizabeth was given at least one dress of a fine fabric similar to the queen's, and according to the Croyland Chronicle Elizabeth played games with the queen which involved them changing their gowns. These 'vain changes of apparel presented to queen Anne and the lady Elizabeth'[149] caused rumours about Elizabeth being closer to the king than was fitting. Such frivolities, and the resulting rumours, overshadowed everything else in all sources describing the festivities, though the Croyland Chronicle rather contradicts itself by stating that '[t]he feast of the Nativity was kept with due solemnity at the palace at Westminster';[150] perhaps it was not the celebrations themselves but simply Elizabeth's part in them which was seen as untoward.

Francis was not entirely focused on the revelries. Before Twelfth Night, on 4 January 1485, his sister Joan's widower Brian was granted permission to remarry,[151] which could very well have awoken sad memories for Francis.

Bastard Niece?

Brian's impending remarriage was not the only personal news Francis received around Christmas 1484, for something else happened which might have taken his mind off Brian and demanded his full attention. In very early 1485, or perhaps late December 1484, Francis's sister Frideswide gave birth to her third child and first daughter, a baby she named Anne, probably after Francis's wife. This was the third of Anne's nieces named after her.

Though it is notable that Frideswide did not choose to name her daughter Joan after her mother and sister, Anne appears to have been a doting aunt and thus had been chosen twice by her older sisters as namesake and probably godmother for their daughters. Frideswide, who had grown up with Anne and was closest to her in age of all the FitzHugh girls, wanted to honour a woman she liked, and also make her a godmother.

However, apart from affection for her sister-in-law, there might have been another reason why Frideswide chose to avoid the name Joan – it was her mother-in-law's name. Frideswide did not appear to be close to her husband,[152] and may not have wanted to name her child in a way that could be interpreted as a friendly gesture to his committed Lancastrian family. However, there are some notable oddities which could point to a rather more scandalous motivation.

Shortly after the birth, on 10 January 1485 Richard made another grant to Frideswide, in addition to the one of 18 August 1484, this time of 'a yearly rent of 100 marks from Easter last from the issues of the honour or lordship of Wallingford',[153] the place for which he had granted her the earlier annuity, dating back to Easter 1484. Curiously, this second grant appears to have been not a confirmation of the first but an addition to it, meaning he granted her a total of an annuity of 200 marks – a sizeable sum, significantly more than he had granted Margaret, Countess of Oxford, who received £100, and even his own mother-in-law, Anne Beauchamp, who received £80 in addition to free board at one of his castles.

These grants and their size would already be notable, but there is also the fact that on the day of this second grant Francis himself was given a 'grant for life [...] of the office of steward of the lordships of Cokeham and Bray [...] with the accustomed fee from the issues of the lordships and all other profits, and authority to grant the office to any person',[154] an enlargement of the grant made to him when his sister received her first annuity. This grant was backdated to Michaelmas 1483.

The most obvious reason for the grants is that Richard wished to please Francis and chose to do so not only by granting him the manors but also giving Frideswide an annuity, perhaps to help her and her family in a rather difficult situation. Her father-in-law, William Norris, had joined the rebellion in 1483 and had consequently been attainted, meaning Frideswide and her husband, still a minor, must have been living in straitened circumstances. Though Francis received many of William Norris's forfeited lands and may very well have used them to support his sister and her family, passing at least some of the income back to them,[155] they would not have wanted to be dependent on such charity. It is probable that Richard wished to remedy that, doing a good turn for his beloved friend's sister.

Many other traitors' widows or wives were supported through small annuities as a matter of course. Frideswide, on the other hand, was given a grant with a vague explanation of services to the king. With this in mind, and given that the second grant was made just after Frideswide gave birth, there is another, rather more scandalous explanation: Richard might have been the father. The annuities could have been provisions for mother and child.

If this was the real reason for the grant, it would be fascinating to know Francis's thoughts. His sister was married, and Richard sleeping with her could be seen as dishonouring her. On the other hand, he amply provided for her and the child, and must have kept the affair very discreet, so that there was no scandal attached to Frideswide's name. In any case, if such an affair occurred, Francis must have known of it from the first, and there is no indication that he and Richard had any serious arguments. This either means that the grants to Frideswide had a more innocent purpose or that Francis accepted, if perhaps not condoned, an affair between the two.

In fact, if this was the case, it would also throw a different light on the grants made to Francis at the same time. It makes little sense for the grants to have been hush money, as this should have been paid much earlier, at around the time the affair took place rather than months later, and Francis was treated with complete trust by

Richard, which would hardly be the case if the king imagined he needed to buy Francis's silence. Much more likely is that Francis provided for his sister in her pregnancy, and perhaps even agreed to take in his small niece and raise her in his household. In the case of little Anne being Richard's child, this might have been seen as the best course for everyone involved. Francis and Anne, still childless after nearly a decade of living as man and wife, may well have been happy to have a child to raise, while Francis's closeness with both Richard and Frideswide would have meant the child's mother and father could have come to see her whenever they wished.

Of course, little Anne being Richard's, and Frideswide giving birth to the king's illegitimate daughter at the time of the Christmas festivities, would encourage a rather different interpretation of events at court. It would certainly go some way towards explaining Richard's apparent exuberance and good spirits, lamented in the Croyland Chronicle;[156] the expected birth of a new baby would have been a comfort after the death of his son.

It might also explain the rumours of Anne being 'neglected' despite being present in all court festivities, having all the finery and deference due to her and being treated well, as was her due. Kings siring bastards was hardly unheard of, but it is hardly far-fetched to suggest that Queen Anne would have been saddened at her apparent infertility while her husband's mistress bore him a baby daughter.

In fact, Richard having an illegitimate baby at this time could also explain an otherwise rather inexplicable rumour also circulating at this time connected with Elizabeth of York and hinted at in the Croyland Chronicle as 'other things which are not written in this book, and of which I grieve to speak' and which are said to have been 'so distasteful, so numerous that they can hardly be reckoned, and so pernicious in their example, that we ought not so much as suggest them to the minds of the perfidious.'[157] This rumour was that Elizabeth had slept with her uncle and become pregnant.

This rumour is untrue. It spread nonetheless, and not simply as an exaggeration of the marriage rumours; French chronicler Jean Molinet, writing approximately ten years later, stated outright that Richard seduced and impregnated her: 'There went to court the oldest daughter of his brother, the King Edward, a young girl and beautiful beyond measure; and newly rejected [?] from marrying the Dauphin. He promised her she was next after his wife in standing: He impregnated her and they had a child.'[158]

Elizabeth was very much in the public eye from the Christmas festivities of 1484 to her death decades later, so she could not have possibly hidden a pregnancy, making the rumour rather bizarre. However, as detailed above, the fact that Richard favoured Elizabeth during the Christmas festivities raised some eyebrows and caused gossip; and as John Ashdown-Hill points out, Richard's arrangements for a new marriage with Joana of Aviz also included a match between Elizabeth and Joana's cousin, the then sixteen-year-old Manuel of Beja.

These arrangements could have easily been conflated in the rumours, merging two separate marriages for the king and his eldest niece into one marriage between the two of them.[159] If the birth of an illegitimate child happened at the same time, this could very easily have given the rumours a fresh impetus. Since Frideswide remained obscure, the mother of the baby would have been unknown and naturally some would have suspected the young woman with whom Richard's name was already linked in court gossip.

While some of the evidence is rather suggestive, that is all this is: suggestion. However, it seems clear that whoever the father was, Francis would have been happy to have a new niece. If Frideswide's husband was the father, though, it would have affected Francis far less than if she was Richard's. In the latter case, it would have been pleasing but distant news. If she was truly Richard's, and Francis and Anne agreed to take her in, this would have caused some upheaval in the Lovell household as arrangements were made to ensure the child had proper care, with nurses and others employed to look after her. Sadly, no accounts of the Lovell household survive to confirm or debunk this.

The Beginning of the End

It is possible that the birth of baby Anne required Francis to leave court to oversee arrangements in January 1485, but nothing survives to indicate this. Most likely, Francis spent most if not all of his time in Richard's presence as usual, and witnessed first-hand the sad decline in Queen Anne's health around or shortly after the Christmas festivities. According to the Croyland Chronicle, reporting the rumours about Elizabeth and Richard mentioned above, Richard was planning to make his match 'on the anticipated death of the queen taking place, or else, by means of a divorce',[160] which could mean that Anne was already known to be unwell by Christmas 1484 but not yet certain to die. However, since the Croyland Chronicle was written later and with obvious hindsight, its timeline is not entirely reliable. There is no primary source other than the Croyland Chronicle which puts public knowledge of her illness so early in the chronology of events.

By January 1485, however, either the queen's illness had either already become common knowledge or Richard had sought to divorce her, as he began making preparations for his remarriage, which he could not have done without the advice of his council. In this, the anonymous chronicler at Croyland was correct; he was simply mistaken about the identity of Richard's intended second wife.

We do not know the precise role Francis played in the plans for Richard's remarriage. As lord chamberlain, he would have been expected to have taken care of many details regarding envoys and ambassadors, plus preparation for the inevitable journey to Portugal. As usual, Francis appears to have risen to the occasion without eliciting any comment.

Significantly, as lord chamberlain, Francis would also have had to see to the employment and payment of the physicians who treated the royal couple; this task would have been of utmost importance now that the queen's illness had become public knowledge.[161] Francis would not have chosen the physicians himself, but arranging their employment would have been yet another task added to his workload, and a rather melancholy one at that. Though he himself probably saw little of the ailing queen, he would have been privy to the details of her decline up to her death on 16 March 1485. As so often at medieval courts, these events were not just personal tragedies but also matters of political significance and superstition. Francis would have been troubled by the suggestion of ill omens, in addition to his personal grief. It can be assumed that Francis felt at least some regret for the early death of a woman he had known since childhood, but as he does not appear to have been very close to the queen, it might not have been much more than that.

Not much was written of Richard's reaction to his wife's fatal illness at the time, though in history books it is infallibly depicted as one of two extremes. Depending on whether or not a writer is sympathetic to Richard, he is either described as being gleeful about his wife's death as it freed him up to remarry,[162] or devastated by the loss of a wife more beloved than any other.[163] From what scant evidence there is, it can be surmised that the truth, unsurprisingly, lay in the middle. Richard appears to have shown conventional grief at the passing of his wife but was not crushed. Whatever his feelings, he did what he had to do, organising envoys to his sister Margaret in Burgundy, preparing his ambassador Edward Brampton's journey to Portugal to organise a remarriage for himself, and keeping up the normal workings of the government.

Richard's reaction overshadows all others in chronicles and history books, and as usual Francis merits no mention. However, once more, he must have been deeply involved in the proceedings at court. As lord chamberlain, it fell to him to organise the queen's funeral, just as he had organised that of Prince Edward. He would have been in discussion with Richard about how the ceremony should unfold. Unlike Prince Edward's funeral, however, there is no doubt about when and where Queen Anne's funeral took place. Less than two weeks after her death, the queen was laid to rest in Westminster Abbey, according to the anonymous chronicler at Croyland, 'with no less honors than befitted the interment of a queen'.[164]

For all that was rumoured at the time and later said about Richard, all the claims that he had wanted his wife dead or even poisoned her, it was never said that the funeral was anything but what was expected: respectful, traditional and perfectly organised. In fact, it is notable that all the events at court which it was Francis's task to organise appear to have been perfectly planned and executed. The lord chamberlain clearly had a remarkable talent. Such a knack for organisation was invaluable in a position that required it so much, and it is quite possible that Francis also had a hand in all the planning and organisation necessary following the queen's death, if only taking care of all the minutiae, such as organising the proper transport for envoys and ambassadors.

Almost immediately after Queen Anne's funeral, there would have been something else for Francis to organise, and this time it was something less conventional. In the immediate aftermath of the queen's death rumours abounded that Richard had been happy about her death, perhaps even sped it along, and especially that he intended to marry his niece Elizabeth of York. On 30 March,[165] the king chose to openly deny these rumours in front of the citizens, merchants and aldermen of the city of London.

The Mercers' Company recorded that denial on 31 March 1485, saying that 'the Kyng sende fore & had tofor hym at sent Johnes as yesterdaye the Mayre & Aldermen where as he in the grete Hall there in the presens of many of his lordes & of muche other peple shewde his grefe and displeasure'[166] at the rumours of him being happy about his wife's death, even being involved in it, and wanting to marry his niece. The Croyland Chronicle concurs almost word for word, saying that '[t]he king, accordingly, followed their advice a little before Easter, in presence of the mayor and citizens of London, in the great hall of the Hospital of Saint John, by making the said denial in a loud and distinct voice.'[167]

This was probably less about Richard wanting to save his reputation among his citizens and more about him wanting to make it clear to King Joao II of Portugal that he was still very interested in the matches he had sent his ambassador to discuss with him – one for himself to Joao's sister Joana of Aviz and one for Elizabeth to Joana's cousin Manuel of Beja – and that there was no truth to any rumours that might reach him.[168]

Much like his oath to Elizabeth Woodville a year earlier, this appears to have been interpreted differently by his immediate contemporaries than it was by later historians; at the time it was accepted as a clear statement.[169] Francis presumably organised the details of the meeting in which Richard made his denial, and he was present during it, but that is all that can be said about his involvement.

On 5 May 1485,[170] roughly a month after Richard's denial of the rumours, Francis saw his long-standing quarrel with the Hastings family finally resolved through the intervention and 'mediation of frendes'. These friends were not named in the source reporting the quarrel, but they might have been members of the FitzHugh family, related to both Francis and Katherine Hastings. The conclusion reached was very favourable to Francis. In order to keep the manors and lands Francis had claimed, Katherine was required to make him a one-time payment of 200 marks and to convey to him lands worth that amount annually.[171] This was presented as a compromise, but was so obviously in Francis's favour that David Baldwin suggests Francis must have been after even more.[172]

This claim is based on a mention that the conflict 'cannot finally be appeased during the nonage [non-age, meaning minority] of the said Edward Ld Hastyngs', which Baldwin reads as a threat by Francis – a declaration he was about to make another, harsher, claim once Edward came of age[173] – but there is no evidence to support this. The statement was a fact – once Edward Hastings came into his properties, legal matters previously arranged with his guardian had to be settled again in many cases, especially disputed ones such as this; and there is no reason why Francis, after having made his claim but committed no violence, would after two years suddenly decide to settle for less than he wanted rather than pushing it all through immediately, or simply waiting another year if he thought he stood a better chance once Edward was of age.

Even so, it was a sorry interaction, a very rare instance of Francis ignoring established facts and law to pursue a grudge. It shows him at his worst, acquisitive and greedy. All that can be said in his defence is that he could have acted worse had he chosen to, trying to take the manors and lands he wanted by force. This does not, however, excuse his behaviour towards Katherine and Edward Hastings, which has to be seen as a black mark against his character.

Preparing for War

Francis must have been pleased about the long quarrel with the Hastings family finally being resolved in his favour, but from now on he would have few reasons for cheer. By April 1485, the threat of invasion loomed large over Richard's court, and he began making preparations to defend his crown. Before going to Northampton to coordinate the defence, Richard went to visit his mother Cecily in May 1485,[174] with Francis in tow.

If Francis spoke to Cecily on the visit, it would have been the last time – just as it was the last time Richard saw his mother. Shortly after Richard left her manor, defensive preparations began and Francis left court to fortify the south coast. Though he was only given the task to outfit the ships of the royal fleet and commandeer them on 26 June, he left court before that and was travelling south early that month. On 10 June, while staying at his cousin Henry, Lord Morley's property of Wooburn Deincourt on the way to Southampton, Francis drew up the indenture to make provisions for his wife in the event of his death.

Though there is no indication that Francis wrote a will, or at least no reference to it survives, in a way the indenture seems to have served a similar purpose. Like a will, it also gives the impression of a man thinking about his life and what legacy he might leave behind:

To all those faithful in the Scripture, greetings are given from me, Francis Viscount Lovell. My charter dated at Minster Lovell the tenth day of March in the first year of the reign of King Richard, the third since the conquest delivered and surrendered. In the same charter of mine Thomas, lord Scrope of Upsale, Richard Ratcliffe, William Catesby, Thomas Malyverer, knights, George FitzHugh, clerk, Geoffrey Franke, Thomas Metcalf, Edward Franke and James Walton were affirmed in my manors Thorpe Waterville, Duston, Titchmarsh, Halse, Brakely while at Northampton. They, namely the same Thomas lord Scrope of Upsale, William, Thomas, George, Geoffrey, Thomas, Edward and James, have and hold all said manors, and their rents, lordships and service.

They shall fulfill and assist their duties with their heads to the best of their abilities after my death and according to my counsel, made clear in this charter. However, under this form and condition, if Anne, now the wife of me the said Francis Viscount Lovell, survives me, then that the said Thomas, lord Scrope of Upsale, Richard Ratcliffe, William Catesby, Thomas Malyverer, knights, George FitzHugh, clerk, Geoffrey Franke, Thomas Metcalf, Edward Franke and James Walton, give up and sacrifice their enfeoffeement and affirm Anne the wife of me, the said Francis Viscount Lovell, in all manors and their lordships, rents and services. The same Anne has and holds it during the time of her life, without any inconveniences which may remain for the same Anne after my death.

The same intentions and wishes of me, the said Francis, given clearly, and reminded of by me the said Francis Viscount Lovell, do not hinder forms and prevent gifts made during the time of the life by Anne my wife. I want that my complete deeds and grants about this are shown later to my feoffees, afterwards to give and transfer to Anne the wife of me, the said Francis, my manors of Halse and Brakely and all their etc. at Northampton, to be have and held by the same Anne. She shall fulfill and assist her duties with her head to the best of her abilities. I leave my debt gone and settled. And I am the true lord Francis Viscount Lovell and give my said manors and all their etc to the said Anne. She shall fulfill and assist them in spite of the family speaking and claiming defence.

And for this my gift I want that Anne the wife of me, the said Francis Viscount Lovell, orders two priests of good description, fame and conditions, to celebrate to help me the said Francis gain forgiveness and goodwill, which I want situated in Cambridge or Oxford and read two times a year in their university, for thirty years fully completed. I also want that the said Anne takes my obit once a year during her life.

In the presence of witnesses etc, holding to the Scriptures, I put this to law. Sealed by me and by those appointed to testify, for which I took Alice Ruge, Robert Kyttingale, Edward Franke, Thomas Beston, Richard Rendell and Alys. Dated at Wooburn, the tenth day of June in the second year of the reign of King Richard, the third since the conquest.[175]

What is most notable about this indenture is naturally his extreme generosity to his wife Anne. Rather than giving her lifetime rights to some of his possessions, Francis gave her outright ownership of the two manors Halse and Brakley and their lordships, and effectively made her the liege lady in charge of all other manors mentioned in the indenture, giving her complete control over them.

This meant that, for all intents and purposes, she was their owner during her lifetime. Since these manors and lordships were rich ones – several of which Francis had had gone through disputes to own – this was not only an endowment which would have left Anne a rich woman, it was also one which must have had personal significance for the couple.

This is far from the only point of interest in this indenture. While the generosity speaks to Francis's feelings for his wife, the terms of the endowment allow for some more general observations about his character.

For one, there is a certain insecurity noticeable in the curious request that Anne have prayers said for him in return for his 'gift'. This is a rather strange provision, given that it was the norm for both men and women to have prayers said for deceased spouses, no matter what their actual relationship was like and, as mentioned above, such requests were common without any gift attached to them. Unlike his maternal grandfather, John Beaumont, for example, who included a dry item that 'my obytt be held yerely'[176] in an otherwise fairly emotive will, Francis added this curiously emotive request in a dry indenture not meant to be particularly personal. Added to that is the fact that we know of absolutely no reason which could have given Francis the feeling that Anne would only be prepared to do the bare minimum for him in exchange for generosity, so that this curious addition is more indicative of his subjective feelings than it is of any hard facts.

The indenture confirms that since 1483 Francis had further developed his interest in universities, and that this was why he asked for his obituary to be read in a prestigious university. While Oxford was close to Francis's ancestral home of Minster Lovell Hall, Cambridge was not too far away either. Since he had no preference for either, it seems like proximity was not the motivation; more likely it was the fact of the venue being a prestigious seat of learning.

Perhaps the most interesting feature of the indenture is Francis's implicit certainty that he would never have any children. Anne inheriting two manors means that she would have been able to pass them on to her own descendants. This arrangement could have disadvantaged any children Anne had by him, as any children

Anne had by another man after Francis's death would have a claim to them, so it seems he thought – or knew – that their childlessness was his fault, and did not, as was the norm for the time, blame her.

This might have been directly due to his health; as mentioned above, he may well have suffered from chronic illness. Horribly, it might also be connected to sexual trauma that possibly took place in his childhood, explaining his apparent hatred for his father. It could also be that abstinence was advised by physicians to manage a condition he had. While there were different views on sexual activity and health during the fifteenth century, a widespread opinion seems to have been that too much sex could be detrimental to physical health. For example, upon the early death of Prince Juan of Asturias, son of Isabella of Castile and Ferdinand of Aragon, stories circulated that this was his cause of death, and supposedly there had been concern about it even in his own household before his death. If such medical opinions were held in England at the time, it might therefore be that Francis did not want to risk his already frail health, or was advised not to.

Maybe his conviction that their childlessness was due to him was because of his own insecurity, so obvious in the indenture, and not based on any knowledge of his actions or lack thereof, but on balance this seems unlikely. Unless he was absolutely certain he would have no children, he would have allowed for the chance it might still happen, even if he considered it unlikely. This is another piece of evidence pointing towards possible bad health.

Finally, his anticipation of trouble from 'the family' also throws an interesting light on his relationship with his cousin Henry, Lord Morley. It could very well be argued that despite their joint involvement in the Council of the North, things had not improved since their quarrel in late 1483, and that this shows in the arrangements Francis made for Anne and in his expectations of how Lord Morley would react.

Lord Morley would have had good cause to be angry about the arrangements, for they would have stripped him of some possessions which would have otherwise fallen to him in the event of Francis's death. This was because their grandfather William Lovell, in his will, had created a male entail for his lands; Francis had circumvented it to gain the lands set aside for Anne in the indenture. However, these lands were still only a small part of his vast possessions, most of which would still fall to Lord Morley. That Francis expected Morley to challenge the indenture and try to take the manors from Anne does not point to a cordial relationship. On the other hand, as mentioned above, around this time Francis was a guest at Morley's manor of Wooburn Deincourt, which he had inherited on their grandmother Alice Deincourt's death, so perhaps the men were on good terms. Maybe the clause about 'the family speaking and claiming defence' was just a precaution, with his and Morley's quarrel of 1483 in mind.

Whatever the nature of their apparently complex relationship, it cannot have been on Francis's mind a great deal that summer, except when he had to think about his wife's possible future as a widow. With that settled, he would have been far too busy to spare family relationships much thought, faced as he was with the gargantuan task of managing the royal fleet. This job included ensuring the seaworthiness of the fleet, getting repairs expedited, and seeing that all ships were outfitted, equipped and manned correctly. Francis also had to command the fleet when they took to sea to catch and defeat the invading fleet. It would have been an incredibly difficult task for a man who presumably had never been on a ship before.

In fact, it is rather baffling that Richard delegated this task to Francis, inexperienced and hardly military-minded, rather than John Howard, Duke of Norfolk, who was his Lord Admiral.[177] Presumably, this was because Howard was busy gathering a sufficiently large army in case the invaders made it to England, which might have been considered the more important task, leaving Francis in charge of the fleet. Whatever the case, this is another significant gesture of trust from Richard, with Francis having shown no indication of martial, let alone maritime prowess. It might have seemed a gamble, but Francis rose to the challenge. With his talent for organisation, this might have even suited him better than preparing for battle on land, and he appears to have done all that could be done in his position. Though he did not, in fact, prevent the invasion, this was due to faulty information he received and not a flaw in his own organisation.

Perhaps due to Richard being misinformed, Francis was guarding the wrong location. As the Croyland Chronicle put it, this mistake was due to Richard

> ...being deceived by a quibble on the name of that harbour, which had been mentioned by many as the place of their intended descent. For some say that there is a harbour in the neighbourhood of Southampton, called Milford, just as there is in Wales; and there being some persons endowed, as it were, with a spirit of prophecy, these predicted that those men would land at the harbour of Milford, and were in the habit of looking for the fulfilment of their prophecies to that effect, not at the most famous place, but most commonly at the other one which bore the same name. And then besides, the king, at this period, seemed especially to devote his attention to strengthening the southern parts of his kingdom.[178]

This mix-up and its disastrous consequences cannot be put at Francis's door, and in fact no primary source ever blamed him. His efforts seemed to be accepted as the best he could do. Even the Croyland Chronicle, lambasting the cost of the coastal defence, does not hold Francis responsible for the reckless and useless spending, instead rather absurdly claiming King Richard would not have needed a coastal defence at all. Francis is only mentioned in passing:

> Rumours at length increasing daily that those who were in arms against the king were hastening to make a descent upon England, and the king being in doubt at what port they intended to effect a landing (as certain information thereon could be gained by none of his spies), he betook himself to the north, shortly before the feast of Pentecost; leaving lord Lovel, his chamberlain, near Southampton, there to refit his fleet with all possible speed, that he might keep a strict watch upon all the harbours in those parts; that so, if the enemy should attempt to effect a landing there, he might unite all the forces in the neighbourhood, and not lose the opportunity of attacking them.[179]

Above: Minster Lovell Hall, the manor in which Francis and his sisters were born, and in which he spent the first eight years of his life. As an adult, Francis had the manor renovated. (Courtesy of Hugh Llewelyn under Creative Commons)

Below: St Kenelm's Church, Minster Lovell. Both Francis's father and his grandfather were buried inside this church. (Courtesy of Barry Marsh under Creative Commons)

Above: The tomb of William Lovell, Francis's grandfather, in St Kenelm's Church. (Courtesy of Hugh Llewelyn under Creative Commons)

Below left: Edward IV, who elevated Francis to viscountcy in January 1483. (Courtesy of Ripon Cathedral)

Below right: Richard Neville, Earl of Warwick, Francis's guardian from 1465 to 1469.

Ravensworth Castle, the ancestral home of the FitzHughs. Francis's marriage may have taken place there. His sisters found their home there from 1466 to 1471, and Francis himself lived in the castle from 1469 to 1471. (Courtesy of Andy Waddington under Creative Commons)

The tomb effigies of John de la Pole, Duke of Suffolk, and his wife Elizabeth Plantagenet, Duchess of Suffolk. Francis was their ward from 1471 until he attained his majority in September 1477. John, Duke of Suffolk appears to have been a father figure for him and Francis emulated his lifestyle as an adult. (Courtesy of Deben Dave under Creative Commons)

Above: Middleham Castle, which was a central location in the Wars of the Roses. It belonged to Richard, Earl of Warwick in the 1460s, and later to Richard, Duke of Gloucester. Francis lived in the keep from 1465 to 1469, under the Earl of Warwick's tutelage. Since his own manor of Bedale was very nearby, it is likely Francis often visited Richard of Gloucester in Middleham Castle in the 1470s. (Courtesy of Amanda Slater under Creative Commons)

Left: Elizabeth Woodville, wife of Edward IV. Throughout his life, Francis was embroiled in several conflicts for lands and possessions with Thomas and Richard Grey, her sons by her first husband.

Right: Richard, Duke of York enemy of Francis's grandfather John Beaumont, as well as his father and uncles on both sides of the family. (Courtesy of the British Library)

Below right: Margaret of York, daughter of Richard, Duke of York and sister to Edward IV and Richard III. A power player in European politics since her marriage to Charles the Bold in 1468, Margaret offered a place of safety to Yorkists after 1485. She was prominently involved in the Lambert Simnel rebellion against Henry VII in 1487. (Courtesy of the British Library)

Below: Henry VI, the Lancastrian king. (Courtesy of the British Library)

Fꝛancis vicont Louell ꝯ ꝯ holand
Burnell deputyt ꝯ Grey

Above left: Richard III, Francis's cousin by marriage and closest friend. (Courtesy of the British Library)

Above: The Lovell Garter arms. Francis was made a Knight of the Garter in 1483 shortly after Richard became king.

Left: Henry Stafford, 2nd Duke of Buckingham. He originally sided with Richard after Edward IV's death in 1483. Later, however, he became involved in a rebellion against him. Francis played a role in the suppression of this rebellion. (Courtesy of the Rijksmuseum)

Above: A field purported to be the site of the Battle of Bosworth, where Richard III was defeated in 1485. Francis's presence there during the battle is likely, but disputed. (Courtesy of Nilfanion under Creative Commons)

Right: The gatehouse of St John's Abbey in Colchester. The abbey itself has been destroyed. It is here that Francis fled into sanctuary after Bosworth, together with Humphrey and Thomas Stafford, and stayed until March 1486. The abbey had extended rights of sanctuary, so that they did not have to leave after the usual forty days of safety sanctuary allowed. (Courtesy of Saltmarsh under Creative Commons)

The marriage between Henry VII and Elizabeth of York is sometimes thought to have been the end of the Wars of the Roses. However, the Battle of Stoke, or Stoke Field in 1487 represents the last engagement of the conflict. (Courtesy of the Metropolitan Museum of Art)

The field on which the Battle of Stoke is meant to have taken place. Francis vanished after the battle, though family and friends did look for him.

Francis seems to have done well in all that was expected of him but, as so often when he was involved in military proceedings, he eventually failed. On 7 August, Henry Tudor and his men landed in England and began marching towards the royal army.[180] The news reached Richard very quickly; in fact, it is possible that it was Francis who informed him, realising his fleet was at the wrong Milford and sending word to the king as soon as he could. Certainly, he would have been one of the first to know.

Disaster

As soon as the news arrived, Richard sent out summons for lords and their hosts to come to him and prepare for battle. Whether he summoned Francis from his position in Southampton is not known for sure, though evidence suggests he did. Most who dispute this say that Francis could not have arrived quickly enough, which is obviously nonsense given that people travelled to the battlefield in time from various corners of England. It is also sometimes said that the coastal defence would not have been dismantled quickly enough for Francis to reach Richard in time.

However, this latter argument is also flawed. While it is no doubt true that the defence would take more than two weeks to dismantle, it does not seem that the plan was to dismantle it at this time anyway. The strength of Henry Tudor's French support was unknown, and it would have been foolish to leave no measures in place against the possibility of further support. Moreover, there needed to be defences in place to stop fleeing invaders from leaving England after their anticipated defeat.

It has also been argued that Francis would have had to remain with the fleet, but this is not true. It is known that on 21 August Lord Audeley was in Southampton overseeing the fleet, and while it is possible Francis was there with him, there is no mention of him at that time. It also seems unlikely that two lords would have been kept there, unable to take part in the fighting. Judging by what happened later, Francis must have been present when the armies met at Bosworth.

To the last, the friendship between Francis and Richard held strong. For Francis to have reached Richard in time, he must have ridden hard, and there is a lot of pathos in imagining the loyal friend, a man not given to travelling, abandoning all caution and spurring his horse to reach his king, to be able to stand beside him at the moment of truth. Perhaps he even saw some similarity to a scene not quite two years before, during the 1483 rebellion: Francis arriving in Richard's presence dishevelled, having done all to serve him well, yet having failed to keep the danger away from Richard; having to report failure, yet being received with affection by the king who loved him.

If the two men thought of such similarities, they must have hoped and prayed that the outcome would also be similar. Like any before a battle, both would have been apprehensive, aware of the proximity of death. Francis was clearly willing and ready to die for Richard, but it appears to have been a thought Richard could not stomach. Little is known about the tactics of the battle, but Francis was apparently kept away.

The only directly contemporary source indicating Francis's whereabouts during the battle is an announcement made by the new king, Henry VII, afterwards. Francis was listed among the dead.[181] This was incorrect – he was alive – but it could well indicate that Francis was in fact at the battle and at first assumed to have perished alongside many of Richard's closest supporters.[182] Another possible explanation is that it would have been assumed that such a close friend would have been with Richard, and so if he could not be found he had surely died in the battle. Another theory is that Francis was declared dead to discourage any subsequent rebellions, which is believed to have been why John, Earl of Lincoln was declared dead despite not even being at Bosworth.[183] However, while announcing the supposed death of Lincoln, the Yorkist heir presumptive, had the advantage of sowing confusion and stopping potential rebels from rising in his name, there would have been no such reason for declaring Francis dead.

Just what Francis did during the battle will remain a mystery. All that can be said with reasonable certainty is that he did not ride with Richard in his last charge, for even if he had somehow managed to survive he would have been surrounded by enemy fighters and his capture would have been recorded. Polydore Vergil, writing some twenty years later, states Francis was at the battle but fled to sanctuary after the defeat, and gives no further details.[184] His version might be true, but given Vergil's many provable mistakes and deliberate departures from known facts in his report of the battle, he is an unreliable source.

Everything in the historical record suggests that Francis was not really involved in the fighting. This might have been down to political considerations, with Richard wanting Francis nearby to fulfil some duties for him in the event of his death,[185] though if so he would have been at some remove from the fighting, safe from the risk of being taken prisoner or caught by stray arrows. More likely is that Richard simply wanted Francis to live, no matter what the outcome of the battle, for personal reasons – a last gesture of affection towards his beloved friend.

As history records, Richard lost the battle and his life, fighting valiantly until the end, as even those slandering his name after his death conceded.[186] Francis must have watched, helpless, as enemy fighters engulfed his friend and king, who fought without hope of survival, who died as Henry Tudor's army won the day.

By noon of 22 August 1485, the battle was decided. Many had lost their lives. Among the dead were several influential courtiers and men of the king's household, men whom Francis would have known well: John Howard, Sir Richard Ratcliffe, Sir Robert Percy and Richard's main secretary John Kendall, among others.[187] King Richard, third of that name since the Norman conquest, was dead. Francis, Viscount Lovell, was left a broken man.

'... convicted and attainted of high treason'

The aftermath of the Battle of Bosworth was brutal. Henry Tudor, now King Henry VII, treated the Yorkist survivors and dead with incredible, uncharacteristic cruelty. Men like the Earl of Northumberland – who had not even engaged in battle – and Thomas Howard, Earl of Surrey, were taken prisoner,[1] the latter sentenced to three years' imprisonment.[2] Though later generations have sometimes tried to distort Henry's treatment of the enemy side into something justifiable and even kind,[3] contemporaries were unimpressed. In particular, people were horrified by the barbaric way Richard's body was treated; he was stripped, flung over a mule with a felon's halter around his neck and brought to Leicester to be exhibited entirely naked for two days. This act was even referenced with disgust by accounts written during the Tudor dynasty.[4]

It can be hoped that Francis never heard about what was done to Richard's body. Certainly, he would not have witnessed it first-hand; knowing that he had to avoid being captured by enemy forces, Francis did not wait around after the battle, fleeing as soon as he could in the company of two of Richard's archers, Humphrey and Thomas Stafford. The Staffords, despite being cousins to Harry, Duke of Buckingham, had already shown great loyalty to Richard during the 1483 rebellion,[5] and they did not waver after Henry VII's victory. Like Francis, the Staffords clearly had no interest in throwing themselves upon the mercy of the new king; perhaps they doubted they would be treated with mercy.

We do not know exactly where the three of them, perhaps accompanied by some servants, went immediately after the battle, but eventually they arrived at St John's Abbey in Colchester and claimed sanctuary there.[6] It is most likely they went there as soon as they could; Francis would have been aware that he was a wanted man once Henry Tudor discovered he had survived. Desperate and grieving, he had nowhere else to go. His own possessions were not safe if he did not want to be found.

It was presumably when they were already at St John's that they received more bad news, and this news might have personally affected Francis: three days after the Battle of Bosworth, Richard's lawyer Sir William Catesby, the 'catte' in the Collyngbourne rhyme, had been executed without a trial. Catesby was allowed to draw up a will before his death, which has since excited considerable speculation because in it Catesby states that Henry VII is 'callid a full gracious prince' and goes on to claim that he 'never offended hym by my good and Free will; for god I take to be my juge I have ever lovid hym.'[7]

This might indicate that Catesby was plotting against Richard, though it would make little sense given his execution almost immediately after Bosworth. It could also mean that Catesby was simply afraid for the future of his family, which is very much supported by the fact that the above-quoted statements were made in direct connection to his expression of hope Henry would treat them well. Catesby would not have been the first, nor the last, to suppress his real feelings and offer fealty to authority to protect his family, and a claim to have worked for Richard under duress, while not borne out by what evidence we have of his actions, could not be contradicted by anyone still alive and in a position to speak up.

Whatever Catesby's motivations, his will shows that in the hours before his death he was thinking of those he was leaving behind and worrying about his immortal soul. In this context, William, Thomas and George Stanley are mentioned, in another controversial sentence which seems to accuse them of not trying to prevent his execution. Finally, Francis is mentioned also. Near the end of the document, Catesby expressed his wish that 'my lord Lovell come to grace than that ye shew hym that he pray for me.'[8]

Despite this mention of Francis seeming rather rushed or an afterthought, it is informative. For one, it shows that Catesby was certain Francis was still alive at the moment of writing, which suggests that he survived physically unscathed. Also, the relationship between the two men must have at least been cordial for Catesby to wish for Francis's prayers. This is supported somewhat by the fact that his mention of Francis is not accompanied by a complaint, unlike the reproach against the Stanleys that they had not tried to '[pray] for my body as I trusted in you', and the somewhat passive-aggressive plea for his uncle John to 'remembrer my soule as ye have done my body; and better'.[9]

It is of course possible that Catesby had no such complaints against Francis because the two men were not close enough for Catesby to have expected any help from Francis. However, the evidence from Richard's reign, when they were both in positions of power, suggests that they often worked together and that their relationship, whether businesslike or personal, was fruitful.

In fact, it is quite possible that the two men knew each other and were linked in some way before Richard became king, while he was still Duke of Gloucester, Francis not yet a viscount and Catesby primarily connected to William Hastings.[10] Certainly, there were family ties: in his will, Francis's grandfather William Lovell mentioned William Catesby's father as one of his feoffees alongside men like Thomas Bourchier.[11] However, we do not know if William Catesby the younger and Francis continued the connection at any point before 1483.

Nonetheless, as soon as Richard was king the two are often found in accounts together. Notably, Francis included Catesby in a list of feoffees of some of his estates alongside men he is known to have been close to, such as the brothers Franke and his brother-in-law George FitzHugh. Catesby was also one of the men Francis entrusted to transfer some of his manors and lands to his wife, Anne, in his indenture. The two men were also granted the constableship of Rockingham together,[12] and Francis, with conventional expressions of love, passed a manor granted to him on to Catesby.[13]

It is intriguing that Francis and Catesby were thrown together in William Collyngbourne's famous rhyme, but it is most likely that this had nothing to do with any relationship between the two men, and everything to do with their individual ties to the king. Again, as so often with Francis, at the time his actions mostly seem to have been considered unremarkable and above reproach. Catesby's request for prayers suggests that, whatever their relationship, he too had no cause for complaint when it came to Francis. If they were friends, news of Catesby's death would have been an additional blow to Francis, but even if they were not, his execution certainly would be.

It is hard to imagine what Francis must have gone through in those first weeks and months after the battle. Bereaved and hunted, he arrived at St John's Abbey a broken man. One can envision him, still a month shy of his twenty-ninth birthday, arriving at the abbey looking suddenly old, his face ashen, his hands shaking, a husk of the man he had been just weeks ago.

There is a lot of speculation as to why Francis and the Staffords chose to go to Colchester to claim sanctuary. It is sometimes postulated that Francis had some secret orders to carry out in the event of Richard's death but that he was prevented from doing so, having to go on the run again and taking sanctuary in the nearest possible place.[14] Another theory is that the abbey itself held some secrets, the most popular suggestion being that the so-called Princes in the Tower had been hidden there and that Francis went there to see to it they were sent abroad. This theory is detailed in Matthew Lewis's book *The Survival of the Princes in the Tower*,[15] and also in David Baldwin's *The Lost Prince*.[16] According to the theory, Richard entrusted the boys to the Yorkist abbot Walter Stansted, who was perfectly placed to take care of them, as his abbey lay in a part of the country infallibly loyal to him.

Some oddities and mysteries shown in the aforementioned books may indeed point towards there being a secret connected to St John's Abbey in Colchester, but the theory that Francis went there to see Richard's famous nephews is based on a fallacy connected with the fact that Francis stayed there for longer than the forty days someone was allowed to stay in sanctuary before the rights of sanctuary expired. For Francis and the Staffords to stay in the abbey for as long as they did – well over half a year – it is assumed that Henry VII must have allowed them to do so, and his reason for doing so is then assumed to be that he is in negotiations with Francis about the fate of the erstwhile Edward V and his younger brother, Richard of Shrewsbury.

This overlooks the history and rights of St John's Abbey, however, which included extended rights of sanctuary, meaning a person could take sanctuary there as long as they wished, not simply forty days. Westminster Abbey also had such rights, which was why Elizabeth Woodville had been able to stay there with her children for several months in both 1470/1 and 1483/4.

For St John's Abbey, these rights had first been granted as early as 1109 and reaffirmed on 13 May 1453 by Henry VI.[17] Having been so recently reaffirmed, they were not open to doubt. During the Lancastrian readeption in 1470/1, John Howard had stayed in the abbey from October 1470 until April 1471.[18] Knowledge of Howard's stay might have been the impetus for Francis and the Staffords to go there, rather than any secrets connected with the abbey.

Whatever their motivation, the very fact that the abbey was led by an abbot with Yorkist sympathies[19] was to be of great help to Francis and the Staffords once they started plotting against Henry VII some months after the Battle of Bosworth, and it may have been a comfort when they first arrived. Due to Francis's high standing, it may have been the abbot himself who greeted them when they took sanctuary, and perhaps Abbot Stansted even afforded the stricken viscount some comfort.

For the first two or three months of sanctuary, Francis and the Staffords appear to have done nothing at all. Maybe grief and stress made Francis physically ill once again, or perhaps he was prostrate with grief and what we would today call depression and survivor's guilt.

At some point after the battle, probably around the time of his birthday, Francis received an offer of a pardon from the new king.[20] That he even needed a pardon, despite having been on the side of the anointed and lawful king at Bosworth, was due to Henry VII having backdated his reign to a day before Bosworth, meaning that fighting for Richard was retroactively declared treason.[21] This was a very unpopular move, and would cause Henry trouble in the years to come,[22] but anybody wishing to prosper under him had to accept it for now, if perhaps grudgingly.

It would have been the normal course of action for Francis to swallow his pride and accept Henry VII's pardon. Even if he had no intention of actually staying loyal to the new king, he only had to pretend. The history of the Wars of the Roses is replete with men doing just that – Edmund Beaufort during the early reign of Edward IV, Harry, Duke of Buckingham during the reign of Richard III, and John, Earl of Lincoln during the reign of Henry VII are just three examples.

Francis would have had every reason to accept the pardon, and even to accept Henry VII as his king while he tried to live his life as best as he could, tolerating if not enjoying the status quo. He had a loving wife, a sister he cared for, plus hard-won wealth and possessions. If he took the pardon he would even have had the chance to meet his uncle William Beaumont again, possibly establishing himself as his heir.

It would have been the expected course, sensible and not shameful at all. It would not have been in any way a betrayal; in fact, by seeing to it he would survive, Richard surely expected, even wanted, that upon his death Francis would accept Henry VII, continue living the best life he could, and try to be happy.

But Francis was an unconventional man, quietly emotional and unwilling to forgive. He did not want to take the normal course of action, which would have required him to swear fealty to the man who had killed his friend. No moral obligations, no dangers, prevented him from swearing fealty to Henry. His situation was better than that of others who had fought for Richard like Thomas Howard, Earl of Surrey, or Henry Percy, Earl of Northumberland. While these two were taken prisoner, Francis had the advantage over them. He could have thrown himself on the victor's mercy with the expectation of leniency; the incarceration of Surrey and Northumberland had already caused some unhappiness,[23] and mistreating someone who came to terms with Henry of his own volition would have been bad for his reputation and completely unnecessary. In fact, to have Francis at his court, a man who was known to have been high in Richard's favour and moreover fairly well-liked, would have benefited Henry and supported his claim of wanting to unite the warring Yorkist and Lancastrian factions.

Henry was clearly aware of this, hence his offer of a pardon to Francis. Perhaps he wanted to show some goodwill, or perhaps he and his men expected Francis, who seems to have been a calm and relatively peaceful man, to accept the pardon to save his wealth and thereby provide credibility to Henry's stated claim of wanting peace.

There would have been no danger for Francis. Though it is often pointed out that the pardons for the Yorkists were full of restrictions,[24] there was nothing Henry could have done against Francis, even if he had been unaware of the man's propaganda value. Francis's ties with the FitzHughs would have made him untouchable – turning the FitzHugh family against the crown could have meant open rebellion in the north.[25] In such a case, as later events would show, it is quite possible that there would have been instances of unrest all over the rest of the country.[26] Even if Henry had not considered the FitzHughs important enough to cause him trouble, Francis's close connection with the Duke and Duchess of Suffolk and their son the Earl of Lincoln would have prevented the king from doing anything that could turn the Suffolks against him.

Henry would have been well aware of his precarious situation in the early months of his reign. He was not stupid or short-sighted, and would never have dared move against Francis had the latter accepted him and sworn fealty to him. Of all of Richard's men who were offered the chance to enter Henry's court – and potentially his government – Francis was in the best position to do so on terms that suited him. Given his previous lack of interest in politics, presumably an agreement could have been reached which did not give Francis too much advantage and therefore risk alienating those who had fought with Henry and won him the throne.

The exact details of the offer made to Francis are unknown, but a claim sometimes brought forward is that Francis was offered a place in Henry's coronation, as there is reference to his presence in a record of attendance and honours to nobles at the coronation. However, this record was clearly a barely modified version of that for Richard's coronation, and included John Howard, Duke of Norfolk, who had died at Bosworth, and moreover lists as Francis's task carrying a sceptre in the queen's train[27] – which originally was meant to be Francis's part in Richard and Anne's joint coronation – despite Henry not even being married when he was crowned.

There is in fact no evidence at all that Henry intended to include Francis in the government in any special capacity, though including him, or anyone else who had been involved in Richard's government, might have helped him to make the transition between governments more smoothly.[28] However, Henry did not seem overly concerned with this transition, and in fact in some instances he appears to have sought to make a definite distinction between his government and Richard's, even abolishing some of Richard's innovations, such as the Court of Requests[29] – not a very kind-hearted move by the new king. It seems likely, therefore, if by no means certain, that what was offered to Francis was simply the restoration of most of his wealth and his titles. Though he would have lost those lands and possessions granted to him by Richard after the 1483 rebellion, which had been given back to their original owners who returned with Henry VII, he would have still been a rich man had he taken the pardon.

But Francis did not want to bend the knee. When offered this pardon, Francis made his choice. He would not accept. Not even to help his plans of rebellion would he swear an oath to Henry VII. Loyal and loving to the last, Francis rejected the pardon.

The Traitor

Francis's decision had major consequences, and they came swiftly. On 9 December, in Henry VII's first parliament, which also passed an official decree making Henry king in law as well as in practice, Francis was attainted.[30] All his lands, possessions and titles fell to the crown, and he was declared a traitor, meaning that if he was caught by the king's men he would be executed. Even venturing out of sanctuary was to risk his life.

His fall from grace was complete. Within five months he had gone from the king's closest friend, with immense power at his fingertips, honours manifold and riches untold, to a penniless fugitive for whom every action was fraught with danger. He had had everything to lose, and chose to lose it all.

Destitute, powerless and cut off from all he loved, Francis had two choices left after December 1485: go into exile, or stay in

England and start a rebellion without foreign assistance. Francis chose the latter, supported by the Stafford brothers, and perhaps also by Walter Stansted.

Everybody involved must have known that this was an incredibly dangerous decision. Sequestered in sanctuary, with every journey outside a risk, Francis chose the most immediate but also the most dangerous way to begin a rebellion. Clearly, he did not want to be a supplicant at foreign courts, begging for support, if he could avoid it. Nor does he seem to have had much of an interest in the political side of rebellion. As ever, his motivations were apolitical, and he started the rebellion with one goal, and one goal only: to avenge Richard's death by killing Henry VII. This was the cause he advertised from sanctuary after the first few months of recovery. This was what he planned for.

An organisational genius, he succeeded in contacting men ready to support him even while staying in sanctuary, all the while apparently remaining undetected by the king and his government. A row of pardons issued to men from Colchester in summer 1486 for suspected or known involvement in this rebellion shows the success Francis and the Staffords enjoyed.[31] Presumably, Abbot Walter Stansted helped find those who would potentially be interested while avoiding the attentions of those likely to alert the new king's men. His help would not only have made finding support easier, but would also have made establishing contact with them far less dangerous. The abbot's involvement is uncertain, but after the rebellion was over he was at least suspected by Henry's government.

In late 1485, Henry had no reason to suspect anything was going on in the abbey. In any case, he was still so unsteady on the throne that he could not have afforded to act against a Church institution without hard evidence. It is possible he did not even care what Francis was doing in sanctuary, thinking that he could do little now that he was stripped of his wealth and isolated; the Staffords, for their part, may not have been significant enough for him to worry about. In any case, Henry would have been too busy to give much thought to three men who had so far done nothing to move against him, and whom he presumably thought were completely powerless.

If so, this was a miscalculation. We do not know when, but at some point during his stay in the abbey Francis started to make his plans. As he might have hoped, he found support and help in the abbey and the town of Colchester. The men contacted appear to have been mostly commoners or members of the gentry, nobody of higher standing than a knight. For example, one Sir Thomas Pilkington was the recipient of one of the pardons mentioned above.[32] He is described in it as 'alias late of Colchestre', but not given any other distinguishing mark connecting him to anyone of higher standing. The same holds true for several other men connected with Francis or the Staffords during the rebellion.

Presumably, Francis, Stansted and the Staffords knew perfectly well that Henry was powerless to act against them without proof, and also that he assumed they were no threat. If they all worked together, pooling their ingenuity, they could make planning the rebellion a far easier, less dangerous task than it would have been for Francis and the Staffords alone. Walter Stansted was never punished, but St John's Abbey was subject to heavy restrictions in the aftermath of the 1486 rebellion, arguing that a collaboration between Stansted and Francis did occur.[33]

After the rebellion there were hints and suspicions that some more significant personalities were involved, but such rumours were par for the course after any rebellion, especially under the famously paranoid Henry VII. John, Earl of Lincoln is the only such man who can be proven to have had contact with Francis,[34] although this contact does not appear to have been made until after Christmas 1485.

There can be no doubt that Francis would have paid close attention to court gossip in order to glean the mood there as well as among the common folk, and to work out if anyone at court would be ready to support him. On the whole, the population was not too pleased about Henry taking the throne, and he had to contend with several small disturbances. Most notably, there was trouble in the north of the country, where Richard had been most popular. In fact, in October 1485 Henry had been compelled to send reinforcements to the north because the lords charged with keeping the peace there, Francis's brother-in-law Richard FitzHugh among them, were not able to cope with the marauding Scots at the border,[35] who had been invited to invade by angry northerners.[36] Given what we know of Richard FitzHugh's later movements, it is even possible that he did not try too hard to prevent these incursions, giving the impression of enforcing the king's rule but actually turning a blind eye to the Scots.[37]

The north was not the only part of the country where there was disquiet, and a look at the details of Henry's early reign show quite clearly that while the south of the country appeared mostly quiet, there was actually no part which was completely pacified. Shortly before Francis's rebellion started, in February 1486, Henry was even forced to send his uncle Jasper Tudor, Duke of Bedford, into Wales.[38]

It is quite possible that Francis and the Staffords were in contact with these early rebels, especially in the unsettled north, where Francis had connections. Some actions reported in and around York in late 1485 give an impression of unbridled rage among the populace, uninfluenced by outside forces. One such example would a recorded instance of violence in which one John Eglesfield 'beat and sore wounded in peril of death' the Earl of Northumberland's 'servant Robert Robinson, bailiff of [Northumberland's] lordship of Ulvyngton'.[39] This violent incident illustrates that the north was unsettled and volatile, and Francis must have felt that he was likely to find plenty of support for his endeavour there. Such incidents might have prompted Francis to make contact with several northerners.

Even if he did not yet make contact, certainly he would have been cheered to hear of such incidents, which might have gone some way towards helping him through his grief. He would have tried to get news from the court itself, and would have learnt of the new king's coronation, which, while expected, must have left a bitter taste in his mouth. More welcome would have been news of a riot that broke out in Parliament in December 1485 in protest at some of Henry's actions.[40] He would probably also have heard of the new king's apparent reluctance to marry Elizabeth of York,[41] followed by him relenting and making preparations,[42] although this might not have meant a lot to him.

It must have been a bleak Christmas and New Year for Francis, especially compared with the dazzling festivities of the two previous years. There would have been festivities in the abbey, which was a wealthy institution, presumably with good food and other luxuries, but it cannot have been much comfort for Francis, who had shown in the path he chose that possessions did not mean anything to him in comparison to his loyalty and love for Richard.

If anything gave him comfort it would not have been festivities and finery but prayer and the religious significance of Christmas. Even that might not have helped him, however; his actions during the rebellion would show how little he valued his life at this point. Indeed, his choice to stay in England to arrange a rebellion already speaks to this lack of regard for his safety, and it is most likely he was a downcast presence during the festivities. Broken and depressed, with only vengeance left to him, did Francis even have hope to die in the course of a successful rebellion?

Even if Francis hoped for death, he did not court it. He knew that if he wanted to see the king dead, he would have to be cautious. He sincerely intended for his plan to succeed. It was not a statement of his dislike of Henry VII like the small skirmishes in the aftermath of Richard's death,[43] nor was it a small rebellion planned to distract from a bigger one, like his father-in-law Henry FitzHugh's had been fifteen years earlier. It was a deadly serious attempt to kill Henry, and it appears that no thought was given to his replacement.

Naturally, the lack of an alternative ruler to rally around was a strong hindrance to recruitment. Perhaps Francis hoped that this problem would solve itself, that once Henry was dead Richard's heir John, Earl of Lincoln, would in the natural course of things take the throne. We will see that Francis may have made arrangements with this in mind, but most likely he did not particularly care who took the throne if he was successful. There are no indications that he ever addressed the matter during the rebellion, only some clumsy attempts by the Staffords.

It was clear where the focus of this rebellion lay, and this was where Francis and the Staffords channelled their efforts. Though the rebellion can seem under-planned, lacking as it did any figurehead or foreign support, it is clear that a lot of thought was given to how best to reach Henry VII and kill him.

Everyone involved in the rebellion was aware that for it even to have a chance, for Francis to come close enough to Henry to attempt an assassination, the plan could not be carried out in winter while Henry VII was safe in London. This is likely why Francis and the Staffords stayed in sanctuary, presumably planning what to do once the rebellion began in earnest, and how to employ the men they had gathered to their cause.

The Rebel

We do not know exactly when Francis and the Staffords left sanctuary and started their rebellion, but the threat of rebellious activity was raised early in 1486. On 15 February that year, Sir Robert Plumpton received a letter which illustrates the king's fear of activity in the several parts of the country, specifically in the north, presumably Yorkshire, and in Wales:

> Also, Sir, the King proposeth northward hastily after the Parliament, and it is said he purposes to do execution there on such as have offended against him ... Also, Sir, these lords and gentlemen that was attainted, they 'gyt' no grace, as it is said ... Also, Sir, the King cometh with great company: as it is said, with 10 hundred men in harness, and with him 5 or 6 score lords and knights. Also, the Duke of Bedford is gone into Wales to see that country. Also, it is enact that all manner of prophecies is made felony. Sir, other tidings, I know none as yet that be certain.[44]

The letter writer was correct about the movements of Jasper Tudor, Duke of Bedford. However, he may have been mistaken about Henry's planned actions. It seems a good guess that Henry would have taken bodyguards, but the letter appears to exaggerate in other aspects as Henry, while accompanied by many of high standing during his eventual progress, was not in fact accompanied by over a hundred 'lords and knights'.[45]

The letter is accurate in that once Henry began his progress he chose to travel northwards. There need not be anything significant in this, as it was a quite normal route for a royal progress to take, starting in Westminster, and Henry appeared to model his first progress closely after Richard's, perhaps for convenience.

Before Henry set off, on 2 March 1486,[46] he rewarded his uncle Bedford with Francis's ancestral manor of Minster Lovell Hall, which had been in his hands since Francis's attainder three months earlier. Depending on when Henry learnt of Francis's intention to rebel, this could have been a precaution, occupying a place that might otherwise have offered a safe haven to Francis, but it could just as well be a coincidence, the grant of the manor a reward for good work done to quell discontent in Wales.

Whatever Henry's reasons, by the time Bedford received the grant, Francis had not yet started his rebellion. It was only around mid-March, after Henry had left for his first royal progress, that Francis and the Staffords left sanctuary and began their ill-fated rebellion. The stops on their journey were likely chosen for their proximity to known supporters but also for their likelihood to produce new support.

Though there is plenty of evidence that the rebellion gathered support, their movements after they left sanctuary suggest a lack of planning beyond their basic route. The actions of the Staffords in particular reflect a lack of proper planning after they arrived in the Midlands, where they had probably chosen to go to because their family had ties there.[47] Once they arrived, they relied on a mixture of misinformation, contradictory claims and their own presence to win support. The brothers first attempted to enter Worcester on the pretence that they had been pardoned by Henry VII, a ruse that apparently succeeded.[48]

Once this was accomplished, they either spread rumours themselves or were supported by rumours springing up independently – perhaps encouraged by the chaos of rebellion – that Richard's nephew Edward, Earl of Warwick, son of the late Duke of Clarence, had been freed from the Tower of London, where Henry had put him after the Battle of Bosworth, and was in the company of Francis in the north of the country.[49] Another rumour spread that Francis had taken Henry VII prisoner, and this was used by the Staffords to encourage men to 'assist Lovell in the destruction of Henry VII'[50] – a rather strange move considering that they had, apparently, only been able to enter the city with assurances that they were the new king's 'true liegemen'.[51] While the two brothers met with more success than should have been possible with such amateurish attempts, their movements nonetheless suggest that they had not been properly prepared beforehand, and that the bulk of the planning in sanctuary had pertained to Francis's actions.

Perhaps because of this, Francis, who had gone to Yorkshire on his own, was more successful at first – or at least not so reliant on improvisation. Superior organisation might have played a part, but presumably he also benefited from the greater Yorkist sympathies in the north. While the Midlands was not a region known for particular loyalty either to York or Lancaster, the north of the country was loyal to Richard, and even chroniclers who were unkind to him, such as Polydore Vergil, acknowledged this. Though Vergil is otherwise at pains to paint the rebellion as little more than a little local difficulty, he states that when in York and faced with the prospect of a rebellion, Henry's fear was mainly down to being surrounded by people 'in whose mind the memory of Richard's name remained fresh'.[52] Even if this was somewhat simplistic, it does seem that Yorkshire on the whole was ready to support Francis and his rebellion.

In fact, Francis may well have chosen the north not only because he had a power base there but because he had heard of the consistent trouble York had given Henry in the time he had spent in sanctuary. It would have helped that Francis had loyal men there, who probably brought him other sympathetic countrymen, but it was Richard's popularity, not his own, which carried the plan. This has little to do with the quality of his scheme; as we have seen with the unusually welcome Scottish incursions, there had been trouble in Yorkshire ever since Richard's death. Francis's rebellion was presumably greeted with the same enthusiasm.

Though this rebellion is often brushed off with one or two sentences in history books, if mentioned at all, it appears to have been similar in size and support to the Buckingham Rebellion. The motives of the commoners involved were much the same, too. Much as the Buckingham Rebellion had relied upon those who had been dissatisfied with Richard's accession and feared loss of favour,[53] many in the north were unhappy with Henry's usurpation and feared losing the power they had established under Richard. Francis found enough support among these people to foment a rebellion that contemporaries considered a significant disruption of Henry VII's progress.

It seems that until shortly before the rebellion started, perhaps shortly before Bedford was granted possession of Minster Lovell Hall, Henry and his men were completely in the dark about the existence of the plot. Henry only appears to have learnt of it when told by one Sir Hugh Convey, who had been privy to the plans. According to Sir Hugh, talking of the meeting in later years, Henry was genuinely shocked:

[T]hat time my Lord Lovell lay in Colchester a trusty friend of mine came to me and showed me in counsel the day and time of his departing, and of all his purpose. I was sworn to him that I should never utter this to man living to his hurt, but yet forthwith afterwards, because of mine allegiance, I came to Sir Reynold Bray and showed him all as is above, and forthwith he said that Master Bray showed the same unto the King's [sic]. Whereupon I was brought before his Highness, and I affirmed all to be true as my said friend had showed; and the King said that it could not be so, and reasoned with me always to the contrary of my said sayings. At last he asked what he was that told me this tale of his departing. I prayed his Highness to pardon me, for I said that I was sworn to him that I should never utter him, to be drawn with wild horses; wherewith the King was angry and displeased with me for my good will.[54]

This is very revealing, not just in the information that there wasn't even a suspicion of the plot at court but also in that Henry thought the idea was completely far-fetched. Though an element of wishful thinking may have played into Henry's initial refusal to believe Convey's claim, there were others at court who would not have dismissed the rumours had they heard them, most notably Henry's uncle Jasper Tudor, Duke of Bedford, and John de Vere, Earl of Oxford, both seasoned warriors and courtiers.

The very fact that proper action had been taken against small uprisings in the country shows that Henry and his men were prepared to do whatever it took to quell dissent;[55] they were not complacent. With this in mind, it seems that Francis and his co-conspirators managed to keep their preparations secret until shortly before they took action.

It is not only this disbelief that is notable about Sir Hugh's statement. He very clearly states that he gave Henry not only 'all of [Francis's] purpose', meaning his plans, but also 'the day and time' of his planned exit from sanctuary. Despite this, Henry's men were not able to apprehend Francis; in fact, they don't even seem to have come close. The obvious conclusion is that either Francis had passed on false information with the express purpose of misleading them – possible but unnecessary while the court was in the dark – or that someone at court, hearing of Sir Hugh's meeting with Henry, told Francis that his trust had been betrayed, enabling him to change his plans accordingly.

Contemporary sources are silent about this, simply reporting the bare facts of the uprising and the alarm it caused in the country. Interestingly, the Croyland Chronicle, written at just the time the rebellion was happening, does not mention Francis in connection to it at all. This may well be because the chronicler had only heard about it in rumours, though most of what he says seems to be correct and is corroborated by other accounts, showing differences only in details like its claim that the men Henry gathered were all unarmed,[56] which no other source corroborates.

Given the correct information included in the Croyland Chronicle's description of the uprising, it is interesting that the chronicler does not identify Henry's enemies. It is of course possible that the instigators of the rebellion were not known to the chronicler given the events were only just coming to light. Even so, it seems unlikely that the chronicler had heard no rumours about the identities of the plotters. Even if rebellions were of uncertain origin, they were often connected with notable enemies of the king or those known to be dissatisfied. An example of this can be found in the repeated rebellions in the north in the years before Warwick openly declared against Edward IV,[57] and in the Jack Cade rebellion, which was connected to Richard, Duke of York[58] even before he ever made any move against Henry VI's government.

In the case of Francis's rebellion, while the Staffords may not have been of high enough standing to be connected with the uprising, Francis undoubtedly was, and what little primary sources report of him shows he was well known to be close to Richard and opposed to Henry. Moreover, it seems that proclamations against Francis were issued well before he reached York to try and assassinate Henry.[59] Surely, then, the chronicler at Croyland would have heard of this, again possibly only from the rumour mill, and either disbelieved it or did not think Francis was important enough for the story he was trying to tell, possibly because his name would not add anything to the understanding, having only been mentioned once before and in a way that doesn't suggest he had a rebellious character. This, perhaps even more than his lack of appearances in chronicles and reports about Richard's reign, shows very well what sort of reputation Francis enjoyed. He was seen as quiet, calm, unobtrusive, not at all the sort of man likely to start such a dangerous and ill-planned rebellion, or really any rebellion at all.

Polydore Vergil, writing some twenty years later, gives a rather confused description of the rebellion, but if his version is taken together with the account in the Croyland Chronicle, the sequence of events can be understood fairly well. It appears that after arriving in the north of the country and securing some support, Francis attempted to organise an army to face Henry.[60] Though this sounds rather ridiculous in hindsight, it was taken seriously by Henry's government. The preparations as recorded by Vergil definitely show this:

> But since this development called for diligence, lest time be given his adversaries for increasing their forces, he commanded Duke Jasper of Bedford to go against the enemies with three thousand lightly armed men, a goodly part wearing leather breastplates, and advised him of his own plans. In the meantime he himself gathered what soldiers he could.[61]

It cannot be said with certainty how many men Henry actually gathered, but it is clear that he did not appear to think that the 3,000 men raised by his uncle were enough. On 4 April, he appointed 'Thomas, earl of Derby, George, Lord of Straunge, William Stanley, knight, the king's chamberlain, William Gryfuth, chamberlain of North Wales, Richard Harper, Andrew Dymmok, and John Luthrington' to a commission to raise men 'in the counties of Chester and Flint, and in North Wales',[62] though there is no indication how successful this was. Perhaps the number of men raised was similar to the number of men raised for Richard III during the Buckingham Rebellion, in which Thomas Stanley, not yet then Earl of Derby, raised a significant number. The Croyland Chronicle claims that many of the men Henry took with him to the north were unarmed, 'seemingly rather to pacify than to exasperate a hostile population'.[63] This could very well have been true, and would not have been a stupid move; in this way Henry himself could have looked harmless while his men were gathered ready to fight if necessary.

With hindsight, it is easy to say, as centuries' worth of history books have done, that there was no particular danger from the rebellion, but this does not reflect the reality. However, as with the so-called Buckingham Rebellion, it did in time become clear that it was not very well planned, and the king's preventative measures worked well. In the end, in another parallel with the rebellion against Richard three years earlier, conflict was avoided without a sword being drawn in anger. Vergil claims that this was because the king's uncle, Bedford, 'immediately ordered his heralds to offer impunity to all who had thrown down their weapons'.[64]

It is possible that the men Francis had gathered were offered a pardon, though if so it was either not extended to all of them or Henry later went back on his word, for in May 1486 there were several trials for rebels.[65] More likely, however, is that Vergil deliberately minimised the threat posed by Francis and did not go by facts so much as by half-truths to give the impression that the rebellion was insignificant, taking the fact that there were several pardons, not least to a number of men from Colchester, and using this as evidence that all those included in the rebellion were pardoned. Certainly, his claims as to how these supposed pardons helped defuse the threat of the rebellion contradict several known facts. He describes Bedford's offer of pardon as 'a thing of great importance':

> For Francis, either not trusting in himself or terrified, furtively absconded from his men in the night. And all of them, perceiving the flight of their general, without delay cast themselves at Bedford's feet, begged for pardon, and surrendered themselves to the Crown. Thus this enemy assault against the king,

which could have led to great slaughter, was settled by Bedford's timely plan, and Francis, more fearful of danger than avid for glory, ran non-stop into the country of Lancaster.[66]

It could be argued that this is what Vergil truly believed to have happened, and therefore it is the way this rebellion was remembered at the time when he wrote, since it is not very flattering towards Henry. In fact, it makes him look like a rather insecure king, for despite Vergil's earlier assertion that Henry's overthrow of Richard was greeted with happiness by almost everyone,[67] the failure of the 1486 rebellion is attributed to Francis's alleged cowardice, not to Henry's merits. It is explicitly said that it was 'perceiving the flight of their general'[68] which caused his makeshift army to disperse.

There are obvious flaws in this. Francis did not flee, before or after his army had dispersed. Moreover, he evidently still had sufficient support to lie in wait for Henry at York. On the other hand, it is perfectly possible that Bedford's offer of pardon convinced enough of the rebels to desert Francis, destroying his chances of raising an army to engage Henry's men.

A lot of the details of this rebellion are shrouded in obscurity, but we know that Henry VII appears to have dealt with the rebellion within a month of hearing about the threat Francis posed. According to Vergil, Henry was at Lincoln when he learnt that 'Francis Lord Lovell together with Humfrey Stafford had quitted the asylum at Colchester, but no man knew for sure where they had betaken themselves.'[69] This could indeed be true, since Henry was in Lincoln during the Easter festivities taking place on 26 and 27 March in 1486,[70] and this would square with him starting to make serious arrangements for an upcoming rebellion by the beginning of April, presumably after he had ascertained the truth of the rumours.

In addition to ensuring that sufficient men were mustered to meet the threat from Francis, another of Henry's first actions was to employ men to find out who was involved in the rebellion. The list of men found to be involved, or at least suspected of collusion, makes for interesting reading and gives an insight into Francis's relationships and connections. Some of the men implicated had close ties to him, a prime example being Richard FitzHugh, brother of his wife Anne. Though his involvement was apparently never proven, in May 1486 he was stripped of his offices of steward, constable and master forester of Barnard Castle on suspicion of involvement with the rebels. He eventually got them back, though he had to swear loyalty to Henry again. It is also possible that the widower of Francis's sister Joan, Brian Stapleton, was involved in the rebellion as he died, apparently unexpectedly, on 28 March 1486[71] and his children did not enjoy their proper inheritance.[72] This is often taken to mean he died in the course of Francis's rebellion, or was even one of the men hanged for it, though no paperwork to confirm this has survived.

Whatever the case, Brian's death did not distract Francis from his desire for revenge. Whereas the defusing of the military threat in Buckingham's rebellion spelled the end of that revolt, this was not the case for Francis's rebellion. Though he appears to have lost a lot of his support, he had not lost everything; he still had some loyal men with him. There was a change of plans, probably hastily arranged and therefore extremely dangerous. It appears that there was some attempt, probably modelled on the rebellions of Jack Cade in 1450 and Francis's father-in-law Henry in 1470, to put forward a strawman rebel, given the everyman name of 'Robin of Redesdale'.[73] There is no evidence this ever went past the planning stage, though plenty of suspicions are recorded.[74] Francis surely would have been involved.

Perhaps not satisfied with this alone, it appears Francis gathered some men to take a more proactive approach. He wanted to wait until Henry was near York, then try to kidnap or kill him.[75] There is no information about how he intended to do this, or even how close he came; all we know is that he failed. The plan was apparently for Francis to gather some of his men to ambush Henry as he was approaching the city,[76] but the plot was so undeveloped it did not even appear to take into account Henry's bodyguards. The Croyland Chronicle, presumably following rumours, conflates this incident with the one which happened later while Henry was *at* York.[77]

There has been some dispute over whether the plan was to kidnap Henry or kill him on sight. The former seems more likely, as simply killing Henry was probably a suicide mission given his bodyguards would be on hand; the best the would-be assassins could have hoped for would have been a quick death, and the worst would have been the slow and agonising death of a convicted regicide. Francis, brave and desperate, was probably willing to take the chance, but some of his co-conspirators may not have been so eager, opting for the (notionally) safer alternative of ambushing the royal party and capturing Henry, giving them a way out, the threat to the king's life being the safe conduct pass.

Had Francis and his men succeeded in taking Henry, it is possible that the conspirators planned simply to kill him once they had evaded his protectors, but this straightforward murder could have effectively martyred Henry, at least in the eyes of his supporters. Therefore, it is more likely that the intention was to keep Henry captive and in his place elevate Richard's nephew John, Earl of Lincoln to the throne; Henry could then be condemned to death for the regicide of Richard III, making Henry's death not an assassination but an arguably legitimate execution. Nevertheless, whatever Francis had planned, it was not to be. Henry and his party escaped, if narrowly.[78]

According to Polydore Vergil, Henry was understandably upset and frightened once he arrived in York. Though Vergil mixes up the timeline, confusng the attempt on Henry's life with the rebellion as a whole, his statement that '[t]he king was unmoved by this first report, since it was uncertain, but when he learned by a letter from his supporters that what rumor had previously announced was indeed true, he was affected by great fear'[79] rings true, as it reflects what Sir Hugh Convey said. Henry's subsequent reaction, and the pattern of Henry's reaction – initial disbelief followed by fear – may well have been the same when he heard of the fresh danger in York at a time when he thought the rebellion was over. There can be no doubt that everyone was on high alert – and with good reason.

Though he had already failed in his attempt to reach and assassinate Henry, Francis was not about to give up, and he and his co-conspirators regrouped. The atmosphere at Henry's court was tense and watchful, though he tried his best to go on as planned and pretend nothing was wrong. Henry continued with the lavish court celebrations he had planned, such as on 22 April, when 'the King heard his evensong in the Minster church, having a blue mantle above his surcote and on his head his cap of maintenance'.[80] This must have been a tense affair; even Polydore Vergil, loath to admit even the smallest positive fact about Richard, states that he was still very popular in York, and none of the citizens would have helped Henry if Francis attacked again.[81] In fact, Vergil explicitly mentions this as a major part of the reason Henry was afraid in the first place. The open celebrations of Mass, with Henry displayed in kingly attire, must have been a way to distract both king and court as well as all spectators, while giving the public the pomp and ceremony required. The festivities planned for St George's Day the next day served the same purpose.

Taking all sources together, it seems the people of York put on a lavish show for Henry.[82] Having already received him with honour, a lot of spectacles were planned, although these displays did not alleviate the tension in the city. The commoners were not showing Henry the adulation that both he and the city elders had hoped for. Several would have been in on Francis's plan to assassinate the king during the St George's Day festivities, and given how close the plan came to succeeding, it is to be assumed that some were involved in organising the festivities in a way that would facilitate Francis's attempt to reach the king.

Francis may well have regarded St George's Day as a suitable occasion, as St George was the patron saint of England. The notion would have appealed to Francis's pious sensibilities – to his mind, he would be killing a usurper and installing a rightful king on England's throne on the day dedicated to the dragon slayer. It was, on a more practical level, also the best opportunity for Francis and his co-conspirators to get close enough to Henry to have a chance of success.

This time, their attempt appears to have been more carefully planned, and again it failed only narrowly, as stated by the Croyland Chronicle:

> While [the king] was at York, however, devoutly intent upon the festival of St George, he was nearly taken by the cunning of the enemy. The earl of Northumberland, however, prudently

hastening to meet these first (stirrings) had some of the instigators
of this rising hanged on the gallows ...[83]

Vergil references Henry's fear of attack in York, though he makes
it sound as if it was still connected to the military uprising, saying
that although Henry 'was affected by great fear since he had no
army, no weaponry with which to arm his followers, and no place
where he could enlist soldiers at that time, in a city which was
hostile, in whose mind the memory of Richard's name remained
fresh',[84] he reacted with 'diligence, lest time be given his adversaries
for increasing their forces'[85] and commanded his uncle to gather
men. Vergil's account combined the two separate attacks into one
event. Henry Percy, Earl of Northumberland, is not mentioned in
connection with the rebellion and its failure within the text. Given
that Vergil's account confuses what happens and when, and given
that the Croyland Chronicle was written at the time of the rebellion
and is, moreover, supported by other evidence, it can probably be
taken as the more reliable version.

If the Croyland account is to be believed, it appears to have
been a matter of luck that Northumberland spotted the rebels; if
he had not done so, the attack might have succeeded. It has been
widely accepted that this was a matter of good fortune for Henry
and bad luck for Francis and his fellow rebels, but there is another
possibility, one which neither Northumberland himself nor his
family in later years would have wished to draw any attention
to, and which the chronicler at Croyland would perhaps have
found too unlikely to record: that, in the hope of support, the
rebels contacted the earl and tried to convince him to join their
cause. Though this seems like a massive risk, it is not as if Francis
eschewed risks during the rebellion, and it is one that could have
paid off. Having someone on the inside might have seemed like the
best way to succeed.

In fact, despite the inherent danger of trying to contact the men
of Henry's court, it appears Northumberland was not the only
one Francis tried to recruit. There was someone else who seems
to have had knowledge of the plot, and for him the evidence is
less speculative. John de la Pole, Earl of Lincoln, was probably
contacted by the rebels, and he proved rather more sympathetic

than Northumberland. In fact, a year later it was claimed that Lincoln was not only ready to join the rebellion but was already fully involved when it took place. This claim is found in the York Civic Records, and was made by none other than James Taite, the man who had housed the Earl of Lincoln when he was in the city with Henry's entourage in 1486.

Though he said nothing at the time, a year after the rebellion Taite was questioned for having supposedly said 'that the Earl of Lincoln wold give the King's grace a breakfast [his just deserts].'[86] During that questioning, he reported that Lincoln had met with two men 'who dwelt around Middleham' and had allowed them to come to Taite's household, where he openly discussed helping the rebellion with them. Lincoln was so careless about the matter that Taite overheard them talking about using his house as a starting point for rebellion, saying, 'Here is good gate for us to Robin of Redesdale over the walls ...'[87]

Since this story was told by Taite in 1487, by which time Lincoln was openly involved in rebellion against Henry, it could well be coloured by hindsight and the knowledge of Lincoln's eventual defection. However, it does not have to be so. In fact, there are several indicators against this. First and foremost, it makes Henry and his government look slow on the uptake, unable to realise they had a traitor in their midst. Moreover, it would be strange for Taite to invent such a story, considering it raised the question of why he had sat on such knowledge for a year.

This suggests that at least some of Taite's story was true, indicating that Lincoln expressed his support even if he was not fully involved. Taite's account is also full of details that would represent strange and unnecessary additions were he concocting a story. One such tidbit was that Lincoln travelled on a white horse with a saddle inlaid with gold and silver,[88] a detail that would have been easy to disprove were he making it up, given others would have remembered.

While Taite may, in the course of a year, have mixed up some facts, or misremembered them, it seems likely that he was honest and told what he thought was the truth, and which very well may have been the complete truth. If all of Taite's story is true, it would indicate that some of Francis's original plan, before the dispersal of his army, was at least discussed and not completely dismissed, and that there were still some trying to stage a distraction for him while he reached the king.

Lincoln's involvement in such plans, which would indicate involvement in Francis's rebellion from the first, would actually answer some questions about the events of 1486. The most important of these, perhaps, is what exactly Francis planned to do once he had Henry. If he was in contact with Lincoln, who had been Richard's heir presumptive until Bosworth, he might have considered him the obvious man to take over the throne, and Lincoln may very well have been eager to do so. It is quite possible that this was agreed upon by the rebels but not openly broadcast since it would have endangered Lincoln, who was at Henry's court at the time.

Even if Lincoln was not the man designated by the rebels to become king after Henry's demise, he may have helped the rebellion. It would explain how Francis knew that his plans for leaving sanctuary had been leaked, allowing him to adapt his approach to avoid capture. Henry would have kept Lincoln close to try and prevent him from getting involved in any rebellions,[89] and this proximity would have placed the earl in the ideal position to learn of the betrayal, while his connections would have been sufficient to send a warning to Francis.

Emboldened by his success in winning over Lincoln, and perhaps misjudging the allegiances of Northumberland, who had reasons to resent Henry VII, it is entirely possible that Francis decided to make contact. If so, it was not just bad luck but a rare mistake that cost Francis and his rebels their success in York and saved Henry's life on St George's Day.

The failure was fatal for the rebels, with several of the conspirators caught. Most likely they were questioned as to their plans and the whereabouts of Francis, who had escaped, but none of them gave him away. The city of York hid Francis well, Henry's men could not trace him. The rebels caught were hanged the same day.[90] The Croyland Chronicle makes it sound as if they were hanged on the spot by Northumberland, but this seems unlikely. Northumberland did not have the authority to order a hanging, and there would have been no necessity for him to assume such powers to neutralise the threat to the king when Henry was nearby and able to give orders. No documents survive to suggest any trial.

Even if those hanged on 23 April did not get a trial, there were definitely legal proceedings in York after St George's Day, and this suggests the proper conventions were observed. Interestingly, one of the documents to survive from the aftermath of Francis's attack is a warrant for the arrest of one Thomas Metcalf, a man sharing the name of one of Francis's feoffees of 1484, 'for certain misbehavings surmised to be done by him against us, contrary to his duty and liegeance'.[91] There must have been others who were arrested or punished in the same way, but Metcalf's case is interesting because he was a chaplain, showing that the rebellion in York reached beyond disgruntled commoners.

This third failure in a short time spelled the end of Francis's rebellious designs, and he fled York and went into hiding. The uprising has gone down in history as barely more than a farce, but this ignores the real danger it posed to Henry and how seriously it was taken by his government. The punishments handed out afterwards, sometimes to people only suspected of involvement, are also telling as to how seriously people took the rebellion at the time.

The rebellion was certainly no joke for Francis; he knew that his capture would mean his death. Though he had shown no particular interest in his own survival during his attempts to kill Henry, he clearly had no intention of being caught and executed as a traitor if he could not kill Henry beforehand. When his plans went fatally wrong in York and some of his co-conspirators were hanged, Francis fled.

However, even now the rebellion was not entirely extinguished. Its aftershocks were felt as late as 5 May, when some men armed with 'diverse signs, viz Ploughs, Rokkes, Clowtes, Shoes and Wolsakkes, and two standards, one of them with the sign of the Red Rose and the other of the Ragged Staff',[92] assembled in Westminster and then made their way to Highbury to attack some of the king's adherents there. However, these men, while possibly contacted by either Francis or the Staffords before the rebellion, most likely orchestrated this attack independently. In fact, notably, their choice of the two standards had no connection to Francis or the Staffords. In fact, the Bear and Ragged Staff had been the badge of Richard Neville, Earl of Warwick,[93] and may have been chosen by the rebels to show their alliance to his young grandson, Edward, Earl of Warwick, son of Richard III's brother Clarence. The significance of the Red Rose is harder to decipher. Though over the centuries it has become associated with the Lancastrian side of the series of conflicts now known as the Wars of the Roses, this was not the case in 1486. The Beauforts were the one family with a Red Rose badge, which makes it a rather baffling choice for a rebellion against Henry VII, whose mother was a Beaufort. Perhaps the banner was simply chosen to cause confusion.

By this point the rebels' actions were little more than an annoyance to Henry and his government, acknowledged but not treated with any concern. Quite naturally, Henry's main interest was finding and trying those rebels who had actively tried to dethrone and kill him, above all finding the instigators, Francis and the Staffords. He was to locate the Staffords in time, but not Francis.

Contemporary records do not agree on Francis's movements after he fled York, which presumably shows he put his trust in the right people, as he had done when planning the rebellion from sanctuary. In addition, he did not make the mistake the Staffords made. When their rebellion failed after the loss of men, they both took sanctuary again.[94]

It is hard to say exactly when this happened. Henry had sent men to arrest them as early as 18 April, though this attempt failed,[95] meaning that they were then still on the run and had not yet gone into sanctuary. By 14 May, however, Humphrey Stafford, and presumably his brother as well, were in Henry's custody. On that day, which happened to be Whitsunday, Humphrey Stafford was recorded as being led to Worcester where Henry was staying. This means that it was some time between 18 April and 14 May that the Staffords had chosen to take sanctuary once more, this time at Abingdon Abbey.[96]

This abbey did not have the extended rights of sanctuary that St John's in Colchester had, but presumably the brothers hoped to come up with some sort of plan during the forty days they had left to them.[97] However, Henry VII was so upset and frightened by the rebellion that he had them pulled out of sanctuary.[98] This was illegal, and this fact formed the basis of the Staffords' defence.[99] Predictably, this failed. While Thomas Stafford was pardoned, perhaps as a concession to the Church,[100] Humphrey Stafford was condemned to a full traitor's death and executed.[101] Shortly afterwards, Henry bought the pope's agreement that sanctuary could not be claimed by those who had committed high treason[102] – a claim that neither Edward IV nor Richard III ever tried to make, though both are regularly accused by historians of having failed to respect the rules of sanctuary.[103]

Since this happened after Francis fled York, it is fortunate that he did not think of taking sanctuary himself. Perhaps he knew not to trust that sanctuary was sacrosanct, preferring to conceal his whereabouts entirely. Perhaps he simply had better options, for which he must have been very grateful when he heard about the fate of the Staffords.

It is hard to say just what options were available to Francis, since contemporary sources only reflect rumours. Later chronicles, such as Vergil's, were more definite about what they allege happened, if not necessarily more correct. Vergil's version is that Francis 'ran non-stop into the country of Lancaster, without having attempted a battle, and came to Sir Thomas Broughton, a man of great authority in those parts, with whom he remained hidden for several months'.[104]

Though the timeline Vergil gives is incorrect, as mentioned above, and he omits a lot, he may have been correct on this point. He is at least correct that Francis would have gone through Lancaster to meet up with Thomas Broughton,[105] an associate who would go on to support Francis again. Maybe the two men stayed at Broughton Tower for a period, but there can be no certainty, as contemporary sources give conflicting information.

On 19 May, Margaret, Countess of Oxford wrote a letter to John Paston, stating that Francis was on the Isle of Ely 'to the entente by alle lykelyhod, to finde the waies and meanes to gete him shipping and passage in your costes, or ellis to resorte ageyn to seintuary, if he can or maie'.[106] While it is known that Francis did not take sanctuary, it is possible that he was trying to leave the country. This would have been a smart move, and distinctly clear-sighted, given that he and Broughton might not yet have learnt of the Staffords being pulled from sanctuary, meaning nowhere in England was truly safe. At the time of writing, the Countess of Oxford must have had no knowledge of the treatment suffered by the Staffords, as she put going into sanctuary on a par with fleeing abroad, in terms of how it would put Francis out of reach.

However, Francis may have had better information than the countess; the Earl of Lincoln might have already informed him of Henry's assertion that sanctuary could not be claimed in cases of high treason. Even if he did not yet know of this, he was presumably wary, and with good reason. The fact that the countess ended her letter on a rather cryptic note, telling Paston not to capture Francis but that 'what pleasur ye maie doo to the Kinges grace in this matier I am sure is not to you unknowen'[107] might in fact indicate that, perhaps for fear of fellow rebels freeing him, Francis was to be killed on sight. Even if this were not the case, or if Francis was unaware of such an order, it would be sensible for him to flee to Burgundy, to the court of Richard's sister Margaret, dowager Duchess of Burgundy.

Certainly, the beginnings of rebellion are to be found shortly afterwards in Burgundy, and by 24 June a future rebel, a boy claimed in Margaret's household accounts to be the 'sone van Clarentie uit Ingelant',[108] the son of Clarence from England – Margaret's nephew Edward, Earl of Warwick – was present at her court, and was given a gift of some wine by her. It is possible that this boy, whoever he really was, had already been at Margaret's court unrecorded, but it is also possible that he arrived with Francis in early summer 1486.

The official account Henry's government released after 1487 claimed that the English rebels brought the pretender to Burgundy, and while the account was dubious in parts, this assertion cannot be rejected outright. Nor can it be in any way confirmed, however. If Francis and Thomas Broughton were at Margaret's court in Burgundy, they left no trace in any source. It is equally possible that the two decided to lay low in England, thinking that Henry's forces would be patrolling the coasts in order to catch him attempting to cross the sea. The Countess of Oxford's letter placing him on the Isle of Ely indicates a belief that he would try to flee the country.

Perhaps it would have seemed that the safest option was to hide out for a while, staying at Broughton Tower with Thomas Broughton over the summer.

It is even possible that, while in hiding there, Francis and Broughton had already contacted those who they thought would help with another rebellion, as Francis had done less than a year earlier from sanctuary. Among those he was most likely to have contacted were Margaret of York herself, as well as John, Earl of Lincoln. Perhaps he also managed to contact his wife Anne, which would have been dangerous for both of them, as she would surely have been watched to see if she was in contact with him or had knowledge of his whereabouts.

Not only had Francis shown by now that he did not shy away from risks, but the timing of Richard FitzHugh losing his offices in May 1486 suggests that the unspecified suspicion of collaboration with rebels may have in fact been based on a belief that he helped Francis to escape and hide, which would have been much harder to prove than that he took action during the rebellion itself. If Richard FitzHugh really did help him, then Francis would have had an obvious way to send word to his wife, and to receive messages from her.

Whatever they did, Anne managed to avoid suspicion for the time being, though she was later suspected to be in collusion with her husband during 1487.[109] In fact, not only is it possible that this later suspicion was true, but Anne may already have been colluding with her husband in 1486. Assuming Margaret, Countess of Oxford, was accidentally passing on incorrect information in her letter, it could very well be that this information had been given to her by Anne, her niece, or Anne's mother Alice, Margaret's older sister. If so, this would explain the suspicion cast on Anne once it was found that the intelligence as to Francis's whereabouts the Countess of Oxford had was wrong. We cannot be sure of this, but it would be in keeping with Alice's character[110] – as well as Anne's, as it would later turn out.

Whoever Francis was in contact with, and whatever his true location, Francis would hardly have spent the summer of 1486 idle. Sadly for us – and fortunately for him – no one seemed to know where he was or what he did at this time. While this proves his success at staying under the radar during this difficult time, it is frustrating for historians.

Henry VII's government was faced with the same problem, which was rather more troubling for them. Despite their best attempts to trace him and learn of his actions, they had no success. This in itself speaks to Francis's character, and perhaps also to his prudence. As a hunted fugitive, it would have only taken one man to betray him and he would have been captured and executed, potentially even tortured for information. That this was all it took had been shown three years earlier during the Duke of Buckingham's rebellion. When the duke tried to hide, one of his own men, Humphrey Bannister, betrayed him for £1,000.[111] He did not last two weeks in hiding. Francis hid for nearly three-quarters of a year, and so effectively that his movements were impossible to trace and remain so to this day. If nothing else, it can be said that he chose his friends well.

By summer 1486, Henry had tried and executed several rebels, his progress possibly hindered by the fact that alongside his trusted men Oxford and Bedford he had appointed Lincoln to a commission of oyer and terminer, charged with finding rebels and trying several of them.[112] Perhaps influenced by Lincoln, Henry appears to have decided that leniency was preferable to the strict punishments he had handed out in 1485, and he pardoned several people connected with Richard who had been attainted in December 1485. Among them were the brothers Edward and Geoffrey Franke, and Thomas Broughton.[113] There were also pardons for several of the rebels; notably, Thomas Metcalf was released from jail[114] and many of those commoners from Colchester whom Francis and the Staffords had recruited were pardoned.

Presumably this was done in the hope of winning support for Henry by his show of clemency, and perhaps also in the hope that somebody would pass on information about Francis. However, nobody did, and in fact several of the men, the Frankes and Thomas Broughton included, appear to have used their pardons to plot against Henry more effectively, swearing allegiance to him with no intent to uphold their oaths. Broughton, and presumably also the Frankes, almost certainly knew of Francis's whereabouts yet they did not give him away.[115]

The next mention we have of Francis dates from January 1487, when planning was already underway for what would later become known as the Lambert Simnel rebellion. In late January, John de Vere, Earl of Oxford, husband to Margaret, Countess of Oxford, who had written about Francis's supposed whereabouts in May 1486, received a letter from John Paston stating that Francis had left the country. Paston clearly thought that this was valuable information, but he was not the only one trying to keep tabs on Francis's movements. Paston obviously trusted the information he relayed, but his confidence appears to have been misplaced. He received a somewhat reproachful reply from the Earl of Oxford, who asserted that Francis had not yet left the country but was still waiting to do so, with exactly fourteen men to support him.

> John Paston, I commend me to you. And as for such tidings as you have sent hither, the king had knowledge thereof more than a seven-night [week] passed. And as for such names as you have sent, supposing them to be gone with the Lord Lovell, they be yet in England, for he is departing with fourteen persons and no more. At the king's coming to London I would advise you to see his highness. And Almighty God keep you.
>
> Written at Windsor, the 24th day of January.[116]

The tone of the letter is almost suspicious, which hints at how Francis and his rebellion had rattled Henry. Oxford was one of Henry's closest men. He had been instrumental in helping him win the Battle of Bosworth,[117] and was one of the godfathers to Henry's new-born son and heir.[118] As such, he would have been privy to the closest workings of the government. That he expressed a suspicion against a man simply for relaying incorrect information about the whereabouts of a rebel who had already proved hard to trace, and had fooled others before, shows the mood at court.

It illustrates that although later chroniclers – Vergil once more foremost among them – tried to minimise the threat, Francis was quite clearly seen as an existential threat with a wide reach. As events unfolded, Francis would prove that he was every bit as dangerous as they feared.

Whether Oxford or Paston were correct about Francis's whereabouts is impossible to say. If he was still in the country at the writing of Oxford's letter, Oxford clearly lacked the vital piece of information, when and where he intended to board a ship and leave. If he and Thomas Broughton – the latter not mentioned by the letter writers, suggesting his involvement was as yet unknown – were still in England and had thirteen other men with them, and managed to leave the country without being caught, this was quite a trick to pull off, once more speaking to Francis's organisational genius. However, that this happened is not certain. All that is known for sure is if they had not already left by late January 1487, they did so soon afterwards.[119] They might have brought other men with them, as Oxford had no need to invent them, but if so they were not of noble birth and standing, not regarded as important enough to mention by name in any source but Paston's now lost letter.

However many men Francis and Thomas brought with them, Margaret of York happily received them in Burgundy. Over the years that were to follow, she would display a readiness to receive all those fleeing from Henry VII, whether they had committed treason against him or not,[120] but Francis and his men were not unexpected arrivals at her court. The rebellion was already brewing, meaning she and Francis must have been in contact before he arrived in Burgundy.

Soon, Henry VII and his government would learn of the beginnings of the rebellion and the repercussions for the king. Only around a week after Francis likely arrived in Burgundy and Paston received the letter that all but accused him of deliberately passing on faulty information, it was to turn out that the fear of Francis's far reach had not just been paranoia. At the beginning of February 1487, according to Vergil on 2 February,[121] a meeting between Henry VII and his privy councillors took place in Sheen to discuss what to do about the incipient rebellion. This meeting would witness a shocking development. John de la Pole, Earl of Lincoln, supposedly attended the council on the first day,[122] but then abruptly left court. Upon investigating this, Henry's men found that he had left the country and taken ship for Burgundy. As stated by Vergil, 'the earl came secretly to Margaret in Flanders, where some days previously Francis Lovell had betaken himself.'[123]

Lincoln managed his escape without anyone noticing, which does not reflect well on Henry's spies. That Lincoln of all men was not suspected despite having been Richard's heir after Prince Edward's death is a little baffling, but is likely that with Lincoln being closely watched, a complacency crept in about his ability to liaise with rebels undetected. The success in getting Lincoln out of the country speaks well of the rebels' talent for subterfuge, and it is easy to believe Vergil's assertion that upon learning of Lincoln's escape Henry 'was very disturbed in his mind'.[124] However, that it was only then that he 'decided that it was now time to prosecute and avenge the insults of his enemies, which he realized he could by no means avoid'[125] seems very unlikely, and is in fact contradicted by Vergil's own earlier words about Henry trying to stop the rebellion by calling the council.

For Henry, worse news was yet to come after Lincoln's defection. Shortly afterwards, Henry and his councillors made the decision to strip the queen's mother, the queen dowager Elizabeth Woodville, of all her possessions and banish her to the monastery in Bermondsey, a decision said to have been reached 'by thadvise of the lords and other nobles of our counsaill for divers consideracions vs and theym moeuyng'.[126] This was said to cause 'much wondering',[127] and has, especially in modern times, often been credited to a suspicion that she was in contact with the rebels.

Especially in recent years, it has sometimes been postulated that Elizabeth herself chose to give up her possessions and go into the monastery,[128] but logic argues against this. Apart from the fact that this would not have required 'thadvise of the lords and other nobles', it is most notable that Elizabeth had already made different arrangements for herself in 1486, having already taken out a lease on a property she intended to live on.[129]

It is hard to imagine that after having made such deliberate arrangements she suddenly chose to place herself in such straitened circumstances that she was to complain in her will about having no money,[130] which would be absurd if she gave it up herself. Moreover, there is no reason why, if it was truly her choice, this should not have been announced by Henry to counter all rumours, or why Vergil, writing with the benefit of hindsight, would not have reported it. Instead he offered the rather flimsy explanation that Henry had banished Elizabeth for having made her peace with Richard, stating that among the measures taken 'whereby the storm could be avoided', it was decided that 'Elizabeth, the one-time consort of King Edward, was mulcted of all her possessions because she had entrusted herself and her daughters to King Richard.'[131]

This explanation was obviously nonsense, as Henry had more pressing concerns during the meeting at Sheen than how to punish his mother-in-law for something he had known since before his invasion and which had not appeared to bother him before that. There has been much discussion among historians as to the reason for Elizabeth Woodville's treatment, but the very fact that it was ruled on in a meeting held to react to the threat posed by the rebels at least suggests that her banishment could be connected to the rebellion. This is supported by the fact that shortly after the same meeting the decision was made to imprison Elizabeth's oldest son, Thomas Grey, Earl of Dorset, allegedly while he tried to lead armed men to join the king's forces, on the grounds that he might do something in future, not even because of a suspicion that he had done anything yet.[132]

Clearly there was concern that Francis's connections might reach even the family of Elizabeth Woodville, and going by her treatment after the rebellion was over, this suspicion may not have been unfounded.[133] It would have been a masterpiece of organisation by Francis to have maintained contact with Elizabeth while in hiding, and a masterpiece of dissembling on her part to keep up this contact while at court and avoid suspicion until the rebellion broke into the open.

In Burgundy, Francis must have heard of the measures taken by Henry to minimise the damage the rebellion could wreak, but it is doubtful it would have meant much to him. Even if Elizabeth was a co-conspirator, at that point she would not have been able to do much. Her main task in such a case would have been to spread misinformation among Henry's men to help Francis and his fellow rebels evade capture. By February 1487, all she could have done, would have been done. It might have worried Francis that she had been found out, but her discovery would have had few consequences for him and the rebellion.

Another decision by the council at Sheen must have worried Francis more: the move to have Edward, Earl of Warwick, son of Richard's brother the Duke of Clarence, paraded through London.[134] Henry had taken custody of the boy after becoming king, and kept him so closely confined in the Tower of London that in 1486 rumours were circulating that he had been killed.[135] The parade was meant to display that he was in Henry's custody, not in the hands of the rebels.

It is possible that this meant more to historians than it meant to Francis, who may have been confused about it. His likely reaction depends on what exactly the rebels claimed, and in whose name they intended to rise – a point of contention that contemporary sources could not agree on and which is still debated today.[136] Edward, Earl of Warwick was an obvious focal point for rebellion, as had already been shown by the Staffords using his name during the rebellion of 1486.[137] On the face of it, rising in his name would therefore have made sense, and Henry's actions were clearly intended to counter any rebel claim that the boy they had with them was Edward, Earl of Warwick, showing that he was instead a pretender, a low-born boy playing a part.

However, while this version has long been accepted by historians, it exhibits several logical fallacies and factual mistakes. The first of these is the supposed identity of the pretender, the boy Henry's government said was claiming to be Edward, Earl of Warwick. The traditional, government-sanctioned story was that he was a low-born boy from Oxford named Lambert Simnel.[138] Trained by a priest, he is supposed to have gone to Burgundy with the Earl of Lincoln,[139] which is in itself impossible: it would mean that in no more than two weeks the boy departed from England, arrived in Burgundy, was announced by the rebels as the Earl of Warwick, was heard about in England, prompted a meeting of council and was subsequently discredited by the parade of the real Edward, Earl of Warwick.

Presumably, the claim that the rebels chose a low-born boy as their figurehead was made to make them look ridiculous, and it might have been inspired by the fact that the 1486 rebellion had had no figurehead at all,[140] therefore indicating that the rebels had no real plan beyond killing Henry.

For Francis this was most likely true, and his 1486 rebellion and assassination attempt bear witness to that. He only cared for revenge. However, this did not hold true for Lincoln and for Margaret of York. Both, and especially the latter, did not share Francis's disregard for political machinations. Margaret was something of a political genius and had been an important figure in Burgundian politics for well over a decade,[141] using her good relationship to her brothers' governments to further Burgundian interests.[142] Those interests were in danger with Henry's accession, as he had invaded England with French help and was thus indebted to France, a situation that could very well have become dangerous for Burgundy, which had long resisted French attempts to absorb the territory.[143] Therefore, a rebellion with the aim of displacing a king with close ties to France and replacing him with one indebted to Burgundy was very much in Margaret's interest.

It would be wrong to think because of this that Margaret's actions were motivated by mere politics, however. For over a decade after her brother's death, Margaret took in rebels against Henry VII at her court, even when they brought her no benefit, such as the man said to be the murderer of the Earl of Northumberland in 1489,[144] a commoner with no useful ties. This suggests that Margaret took her brother's death personally; but compared to Francis her motives are much harder to discern, seemingly a mixture of the political and the personal.

Too little is known of Lincoln's character and personal relationships to say anything about his motivations, but his very presence renders the claim about a low-born pretender bizarre. As mentioned above, Lincoln had been Richard's heir presumptive after Prince Edward's death; in fact, from 22 August to 7 November 1485, he had been *de jure* king. He had a far better claim than Henry, and a better claim than Edward, Earl of Warwick as well. Not only would it already have made little sense for him to rebel on behalf of the *real* Edward, Earl of Warwick, it would have been twice as absurd for him to do it for a low-born boy only pretending to be the Earl of Warwick.

It has often been assumed by those believing that Francis, Lincoln, Margaret and the others rose in the name of a low-born pretender that Simnel was simply a puppet, and that Lincoln meant to take the throne in his own right if the uprising was successful.[145] Again, this makes little sense. Lincoln's pedigree was flawless. He did not have an attainder hanging over his head like the little Earl of Warwick, and he had been Richard's heir. If he had wanted to take the throne, it would have made far more sense for him to simply rise in his own name. In fact, such a course of action might have attracted more men to the rebellion than rising for a child of doubtful ancestry claiming to be a royal heir but kept from the throne by attainder.

The claim that Lincoln intended to take the throne after staging an elaborate and unnecessary uprising that could only disadvantage his cause smacks of an attempt to make Tudor propaganda fit the facts rather than taking all the facts and trying to see what theory they fit. Unfortunately, the obscurity of Francis's plotting in 1486 and Henry VII's need to frame the rebellion as illegitimate and pathetic means that solid facts are exceedingly hard to come by. We can sometimes prove that something was *not* true, but beyond that we are largely confined to making judgments based off the actions taken.

Once in Burgundy, the rebels began perfecting their plan. Several sources report this plotting, but having been written after the events they could not provide any definite facts,[146] relying instead on rumours and guesses. Francis, once again, is hardly mentioned in these reports, despite being one of the instigators of the rebellion. Yet again he managed to be right at the centre of events without drawing much attention to himself or leaving any traces of his actions in chronicles. Neither Jean Molinet nor Philippe Commynes mention him at all, while Polydore Vergil seems to keep forgetting him before remembering his presence when it proves convenient for the narrative he is trying to sell. In fact, he is only mentioned three times, and never in a pivotal role. Though it is said that 'Francis Lovell had betaken himself' to Burgundy even before Lincoln had arrived there, all focus is on Lincoln after his arrival.

Perhaps before Francis arrived in Burgundy, or perhaps afterwards, the rebels made contact with several nobles in Ireland, first and foremost the Earl of Kildare, who had had close ties with the Yorkist governments of Edward IV and Richard III.[147]

Though Francis would not have met him before, maybe the connection to Richard's government was enough for the men to establish a relationship. More likely, however, it was Margaret who made contact with the Irish nobles, informing them of what was going on and eventually visiting Ireland, having far better connections and having no need to hide her movements.

At the same time, with the support of her stepson-in-law Maximilian, future Holy Roman Emperor and King of the Romans, Margaret organised mercenaries for the rebellion from what is today Switzerland,[148] led by the famous Bavarian fighter Martin Schwartz.[149] Seeing to it that they were properly armed, prepared and paid would have taken a while, a fact alluded to by Jean Molinet, who states that Margaret, 'raised a group of Germans [sic]'[150] numbering fifteen or sixteen hundred, among whom [was] the principal conductor and captain, Master Martin Zwatre',[151] going on to state that only after '[t]he preparations [were] done by the Germans, taking the lives and the artillery, dressed and paid well for some time',[152] did they start to move, and it is quite possible that this was the reason for the nearly three-month delay between the arrival of Francis and Lincoln and the rebels making their next move.

Vergil claims that only after arriving in Burgundy did the rebels begin to plan their attack, which is obviously impossible. However, his take on the whole process of plotting is still interesting in that he insists that the whole rebellion was the doing of 'a single mean, wicked fellow',[153] by which he meant Lincoln. Naturally, this was meant to reflect the supposed lack of support for the rebellion, but it is still notable that he did not point out Francis as an instigator, given that Francis had already rebelled against Henry and repeatedly tried to kill him while Lincoln was still at Henry's court, pretending to be loyal. It reflects rather well the difference in the view of the rebellion among contemporary spectators in England, who saw Francis as important, and those writing in later years, and is more proof, if any is needed, that Francis was good at evading notice. Even in texts which had every reason to vilify him and which had shown no hesitation in maligning Richard, Margaret and Lincoln, Francis is not slandered. In fact, he isn't mentioned much more than Thomas Broughton.

A possible alternative reason for Francis's relative absence in Vergil's account is that featuring him prominently would have raised inconvenient questions that he could not answer in his text without calling his entire narrative about Richard and his reign into question. As a loyal and devoted friend to Richard III, Francis contradicted the picture of the king Vergil was striving to present, and therefore had to be treated with caution. By neglecting to mention him in accounts of Richard's reign, Vergil avoids drawing any attention to their relationship, making it easy to present Francis as a straightforward malcontent. However, this creates as many problems as it solves, rendering the narrative slightly inconsistent and Francis's character strangely changeable.

Since Francis is stripped of his motivations of love and loyalty, his actions make far less sense. Vergil does not try to explain why Francis, described as frightened and cowardly throughout, would rebel rather than going into exile or submitting to Henry. Seeing as his close connection with Richard is not mentioned and Henry is presented as a merciful king, nothing in the narrative would justify his course of action. His behaviour is completely inexplicable given that Vergil prominently mentions several of Richard's closest men submitting to Henry. The omission of Francis's friendship with Richard raises questions about him, his character and his motives that would have been answered were their relationship included. However, mentioning their closeness would have caused a different set of problems for the narrative regarding Richard's character and reign; how could this supposed monster inspire loyalty even after his death and the fall of his family? Vergil opted to avoid difficulties in Francis's presentation by mentioning him as little as possible, so that he is overshadowed by the other rebels of Henry VII's reign.

Even with this explanation for Vergil's relative silence on Francis, it is still curious that one of the instigators of the rebellion drew so little attention and had so little known about his actions that he could be all but ignored. Neither Molinet nor Commynes[154] had any reason to hide Francis's actions, credentials or importance to the organisation of the rebellion, but they do not even mention him. This absence is more connected with his long-established ability to remain in the shadows.

A comparison between Francis's obscurity in the narrative and Lincoln's prominence is unavoidable, but Lincoln, having a claim to the throne himself, was in a different position to Francis. Perhaps the more suitable comparison is to Harry, Duke of Buckingham, and the 1483 rebellion bearing his name. Though not even an instigator of that rebellion, Buckingham drew all the attention, at the time and for centuries after. Francis was the very opposite. With no desire for preferment, and having always shunned the limelight, Francis organised his rebellion quietly, calmly and efficiently.

In May 1487, Francis set off for Ireland with Thomas Broughton, Lincoln and their pretender, whoever he really was.[155] According to Molinet, there they were joined by the Swiss mercenaries organised by Maximilian, who had 'parted Holland, and arrived in Ireland where they found the Duke of Clarence, together with the earls of Lincoln and Guldar [Kildare] and the nobles of the country'.[156] This was an important step towards their pretender claiming the English throne, as Ireland was, at least theoretically, English territory, and English kings also held the title 'Lord of Ireland'.

Ireland was therefore symbolically important, but there was more to it than that. It was also geographically convenient, and, perhaps most importantly of all, it promised widespread support for the rebels, from the population and not just the nobility. The Yorkist cause had always been popular in Ireland, ever since Richard, Duke of York, father of Edward IV and Richard III, had used his effective banishment there as Lieutenant of Ireland to rule fairly and effectively, winning Irish support.[157] Many common people could be expected to remember that and so help the rebels, and according to Molinet many did.[158]

It would have been as much to offer a popular spectacle as to give legitimacy to their cause that the rebels chose to crown their pretender in Dublin. In fact, this motivation is suggested by Molinet, and stated to have been successful. In his retelling of the events, the rebels, with 'the agreement of all of the people, did crown him King of England with two archbishops and twelve bishops'.[159]

The very fact that a coronation took place is also a rather important piece of evidence against the traditional version of this rebellion. Though the ceremony could not take place in Westminster Abbey, as was traditional for English kings, the coronation was a solemn ceremony, blessed with the presence of bishop, weighty and important to pious medieval minds. There could have been no question of simply disregarding this coronation to give the throne to Lincoln if that had been the plan, and most likely there would have been no question of even of crowning a puppet, as it would have cheapened the sacrament. This, perhaps more than all other pieces of evidence, speaks to the pretender being someone of real importance, of royal blood, not just a boy pretending.

Contemporary sources could not agree on the boy's identity, claimed or real. Bernard André, working as a tutor to Henry VII's son and heir Arthur, offered that the pretender was claiming to be 'second son of Edward',[160] meaning Richard of Shrewsbury, the younger of the so-called Princes in the Tower. Others, such as Molinet, said he claimed to be Clarence's son Edward, Earl of Warwick, as stated by Henry's government. Notably, all through Molinet's report he calls the boy 'King Edward' and Henry VII 'the Earl of Richmond', which shows he was not particularly sympathetic to Henry and his cause, and so likely portrayed the rebellion to the best of his knowledge, without adding any spin that could profit Henry.[161]

There is another possibility, explored by Gordon Smith in his article 'Lambert Simnel and the King from Dublin',[162] and more recently by Matthew Lewis in his book *The Survival of the Princes in the Tower*: that the pretender was, or at least claimed to be, Edward V, Edward IV's eldest son, disinherited in favour of his uncle in 1483.

This theory is based mainly on the confusion in the official accounts as to the identity of the pretender, and on the behaviour of Henry VII during and after the rebellion. Andrè famously reports that a herald was sent to Ireland when the rebels were there to prove the pretender was not who he claimed to be, only to find himself unable to do so. As Matthew Lewis points out, some of the treatment dished out to Margaret of York by Henry's envoys also points towards this. When, several years later, Margaret supported the claimant to the English throne whom history remembers as Perkin Warbeck, two of Henry's envoys are said to have accused the childless dowager duchess of having 'given birth to two boys aged 180 months',[163] meaning fifteen years. This would fit with the age 'Perkin' is assumed to have been, but not with the age that Edward, Earl of Warwick – and therefore any pretender claiming to be him – would have been in 1487. In fact, nor does it fit the age of the boy later showed off as the captured pretender by Henry VII's government,[164] and as such it is indicative of some knowledge contradicting the official version. Notably, Edward V would have been fifteen in 1486, when the pretender probably arrived at Margaret's court and planning for the rebellion began in earnest.

There were claims that the pretender not only claimed to be but actually *was* Edward, Earl of Warwick, smuggled out of the country by his father in 1477. This theory was believed at the time by Molinet and in modern times was most notably proposed and argued by Dr John Ashdown-Hill,[165] but Edward V might in fact make more sense as he would have been old enough to take the throne himself, with no protector ruling in his name. The little earl would have been just twelve years old, and many preferred a grown-up king, the relative validity of their claims notwithstanding. Moreover, what with Henry VII having overturned *Titulus Regius*, the Act of Parliament that disinherited the Princes in the Tower, Henry had removed all legal obstacles to Edward V taking the throne, while the little earl was still debarred by attainder.

In fact, Matthew Lewis posits that the Earl of Warwick was only suggested as the claimant because the two boys shared the same name, and therefore this could distract from the pretender's identity.[166] It is not known what regnal number the boy took, but both Edward V and Edward VI have been suggested.[167]

If it was Edward V his identity would have been clear, and in such a case Henry would have known that many would not fight against the young claimant, even if they would not have fought *for* him either. If this was the case, as Lewis argues, it would have been in Henry's interest to hide the fact that the boy claimed to be the erstwhile Edward V, not only by claiming the boy was not who he said he was but even distracting from precisely *who* he said he was.

If Edward, Earl of Warwick was in Henry's custody, this would have been the perfect opportunity for him to discredit them, as the rebels' supposed king could easily be misrepresented as claiming to be Warwick. Especially with rumours of the murder of Edward V still circulating, this would have been easy to believe for many.

The true identity of the purported pretender probably didn't matter to Francis. If he was truly Edward V, it would be interesting to know what he thought of his uncle's closest friend. It is hard to believe that the two would have got on particularly well, though any hostility would have most likely come from Edward V, understandably resentful at having been disinherited four years ago, not from Francis, who presumably did not care.

The young claimant was crowned on 24 June in Christ Church Cathedral in Dublin. The coronation was not just an important step for the rebels towards their goal of setting him on the English throne, as detailed above, but also a unique event in English history for two reasons. First, because the boy was not crowned in England itself. Second, while it was not the first time in English history that a new king had been crowned while another king still sat securely on the throne – Henry II had his oldest son Henry crowned while he was still alive for several reasons – it was the first (and last) time that a rebel against the anointed King of England was crowned and anointed while the monarch he opposed was alive and secure on the throne.

There are many questions about this rebellion, and even about the coronation itself, that can no longer be answered unless new evidence is found. The identity of the boy, despite various theories, cannot be ascertained and is as much a mystery as his age, which has been given as variously ten, twelve and fifteen in different reports.[168] As seen above, even what regnal number he claimed has been called into question.

No matter the identity of the pretender, his coronation was not a small affair which could have easily been forgotten. It enjoyed a lot of support from the Irish and was intended to be as impressive as possible. Jean Molinet, writing several years later, claimed that not only the Yorkist rebels took part but also the mercenaries hired by Margaret of York.

Though Molinet is shaky on details and frequently gets them wrong – for example, he neglected to mention that Lincoln himself, together with Francis, only arrived in Ireland twenty days before the coronation – it is interesting that he reported the coronation ceremony as such a popular and grand affair. This shows that at least gossip must have reported it to be so; allowing for exaggerations, this probably means it was quite a spectacle, though naturally without some of the usual elements of a 'usual' coronation of an English king at the time, perhaps including the regalia needed for a coronation.

John Ashdown-Hill points out that such items as a sword, spurs and a ring could very easily have been found for the occasion, and that Margaret of York would have probably sourced such things, although records make no mention of them. There is some information as to the crown used in the coronation, however, which appears to have been taken from a valuable statue of the Virgin Mary which stood in a church by the gates of Dublin.[169]

There are few descriptions of what actually happened during the coronation and afterwards. The ceremony seems to have gone off without a hitch, though sadly we do not know what parts Lincoln, Francis or the other rebels played in it. In sources such as Vergil, the coronation is predictably dismissed as an insignificant affair. In fact, Vergil does not even explicitly state that there had been a coronation, merely implying it, saying that 'at Dublin they treated the boy Lambert just as if he were born of the royal blood and deserving of being crowned king in the traditional way.'[170]

Despite this, the suggestion has survived that when the coronation ceremony in the cathedral was over, the newly crowned boy was carried back to Dublin Castle on the shoulders of 'tall men' so that spectators who had come out to see him could do so.[171] It appears that in Ireland, where the Yorkists were popular, the coronation had a lot of support even among the common people.

Back at Dublin Castle afterwards, the boy, together with the rest of the rebels, entertained members of the Irish nobility sympathetic to his cause, and according to Molinet this meant most of them.[172] Again, that this was meant to resemble a typical post-coronation banquet can be assumed. Francis, like Lincoln, was certainly present, but his role is unknown.

It can hardly be doubted that this occasion would have brought back memories of Richard's coronation for Francis, possibly painful to recall. Perhaps this soured the day for him, or maybe he tried to focus on the future, and his hope for revenge. If he did keep his distance from the coronation ceremonies, this must have been a personal choice; while the pretender, especially if he was truly Edward V, might not have taken to Francis, he was too important to the cause to exclude and offend. It is tempting to assume it was Francis's own choice not to play a prominent part in the proceedings, reflecting his intention not to take a major role in the new king's government should their rebellion succeed, but it is just as likely chroniclers simply ignored Francis and all he did during the ceremony as he had been previously so unostentatious.

Even so, it is certainly likely that Francis opted to avoid a big political role, given how much his position in Richard's government had owed to his personal relationship to him and how little interest he had shown in political proceedings at the time. In fact, there is some evidence that Francis withdrew himself from such matters in 1487. After the coronation, a parliament met in Drogheda,[173] and once again Francis was not even mentioned. It is obvious that no chronicler would have had any knowledge of his previous preferences and inclination to stay out of the political realities of government, and would have simply recorded his presence had he been active there.

However little chroniclers thought of Francis's involvement, Henry VII's government assigned a lot of importance to the man. This is especially illustrated by a fascinating letter written by Sir Edmund Bedingfield to John Paston shortly before the Battle of Stoke:

> Unto my right worshipful cousin, John Paston, Esquire for the Body.
>
> Right worshipful cousin, I recommend me unto you as heartily as I can, letting you [know?] I was with my Lord Stuart as on Monday last past, by the desire of them that I may not say no to. I heard all that was said there, but they gained no advantage, word, or promise of me; but they thought inasmuch as they were the best in the share, that every man ought to wait and go with them.
>
> Whereto it was answered that our master, next the king, having his commission, must needs have gentlemen and the country to await upon him by virtue of the same, but it was thought I ought

not to obey no copy of the commission, without I had the same [without having] under wax, wherein has been great argument, which I understood by report a fortnight past, and that cause me to send unto my lord to have the very commission, which he sent me, and a letter, whereof I send you the copy here enclosed.

As for you, you be sore taken in some place, saying that you intend such things as is like to follow great mischief. I said I understood no such, nor things like it, and it is thought you intend not to go for this journey, nor no gentleman in this quarter but Robert Brandon that has promised to go with them, as they say.

I understood Sir William Boleyn and Sir Harry Heydon were at Thetford in Kent, but they returned into Norfolk again, I think they will not go on this journey, if the king need. Sir Harry was at Attleborrow on Saturday, I ween he had a vice [?] there to return again, wherefore, cousin, it is good to understand the certain what gentlemen intend to go, and be assured to go together, that I may have word; my cousin Hopton has promised that he will be one. As for Wysman, he says he will be of the same, but I can have no hold [certainty].

Furthermore, cousin, it is said that after my lord's departing to the king you were met at Barkwey, which is construed that you had been with the Lady Lovell; but wrath says never well; and inasmuch as we understand my lord's pleasure, it is well done that we deal wisely thereafter. And, next to the king, I answered plainly I was bound to do him service, and to fulfill his commandment to the utmost of my power, by the grace of God, who ever preserve you to his pleasure.

Written at Oxburgh, the 16th day of May. Your cousin, E. Bedyngfeld.[174]

This letter gives a good insight into the confusion and the difficulties of organisation which beset the king's party during the rebellion. It references the journeys which had to be made, the uncertainty about who was reliable, and, most notably, the rumours which had sprung up. Most curiously, however, it shows that not only had John Paston not managed to entirely divest himself of the suspicion levelled at him earlier in the year but also that Anne Lovell was seen as so likely to be involved in the rebellion in some way that associating with her was thought to be dangerous.

Edmund Bedingfield is clearly sympathetic to John Paston and on friendly terms with him, but it becomes obvious from his letter that Paston was himself the target of rumours which cast him in a bad light and presumably threw doubt on his loyalty to Henry VII, rumours which may well have started with him passing on supposedly wrong information about Francis's whereabouts. Bedingfield does not spell out what it is that is being said, presumably knowing that Paston would be able to guess what he meant by 'such things as is like to follow great mischief'. He mentions having himself spoken against such allegations, and seems to have been quite certain Paston was not intending to go against the king, which turned out to be true.

Bedingfield then goes on to detail other men's movements and what they mean to him and will likely mean to the king, before stating, in the last paragraph, that there has been gossip that Paston's recent stay at Barkwey meant he was staying with Francis's wife, Anne. He does not connect this to what he says above about deeds that are 'like to follow great mischief', nor does he even say that this is where those rumours come from, but he makes it clear they are to Paston's disadvantage.

On the face of it, this is perhaps not too surprising. Anne Lovell was an attainted traitor's wife, who was at the head of the rebellion that king and country were preparing for at the moment of the letter being written. It could be argued that it was only because of this that an association with her at that moment was seen to be suspicious, and it does not actually mean she was suspected of anything. However, such general suspicion was not applied to all wives of attainted or even currently rebelling traitors, who were often regarded as innocent victims and were so, for example in the case of Lincoln's young wife. If Anne was presumed to be innocent and loyal to the king, there would have been no reason to consider a rumour of Paston having visited her as detrimental to him. Moreover, if it was truly just about association, the very fact that Anne's husband had planned his rebellion from Burgundy and she would not have seen him for at least several months, possibly almost two years, should have removed her from any and all suspicion and made any visit to her harmless. Furthermore, as James Gairdner points out in his annotated version of the Paston letters, and as is evidenced by a letter from Anne's mother Alice FitzHugh to him a year later, quoted below, Paston was close to Anne's family, so there could have been any number of perfectly innocent reasons for him to visit her.

Therefore, the fact that a possible visit was apparently used against Paston – and that Bedingfield outright dismisses it as invention by Paston's enemies, stating that 'wrath says never well' – shows that Anne was not seen as a mere helpless and harmless wife with no influence on her husband's actions. That Bedingfield then reports that 'my lord' – whom James Gairdner identifies, presumably correctly, as John de Vere, Earl of Oxford, as Paston fought for him at Stoke – advised him to 'deal wisely thereafter', suggesting that such a visit could have been truly damaging, shows that despite all that was said, Anne Lovell was seen at least as a potential threat.

Perhaps viewing her this way was simply exercising caution. After all, Henry VII knew from experience that women could organise rebellions, contact rebels and be involved in invasions, even when watched closely. His own mother, the formidable Margaret Beaufort, had done all this when he invaded,[175] and he might simply have wanted to prevent Anne Lovell from doing the same for her husband. On the other hand, it is possible that Anne really was suspected of being actively involved, and perhaps these suspicions were correct. It is perfectly possible that Anne was in contact with Francis, but no trace survives to prove it save Henry's evident suspicion.

It is not known if John Paston really did visit Anne shortly before the Battle of Stoke took place. If so, it is unlikely that he did so to pass to her any information about the king's plans, which she could in turn pass on to Francis by letter or messenger. Paston fought on the king's side at Stoke, and while he might have wished to have a foot in the Yorkist camp just in case they won, passing on information of that sort would have been extremely dangerous to him. However, this notion does open the intriguing possibility that the misinformation which landed Paston in trouble with the Earl of Oxford beforehand had actually come from Anne – that she helped Francis by deliberately spreading bad intelligence. This might explain why such suspicion was levelled against her and the mere possibility of Paston visiting her was seen as a malicious rumour against him.

The suspicion cast upon Anne is good evidence for a strong relationship between Francis and Anne; perhaps better evidence than anything during Richard's reign. While the indenture Francis made to provide for his wife in the event of his death is a good indication that he held some affection for her, the suspicion with which Anne was treated is evidence that she was known to care for him, so much so that it was considered likely she was not only in contact with her husband, a rebel on the run, but actively supported him. It is intriguing to note that she was never officially accused of attempting to do so, however, and certainly nobody succeeded in bringing any charges against her. Given her high standing and relation to Henry's queen consort Elizabeth of York,[176] it might have been thought preferable to leave her alone.

Bedingfield's letter also gives an indication that despite the most common portrayal of Anne today being that of an abandoned and neglected wife, this was not necessarily accurate. She may in fact have been in complete agreement with her husband about his rebellions, an active and supportive wife who understood his choices completely.

It would be interesting to know if she and Francis were indeed in contact and, if so, whether or not she acted as an intermediary between the rebels in Burgundy and possible supporters in England. Playing such a role would have made organisation of the rebellion much more straightforward, facilitating the landing they made in England on 4 June. They were apparently met there by expectant supporters, among them the Franke brothers, which does argue for a contact in England.[177]

Arrival

Presumably, the rebels separated into several groups shortly after landing. Francis, apparently with a group of 'German' mercenaries, marched 100 miles in six days, arriving at Bramham Moor on 9 June[178] to intercept Lord Clifford leading around 400 soldiers to join more soldiers at York. Clifford does not seem to have been aware quite how close the enemy forces already were. Arriving at Tadcaster near Branham Moor in the afternoon of Sunday 10 June, he stopped there for the night.[179]

The present Yorkist forces, led by Francis, took Clifford and his men by surprise that night. The York Civic Records describe the attack, although they include an inconsistency about where it happened. At first, quite logically, it is claimed that the Yorkist forces attacked the town where Clifford and his men 'loged', saying that 'the same night the Kinges ennymes lying negh to the same towne [Tadcaster], cam upon the said Lord Clifford folkes and made a grete skrymisse ther.' However, then it is claimed that suffering defeat, Clifford 'with such folkes as he might get, retourned to the Citie again', suggesting at some point Clifford and his men had left Tadcaster to meet Francis and his forces in combat.[180]

It is therefore not quite certain what happened that night, except to say that Francis and the part of the Yorkist rebel forces he led made a surprise attack on Lord Clifford and his men and defeated them, causing them to flee.[181] It is unclear whether they attacked the town to get to them or if lookouts saw them coming and Clifford's men rode out to fight them. According to the York Civic Records, Francis and his troops were at one point inside Tadcaster, and some of what is written suggests that the whole skirmish took place within the walls, making this version more likely. It is stated that 'at that same skrymisse were slain and maymed diverse of the said toune,' and that 'thinhabitants ther were spoled and robbed.' The latter was a typical result of skirmishes and battles in or near settlements, but the former definitely states that those of the town who died did so during the skirmish, not in any violence that followed. In fact, whatever devastation was wreaked on the town seems to have been comparatively mild, as there were no records of Tadcaster being burned, of buildings otherwise destroyed, of non-combatant deaths or of rapes, another horribly frequent crime after such skirmishes.[182]

Whatever truly happened, the York Civic Records do not go into detail. Instead, after briefly mentioning the occurrences during the skirmish, the text focuses on the probable reason for the attack, namely the loss of Lord Clifford's equipment and luggage to the Yorkist rebels: '... and the gardewyans and trussing coffers of the Lord Clifford was taken of the brig by misfortune, and had unto the other partie.'[183]

At the same time that Francis and his forces enjoyed this small success, the Earl of Lincoln tried to gather new recruits while slowly moving to meet the army Henry VII had gathered.[184] It is unusual that in this instance Francis was the man of action, with Lincoln busy building connections, though perhaps this was not too surprising. While it is true that Francis was by nature more of an organiser than a fighter, he had already shown that his sole aim was the utter destruction of Henry VII. Harnessing Francis's anger and desire for revenge must have seemed the most appropriate use of his presence.

Though Francis's raid was successful, Lincoln's endeavour was less so. Presumably due to prudence, or the knowledge of being watched, the City of York did not allow the rebels into the city when they approached with their army,[185] and they had to march on. Francis's forces joined Lincoln's on 12 June,[186] and on 16 June their army met Henry VII's near East Stoke, and engaged in combat.[187]

Little is known about the battle itself, even regarding who was present. There is actually more information about who fought for the Yorkist rebels than for Henry VII's forces, which is odd considering that the rebels' motivations, and especially the identity of the boy they fought for, are shrouded in mystery. We know that Francis and Lincoln led the army, together with the Irish earls of Desmond and Kildare and the mercenary Martin Schwartz.[188]

What is known about the king's forces is largely based on assumptions. It appears that his army was led by the Earl of Oxford, the same man who had led his forces at Bosworth with Jasper Tudor. Oxford had been involved in the campaign against the rebels of 1487 from the first.[189] Giving him command of Henry's army was the logical choice, and does not appear to have ever been in doubt.

It is usually assumed that Henry's uncle Jasper also took a leading part, much as he had at Bosworth. He is not mentioned in any contemporary source, but his absence would be hard to explain. It is also not known whether Francis's uncle William Beaumont, another experienced soldier, was present. However, in his case an absence could be explained by the fact that at this point his mental health was already deteriorating. If Beaumont was present, it would have meant he fought against his nephew. Although it is hard to imagine either of them would be very upset by this – they must have hardly known each other – it is possible that William, already being somewhat unstable, was kept away from the battle so that this conflict of interest would not worsen his state, perhaps provoking him to do something that could harm Henry's cause.

Another of Francis's relatives, his brother-in-law Edward Norris, was definitely one of Henry's men during the battle.[190] It is doubtful that Francis was aware of this, but Norris must have known he was facing his brother-in-law on the field. Norris does not appear to have felt any loyalty to his brother-in-law, unlike Francis's other brother-in-law Brian Stapleton. It is fanciful to imagine that Norris and Francis caught a glimpse of each other during the battle. Whatever Norris did he did it well, for he was knighted after the battle.

Though the actions of individual fighters are not recorded – in fact, even the tactics are a mystery to us – what is known is that the battle lasted longer than that at Bosworth two years before. It has been estimated that the Battle of Stoke lasted around three hours,[191] and hung in the balance for a while. Eventually, the Yorkists were defeated and Henry VII's forces won the day.

There has been much speculation as to why the Yorkists lost. Polydore Vergil, writing years later for Henry VII and his son, claimed that Kildare's Irish forces had only old-fashioned weapons, which meant they were quite easily defeated by the more modern weapons of the royal forces[192] and that without Irish support the rest of the rebel forces were outnumbered and eventually defeated. It has also been claimed that the opposite was the case, that the Swiss mercenaries' state-of-the-art firearms backfired and that many fighters were thus killed by their own weapons,[193] fatally weakening the Yorkist army.

Whatever the case, most of the rebel leaders were killed during the battle. Vergil claimed that they died bravely, standing their ground in the face of defeat, but this cannot be verified. What is certain is that Martin Schwartz, Thomas FitzGerald and John de la Pole, Earl of Lincoln died during or just after the battle. There is an uncorroborated legend that Lincoln was found fatally wounded but still breathing under an oak tree after the battle and was killed with a stake through the heart by the enemy fighter who found him, later being buried on the spot where he had died.[194] It has also been claimed that Henry VII was angry that Lincoln had not been brought to him alive so that he could question the earl about his reasons for rebellion[195], but there is no supporting evidence.

However, one man was absent from the lists of dead rebels: Francis Lovell.

Once more, Francis was the only leader standing after a battle that ended in devastating defeat for his side. His fate afterwards is unknown. The York Civic Records state that he was 'discomfited and fled',[196] but there is no further information. As the dust settled, Francis would have seen only destruction. Perhaps even then separated from Edward Franke, who would try in vain to find Francis in the coming months, Francis was alone, his hopes of revenge crushed. With his supporters dead or captured, Francis had to flee or face the same fate.

Shortly after the Battle of Stoke, it became known that the rebel pretender had been caught by Henry VII's forces.[197] Since he was apparently only a ten-year-old boy, he was pardoned. However, the identity of the boy has since been doubted, and many speculate that the captured boy, who subsequently worked in Henry VII's household, was not in fact the boy the Yorkists fought for; that their true figurehead fell in battle.[198]

Though there have been claims that Francis's flight from the battlefield shows a disregard for the boy who would be king, this argument can easily be debunked. If all happened as is claimed in the traditional narrative, the boy was already captured when the battle ended. There would have been nothing Francis could have done for him; any attempt would have only led to his own capture and execution. If, however, the boy had in fact died in battle, and truly was Edward of Warwick or Edward V, there would have been no reason for Francis to remain. The rebellion would have lost all purpose.

The claim in the York Civic Records apparently accepted Francis fleeing the battlefield as the natural reaction after such a defeat, and this is indeed the most likely scenario. The story most often told is that Francis, with most of his fellow rebels dead, was last seen on his horse crossing the River Trent to escape from Henry's men.[199]

Broken, defeated and alone, Francis, Viscount Lovell, vanished into history.

12

'Discomfited and fled'

Though Francis was never seen after 16 June 1487 by anyone who could prove it, he was far from forgotten. Both friends and foes remembered him and tried to discover his whereabouts. There are several theories as to what happened to him. Polydore Vergil claims that Francis died in battle[1] but he is the only chronicler to do so, even among the later chroniclers. Not only does this contradict what was written at the time in the York Civic Records, but it also fails to take into account that at least for a short time afterwards Francis was assumed to be alive by allies such as Edward Franke, who fought at his side during the Battle of Stoke and in 1488 was said to have no idea where Francis could be.[2]

It is possible that Francis died fleeing after the battle. The chroniclers Edward Hall and Raphael Holinshed claim so,[3] which shows that this rumour had arisen by the middle of the sixteenth century, and it's at least somewhat more likely than Francis dying in battle. For one, it does not directly contradict the statement made in the York Civic Records, because, after all, there is no information about what happened during or after the flight. Crossing a river in full armour after an exhausting battle, with a horse that was likely in full armour as well, could easily have killed him. However, like the possibility that he died in battle, this theory leaves several questions open, such as why men like Franke did not know of his death, and why he was not listed as a casualty of the battle if he died immediately afterwards, in direct consequence of it.

The most popular and widespread version of Francis's death is that he escaped the battlefield, went to his ancestral home and died at Minster Lovell Hall. This theory was reported as a rumour by Francis Bacon[4] nearly a century later, and is said to have been confirmed by the discovery of bones in a secret chamber at Minster Lovell Hall in the early eighteenth century. However, this discovery is the only piece of evidence to suggest he might have gone there. The story, as it is usually told, is that these bones fell to dust immediately after the chamber was opened, and we have no first-hand account of the discovery and subsequent destruction of the bones.[5] Even if it did happen, though, it seems unlikely that the bones belonged to Francis, as there would have been no conceivable reason for him to go there. If he had been injured, which is sometimes speculated, he would not have ridden about 100 miles so he could hide in a secret chamber in a house which was at that point owned by the new king's uncle, and where he would have been in no position to receive any treatment for wounds. If he was not injured, he could have easily found better hiding places than a manor closely associated with him, and it seems crazy to imagine he would choose to go there just so he could hide away in a secret chamber and never leave it again.

Another theory, and one which has gained some traction in recent years, is that Francis escaped after the battle, went to his mother Joan's castle at Stoke Bardolph and died there soon afterwards of injuries sustained during the battle.[6] This is somewhat more plausible, as the castle is closer to the battlefield than Minster Lovell Hall and may have been the nearest place where he could seek treatment for wounds without being sold out to the king's men. This theory is based mainly on a grave discovered in Gelding Church in the nineteenth century that was dated to about the right time and whose effigy was said to be that of a knight who fought at Stoke.[7] This purported lead is in fact the greatest flaw in this theory. The grave would have been nameless so as to ensure Francis remained buried on hallowed ground, rather than his body being found and publicly displayed. It would therefore be somewhat paradoxical to add an effigy to it which could be recognised as that of a rebel knight who had fought at Stoke. It defies belief that Henry's men would not have made the fairly obvious connection. While this theory cannot be dismissed out of hand, it would nonetheless leave such questions unanswered.

Another possibility, perhaps the most likely, is that Francis did not die in England, but escaped after the battle and once more fled to Burgundy, where he died between the summer of 1487 and the summer of 1488. This is especially likely if he sustained a minor injury at Stoke. Lacking proper care, even a comparatively minor wound could have become fatally infected on the way to Burgundy. Francis being present in Burgundy after the battle would explain his inclusion in a list of rebels to be given safe-conducts to Scotland by the new Scottish king, James IV, on 19 June 1488.[8] Since there is an indication that Margaret of York was involved in securing those safe-conducts,[9] it seems likely she knew Francis was still alive when she asked for them. This would also explain the total lack of any indication of his death in English sources. Men like Edward Franke would only have known that he was alive when they last saw him, and Margaret would have had no reason to announce his death to anyone; there would have been nobody to tell. Perhaps she even thought it prudent to keep Henry's government in the dark as to the number of rebels at her court and roaming Europe.

Another popular claim about Francis's whereabouts after the Battle of Stoke is that he escaped after it and fled to Scotland, possibly via Burgundy, and died before 1492. This is a theory proposed, among others, by David Baldwin in his article 'What Happened to Lord Lovel?',[10] and is, in fact, quite plausible. After all, a safe-conduct was issued to him, and Scotland would have been the obvious place for him to go. However, unlike several other rebels of prominence who received a safe-conduct, among them Thomas Broughton,[11] there is no indication Francis ever arrived in Scotland. The only potential evidence is that a 'poor and simple man' of York said in 1491 that he had spoken with Francis and with Thomas Broughton. However, the man later recanted,[12] and there is no explanation offered as to how he would have managed to go to Scotland to speak with them in the first place.

It has been suggested in many popular history books that Francis escaped after the battle and lived in hiding for the rest of a life that extended beyond 1492, possibly in Burgundy, Scotland, or – with Maximilian's help – the Holy Roman Empire, leaving England behind. This possibility cannot be contradicted by what we know, but it is unlikely. It would be the total opposite of what Francis had been doing during the previous years, and it seems unlikely that he would suddenly decide to settle down peacefully and accept the status quo, not even joining the later rebellion of Perkin Warbeck, which would have seemed extremely promising. To explain this there are theories that Francis vanished with Richard's bastard son John of Gloucester, whose whereabouts after 1487 are unknown, and that the safety of Richard's son was more important to him than seeking revenge. However, while this is plausible enough, it seems far-fetched that Francis could get to John of Gloucester, who was probably watched, and vanish with him without there even being even a rumour of it. Nor is there any indication Henry VII made any search for John of Gloucester, which would have been the natural thing to do had he truly vanished. It also wouldn't explain the total lack of any mention of Francis or John in any surviving documentation.

Finally, it is also possible that Francis escaped after the battle and lived in hiding somewhere for the rest of his life, staying out of future conflicts because he had sustained a disabling injury, perhaps the loss of a limb or his eyesight. However, while Francis might have been injured, such a major injury would presumably have needed immediate medical attention, so his flight over the river argues against it. This theory is only plausible in the case of a minor injury that became infected after he had already fled to safety and required amputation. He would have been extremely lucky to survive such an operation at the time, and if this was the case we would still expect to hear of him in the historical record.

It is obvious that no one at the time knew what happened to Francis any more than we do today. However, many tried to find out, most notably Anne Lovell. In a rather impressive act, she tried to find him in 1488, as can be seen from a letter his mother-in-law Alice FitzHugh wrote to John Paston some eight months after the battle, in which she mentions that her daughter has so far been unsuccessful in finding out her husband's whereabouts:

> To my right trusty and well-beloved son, Sir John Paston, be this delivered.
>
> John Paston, I recommend me to you in my most heartily manner. And where I understand by [from] my daughter Lovell,

you desire to know whether I will have the bargain you made for me in Norwich or not, and if I will, I must content [pay] for it now in marks. Son, in good faith it is so, I shall receive no money of the revenues of my livelihood before mid-summer, and also I have paid according to my promise to Sir William Cabell a great payment, the which you know well was due to be paid, so that I cannot be of power to content [pay] therefore, for the which I am right sorry, for I know well I shall never have such a bargain.

Also my daughter Lovell makes great suit and labour for my son her husband. Sir Edward Franke has been in the North to inquire for him, he is come again and cannot understand where he is. Wherefore her benevolers will her to continue his suit and labour, and so I cannot depart nor leave her as you know well, and if I might be there, I would be full glad, as knows our Lord God, who have you in his blessed keeping.

From London, the 24th day of February.

Your loving mother, Alice, Lady FitzHugh.[13]

This letter, though on the face of it fairly straightforward, has been interpreted differently over the years. Since the year it was written is not given, even that has been disputed. James Gairdner argued that the year had to be 1486,[14] since there was no knowledge of Francis after 1487. However, this is almost definitely incorrect. For one, Alice addressed John Paston as Sir John; given that he was only knighted after the Battle of Stoke, this means it cannot have been written before 1487. James Gairdner mentions this but dismisses the address as a mistake, without explaining further why he thinks so.[15]

It is not, however, just the address that shows the year it was written has to be 1488. In 1486, the year Gairdner dates the letter to, Francis's whereabouts in sanctuary in Colchester were no secret. Moreover, Edward Franke was one of Francis's co-conspirators in 1486, and would not have to have been sent by Anne Lovell to find him. It is must be, therefore, that the letter was written in 1488. This is quite interesting in itself, as Edward Franke was himself a traitor by that point, and associating with him could have been dangerous.[16] However, it seems that neither Anne nor her mother were afraid of any possible consequences.

It is also interesting to note that Anne Lovell apparently had several 'benevolers' who supported her in this and were in fact urging her to further try and 'continue her suit and labour', arguing that she was a popular woman who, even in these dire circumstances, was not abandoned or even merely tolerated by her social circle. It perhaps suggests as well that Francis's cause had not died with his disappearance; that there were those still wishing to find him.

The exact nature of Anne's 'suit and labour' has been similarly disputed over the years. The word 'suit', and the fact that at the time of her mother writing this letter she appears to have been in London, has led some people to argue that she was trying to secure a pardon for her husband.[17] However, this seems unlikely, as Francis had already rejected a pardon in 1485, and none of his actions since then give any indication he had changed his mind. With the couple out of contact he could not have told her he wished for a reconciliation, another reason it seems unlikely Anne was trying to secure him a pardon. Also, given that Francis had at this point been responsible for two rebellions, one kidnap attempt and one assassination attempt on Henry VII, the likelihood of him being granted a pardon would have been negligible, even without him having already rejected one.

Moreover, Anne trying to have her husband pardoned does not make sense considering Alice's statements in the text, as she explicitly says that Anne's supporters were encouraging her to continue her search because Edward Franke had failed to find Francis. If she had tried to get him pardoned, she would maybe have tried to continue doing so *despite* Francis not having been found, but not *because* of it. The only way this could make sense would be if she was seeking a pardon for herself and hoped to dissociate herself from Francis, but this directly contradicts both her actions and Alice's words. If she had wanted to dissociate herself from him, Alice would never have said she was doing it for her husband, and Anne would not have associated with traitors like Franke in the process.

Instead, Anne's 'suit and labour' almost certainly refer to her trying to find Francis. Why she did so, and what she hoped would happen if she found him, is a mystery. What is notable is that Alice clearly supported Anne and does not display any grudge towards Francis despite his actions putting her daughter in a perilous position. On the other hand, she explicitly referred to him as her son, even when 'my daughter's husband' would have sufficed. She also referred to Anne not as 'my daughter Anne' but as the conventional 'my daughter Lovell', suggesting they were both happy to remain associated with Francis.

We do not know if they ever found out what had happened to Francis. By December 1489, Anne clearly either knew Francis was dead or thought it likely, for by then she had taken a religious vow. This is known because of a small annuity of £20 made to her in December 1489,[18] in the grant for which Henry VII's government referred to her as 'our sister in God'.[19] This was quite common for noble widows, but it suggests that she knew her mind well and had, by the age of twenty-eight or twenty-nine, already decided she did not want to marry again; in doing so, she also gave up the chance to have children. Though of course her marriage prospects were diminished significantly due to her being a traitor's widow, she was still of high birth and a relative of Henry VII's queen, so it is likely she could have found someone willing to overlook her first husband had she wished. Another option would have been for her to contemplate marrying for her own pleasure, but she clearly had no interest in this option either. This can be taken as yet another indicator of her strong affection for Francis.

Since Anne appears to have helped to take care of Francis's nephews by his sister Joan,[20] it seems unlikely she became a nun. She may instead have chosen a quasi-religious life as her great-aunt Cecily Neville did in her last years.

The last mention we have of Anne Lovell, from a date when we know she was still alive, is from 1495, when she was mentioned in Francis's second attainder, in which her rights were protected, showing that she was still alive then, at thirty-five years of age. We do not know when she died, only that it must have been before January 1513, when, on the death of her brother Richard, the FitzHugh barony fell into abeyance between Anne's older sister Alice and her sister Elizabeth's children.

It is possible, though, that the name of Elizabeth's youngest child gives a hint as to when Anne died. Elizabeth remarried soon after Francis disappeared, and had three more children with her new husband, Sir Nicholas Vaux. As she had done with her first husband, Katherine chose to name these children after her and her husband's close relatives, their first daughter after Sir Nicholas's mother Catherine, the second after her own mother and/or older sister Alice, and her youngest after Anne. Why she decided to do so, rather than name the child after Sir Nicholas's sister Joan, for example, is uncertain – especially since her oldest child, by Sir William Parr, was called Anne as well. The Anne begat by Parr was still alive, so it cannot have been done in her memory. Possibly this youngest daughter was so named because she was her older half-sister Anne's godchild, but it is also possible that Elizabeth named her after Anne Lovell. Anne Vaux was born after 1495, the latest date we know Anne Lovell was still alive, so it is possible that Elizabeth had her soon after Anne's death and chose to honour her sister in this way. If so, Anne was around thirty-eight years of age when she died.

Francis's sister Frideswide appears to have mended the rift with her husband after Richard's death. She had another child in 1486, a girl called Margaret, presumably after her husband Edward's sister. As mentioned above, a year after Margaret's birth, Edward Norris, as well as his father William, joined Henry VII's forces against her brother Francis and the Yorkist rebels, and defeated them at the Battle of Stoke, after which Edward was knighted for his services to the king. Edward did not get to enjoy his knighthood for long; he died later in 1487, of causes unknown, perhaps of an injury sustained during the battle. He was only twenty-two years old, and left Frideswide a twenty-three-year-old widow. She did not remarry, but little else is known of her life. It is possible that she took care of her older sister Joan's orphaned children, as the younger of them, George Stapleton, would go on to name a daughter after her. Frideswide died before 1507, when she is listed as deceased in her uncle William Beaumont's inquisition post mortem.[21]

When all those who had known Francis died, his name became a part of history. He became little more than a cipher, often misunderstood. As in his life, in death Francis remains in the shadows, overlooked in favour of more ostentatious contemporaries. It is hoped that this narrative might indicate that Richard III's personal motto, *loyalté me lie* – loyalty binds me – would have suited Francis perfectly.

APPENDIX 1

Sir William Stanley's Son

In John Seacome's *The History of the House of Stanley*, Sir William Stanley, who was for a short time married to Francis's mother Joan Beaumont, is said to have '[b]y Joyce, his wife, daughter of Edward, Lord Powis, [...] had issue one son, named William'.[1] However, William Stanley is only known to have been married twice: first to Francis's mother, Joan Beaumont, from sometime after 12 November 1465 until her death on 5 August 1466, and then to Elizabeth Hopton from around 1471 until his own death on 16 February 1495. Unless he had another marriage in his youth of which no mention has survived, any legitimate child would therefore have been born to one of these two ladies. In the case of William having a son by his first wife, this child would also have been a half-brother to Francis.

Notably, there is no certainty in most history books if William Stanley even had a son, much less by whom. The *Complete Peerage*[2] only lists one child by him, Jane or Joan Stanley, born after 1471 to his second wife Elizabeth. Several other sources, including Seacome's *History*, claim he had three children: a son named William and daughters Jane/Joan and Catherine. Modern historians have by no means accepted the existence of all these children, and even when they are assumed to have existed, there are differing assumptions as to their maternity.

Barbara Coulton, in her article 'The Wives of Sir William Stanley: Joan Beaumont and Elizabeth Hopton',[3] claims they were all born to Joan Beaumont. However, the problem with her claim is that it does not fit the time frame of William and Joan's marriage. Coulton states that Joan died on 24 August 1469 but does not give any source for this claim, and all contemporary sources place her death three years earlier. Her marriage to William did not even last a year, and while they were married just long enough for her to have given birth to a slightly premature child conceived in wedlock before her death, she could not have possibly given birth to three unless she gave birth to triplets, an extreme rarity that would have been commented upon. Jean M. Gidman, on the other hand, in her article 'The wives and children of Sir William Stanley of Holt',[4] claims that all three children were Elizabeth Hopton's. Though Elizabeth might have been nearing the end of her childbearing years by the time she married William, having given birth for the first time in 1448, this is completely possible, though Gidman also offers no evidence how she came to the conclusion that they were all Elizabeth's. J. M. Williams, in her article 'The Political Career of Francis, Viscount Lovell (1456–1487?)',[5] seems to assume that William's son was Francis's mother Joan's, but apart from mentioning him as Francis's half-brother in the family tree, she does not elaborate on this theory.

Though most casual retellings of William's life include only his daughter Jane/Joan, most in-depth accounts seem to agree on the existence of his son William. Born in August 1466 at the earliest, and quite possibly after 1471, this son was either too young to fight at Bosworth and Stoke or else fought at his father's side and, as a minor of little importance beyond his parentage, was not mentioned. He was, it seems, mentioned in a grant made to his father on 19 February 1489, of the constableships of Flint and Ruddlan Castles, with, as Gidman put it, 'the promise that his son would obtain the later'. He is also sometimes said to have succeeded his father as sheriff of Chester at around the same time, though Seacome points out that there is some confusion on this point, as another Sir William Stanley, of Hooton, was sheriff of Cheshire. The similarity between 'Holt' and 'Hooton' and 'Chester' and 'Cheshire' did, according to Seacome,[6] cause enough confusion to throw doubt on whose son the third William Stanley – not a knight – was.

This William Stanley married Joan Massey, only child of Sir Geoffrey, of Tatton, and had a daughter with her, also called Joan.[7] He disappears into obscurity towards the end of his life, and seems to have died comparatively young in December 1498. If it is accepted that he was indeed Sir William Stanley of Holt's child, then that poses the question of who his mother was, and if he was indeed Francis's half-brother and second grandson to John, Viscount Beaumont.

While Seacome assigns William Stanley the younger's maternity to a woman named 'Joyce, daughter of Edward, Lord Powis', who was never married to William Stanley of Holt, the link between the Lords Powis and the Tiptofts – John Tiptoft was the second husband of William's second wife – points to Elizabeth as the mother. However, given that name and paternity are stated wrongly, it would perhaps be a mistake to attach too much weight to this. It is of course entirely possible, but more confusion could be caused by the fact that even if William the younger was Joan Beaumont's child, he would have grown up with Elizabeth Hopton's children from the age of five and probably have politely referred to her as mother. This could be especially confusing as Sir William's first marriage was only of short duration and came at a time when he was not yet the widely known government figure he was remembered as when Seacome's *History* was written.

To try and identify the mother of Sir William's child, it is therefore not very revealing to look at people's assumptions, particularly since these assumptions were made at least two centuries after the event, but instead try to find clues in the primary sources. Sadly, there is nothing in the little paperwork we have for Francis to indicate that he might have had a half-brother; nor can we glean from it that he definitely did not. In fact, there isn't even much about his relationship with his full sisters, whom we know existed. We do know that he had business transactions with Sir William in the 1470s, but these do not shine any light on their personal relationship, nor do they imply anything about the nature of the transactions. What survives is a series of dry facts of the transactions. Furthermore, nothing in the few actions known of Elizabeth's Corbett sons suggests that they had a younger brother, but there is also nothing to indicate any sort of care for Edward, Earl of Worcester, who was definitely their brother and who died aged sixteen in August 1485. This does not mean there was no care taken of William the younger by either Francis or the Corbetts, it just means that no evidence for it survives.

The matter is made even more tricky by the fact that whoever young William's brother(s) was/were, it is quite possible he didn't have much to do with them. In the case of Francis, he would have been almost exactly ten years older than his younger half-brother and never would have lived in the same place as him, while in the case of the Corbetts they would be over twenty and around twenty years his senior; the oldest one was already married with a child by the time of William the younger's birth. Looking for any close brotherly relationship between young William and any of these men might therefore prove fruitless.

Perhaps more telling is the fact that when Elizabeth Hopton died in November 1498, no mention of a son named William is made in her inquisition post mortem.[8] However, this might be because he died only a month after her, and was dead by the time the inquisition post mortem was made. It might also be explained by the fact that her youngest son, with his older brother already having his own heir, was not expected to inherit anything of her possessions.

Equally, there are reasons why the Beaumont lands which were not under attainder went to Francis unchallenged. During the reigns of Edward IV and Richard III, William the younger would have still been a minor and unable to challenge Francis, and even after attaining his majority he might not have had much of a chance; apart from the fact that Francis, as the older brother, would very likely have been entitled to hold/inherit all of it unless otherwise stated, after 1483 his position as the king's chamberlain and closest friend would have made challenging him a pointless endeavour. However, in this case, young William might have been seen as Francis's heir to the Beaumont lands he held. Unfortunately, we do not have any paperwork to dismiss or confirm this. When Francis's uncle William Beaumont died without heirs in 1507, his viscountcy would have fallen to his oldest nephew by his sister Joan, but not only was Francis attainted and most likely dead by this point, young William too was dead and had left only a daughter, so that the title falling into abeyance does not provide anything conclusive about whether or not William the younger had Beaumont blood.

With Francis's attainder, the fact that William the younger, if he was indeed his half-brother, would have been heir to some of his lands became insignificant. All his possessions were forfeit to the crown, and many of them were granted back to William, Viscount Beaumont, whose attainder was overturned when Henry VII came to the throne. However, it is notable that Sir William Stanley did receive a lot of Francis's lands, even some of the lands that had belonged to John, 1st Viscount Beaumont. This, of course, was presumably because of the significant role he had played in helping Henry VII win the throne, but it may have also served the purpose of pre-empting any suit by William's son once he reached majority, when he could try to get back some of the Beaumont lands by claiming that not all of them had been Francis's by right and therefore should not have been subject to the attainder. The Earl of Oxford regained some family lands which had fallen to the crown in the 1490s in a similar fashion, claiming his mother had lost them by coercion. Granting some of the lands his son might have an interest in to Sir William, so that William the younger stood to inherit them at his father's death, would have dodged such a claim while at the same time avoiding the anger that might be incurred by taking something away from the son of one of Henry's most important supporters.

Of course, this is only speculation. Perhaps the most telling route to identifying William the younger's parentage is his age. Clearly, whether he was born in summer 1466 or after 1471, he was still a minor during the battles of Bosworth and Stoke, though if he was Joan Beaumont's son then he was almost of age when Stoke happened. This might not have stopped him from fighting – Edward Hastings, son of William, born in 1466, fought in both battles – but it could well mean he did not have too much significance yet and so there was no reason to mention him fighting alongside his far more important father. It does not mean he wasn't there – though if he was born after 1471, he likely would not have been as he would have been too young – but if he was, it shows he was not considered of particular interest.

On the other hand, by 1489 he was apparently old enough to be included in grants, and to be acting alone as sheriff. This may well have been possible had he been born in 1472 and around seventeen, but if so it would probably have been mentioned that he was still a minor. If he was born to Sir William and Joan Beaumont in August 1466, however, he would have come of age between the Battle of Stoke and this arrangement, which fits with what we know about both these instances.

Finally, Sir William already having had a son by his first wife could well explain why he waited so long after her death to remarry, though of course there could be any number of other reasons for this. Nonetheless, in the face of such a lack of evidence for when and to whom William the younger was born, anything that might illuminate the issue should be considered.

If William the younger was indeed Joan Beaumont's son, it seems she died in childbed, or just after his birth of childbed fever. Her older son Francis was by then in the care of Richard Neville, Earl of Warwick, and it seems that when she died her daughters by John Lovell were given into the care of their brother's mother-in-law, Alice FitzHugh. William the younger would have presumably stayed with his father; at least, he definitely didn't grow up with his half-siblings in either the Warwick or the FitzHugh household. How well he and his Lovell half-siblings would have known each other is hard to say, but most likely they would have been distant, having almost nothing to do with each other until Francis and Joan Lovell were grown up.

All that can be said is that evidence suggests Sir William Stanley had a legitimate son, and that circumstantial evidence shows it to be somewhat more likely he had this son by his first wife, meaning that Francis, and his sisters Joan and Frideswide, had a Stanley half-brother.

Full Text of Original Letters and Wills

Will of William Lovell, 7th Baron Lovell, 1455[1]

In the name of the blessed trinity, Father and Son and Holy Ghost, I, William Lord Lovell, Burnell and of Holland, whole of mind and of body, make my testament in the manner and form that follows:

First, I bequeath my soul to Almighty God my creature that bought me with his precious blood, and to his blessed Mother, Saint Mary, and to all the holy saints of heaven, and my body to be buried at the Greyfriars in Oxford in such place as I have appointed.

And I will that within eight days after my death, a 1500 masses be done for my soul.

Also I will that my feofees in and of all my manors, lands and tenements, with the appurtenance, In Acton Burnell, Wotton, Croston, Sutton, Holgote, Abbeton, Millynchop, Ewdon Burnell, Acton Raynard, Longedon, Uppynton, Rowton, Ambaston, Chatwall, Wolstauton, Smethcote, Russhebury, Hopebowdelere, and Condour, with the members of the shire of Salop and in all my lands and tenements in Nantwich in the shire of Chester not appointed to my son Harry, the which I have enfeoffed upon great trust, I will that my said feoffes occupy and have all my said manors, lands and tenements with the appurtenance after my decease by the term of nine years and that there be a sufficient person ordained by the advise of my said feofees and executors to receive all the issues and profites of the said manors, lands and tenements and therewith to pay 222 pounds, thirteen shillings, four pennies that I owe to diverse persons, as it is contained in a paper, unless than I pay it in my life.

Also I will that a chapel and a tomb be made for me and my wife, convenient to our estate that God has called us to, of the same issues and profits, in the place where we shall be buried.

And where I have appointed twenty pounds of livelihood to be purchased with the same issues and profits (unless I purchase it myself in my life) to be amortised for two priests to sing perpetually for the souls of me, my wife and our ancestors. I will that, of the same issues and profits, all the costs about the said amortisment be had and borne.

Also, I will that the same Greyfriars shall have 200 marks of the value. Whereof part shall be in ready money and the remnants in ornaments of their church (by the discretion of my wife, my feoffees and executors or the more part of them) to pray specially for the souls of me and of my wife.

Also, I bequeath to the other three orders of friars in Oxford to each of them 100 shillings to pray specially for the souls of me and my wife and our said ancestors.

Also, to the abbot and convent of Brewer 11 pounds.

Also, to Anne Ogard, my daughter's daughter, to her marriage if she be married worshipfully and to such as is or shall be a lord of name 200 pounds, of the same issues and profits.

And I will that he that so shall receive the issues and profits of the said manors, lands and tenements, yearly account of them before such auditors as shall be assigned by my wife, executors and feoffees or the more part of them.

Also I will that anon after the said nine years after my decease determined that my said feoffees make estate of all the said manors, lands and tenements with the appurtenance to my next heir and to the heirs of his body lawfully begotten. And for lack of such issue the remainder thereof to my right heirs.

And in the case that the said chantry be founded in my life, then I will that after the term of six years next after my decease determined that my said feoffees of the said manors, lands and tenements make estate unto my next heir and hold to him and to the heirs of his body begotten. And for lack of such issue the remainder thereof to my right heirs.

Also, I will that my feoffees in and of all my manors, lands and tenements that they be enfeoffed to my use and profit (except the manors, lands and tenements appointed to William, Robert and Henry, my sons, and my manors, lands and tenements in Oxfordshire) anon after my decease make estate unto my next heir and the heirs of his body begotten. And for lack of such issue the remainder thereof to my right heirs.

Also, I will that my feoffees of all my other manors, lands and tenements in the shire of Oxford, except before except, after my decease, of the issues and profits of the same, pay 20 pounds yearly to the sustaining of my said chantry and anniversary unto the time my said chantry be full established and founded, and suffer my next heir to have the issues and profits of all the same manors, lands and tenements over that 20 pounds.

And after the said chantry established and founded of 20 pound of livlihood, I will my feoffees of the same manors, lands and tenements in the said shire of Oxford, except before except, make estate to my next heir and to the heirs of his body begotten, and for lack of such issue the remainder thereof to my right heirs.

Also, I will that my good moveable and unmovable be disposed, after the good discretion of my good executors, by the oversight and survey of my wife.

Also, I charge all my sons, upon my blessing, and as they will answer to God, that they be helping and assisting to my executors to the executing and performing of this my testament and last will.

And executors of this my testament I make Thomas Bylling, sergant of the law, Lucas Laucok, clerk, William Marmeon, William Brawnston.

Also, I will that my wife, in whom I put my most special faith and trust, be surveyor of this my testament, praying and requiring her that she will do her true diligence and part that my said testament may be truly performed, according to my intent. And require and charge my executors that none of them do any great thing touching the execution of my said testament, without they ask advice of her before.

In witness whereof, to this present writing I have put my seal, evening the 18th day of March, the year of our Lord 1455. And the year of the reign of King Henry the Sixth after the conquest 34th.

(First Codicil)

In the name of God, Amen, I, William Lord Lovell, Burnell and of Holland, whole of mind, the 5th day of June, the year of our Lord God 1455, and the year of the reign of King Harry the Sixth after the conquest 34th, declare my last will and advice contained in my testament bearing the date of 18th March of the year of our Lord God 1455 and the reign of our sovereign lord the king 34th, and also add to the same testament in manner and form as in this codicil follows:

First, that where I, in the said testament and last will, ordained, disposed and willed that my feoffees in and of all my manors, lands and tenements with their appurtances in Acton Burnell, Wotton, Croston, Sutton, Holgote, Abbeton, Millynchop, Ewdon Burnell, Acton Raynard, Longedon, Uppynton, Rowton, Ambaston, Chatwall, Wolstauton, Smethcote, Russhebury, Hopebowdelere, and Condour with the members of the shire of Salop and in all my lands and tenements in Nantwich in the shire of Chester not appointed to my son Harry, should occupy and have all my said manors, lands and tenements with the appurtenance after my decease by the term of nine years to perform my said will and testament, as is in the same testament expressed, I will that my said feoffees occupy and have all my said manors, lands and tenements with the appurtenance after my decease by the term of eleven years then next and continual following, to execute and perform with the issues and profits thereof my said testament. And that my last will, under form as in the said testament is and in this my codicil shall be declared.

Also where I, in my said testament, have appointed 20 pounds of livelihood to be purchased with the said issues and profits, to be amortised for two secular priests to sing perpetually for the souls of me, my wife and my ancestors, I, in this my codicil, will and declare that the said purchase and mortisment be so and in such form that it be 20 pounds clear above all manners of charges, and such livelihood as shall be of no less clear yearly value be liklihood hereafterward: of the which 20 pounds I will that my said two priests have yearly twenty marks. And I will that the warden and the convent of Greyfriars of Oxford have yearly the residue of the said 20 pounds therewith to keep my yearly obit and to re-apparell my said chapel after time it is sufficiently belit and performed.

And pay yearly to the chancellor of Oxford for the time being and offering at my obit five shillings, seven pennies. To his commissary so offering in his absence two shillings, three pennies, and to either of the proctors of the university coming with the said chancellor or his commissary and offering at my said obit twenty pennies.

And to the mayor of Oxford for the time being two shillings, three pennies, and to either of the baileys twenty pennies, in case be that they come and offer at my said yearly obit.

Also, I will that my said executors and feoffees, over the said 20 pounds, purvey books, chalices, and vestements, with other ornaments necessary to the said chapel, and also for bread, wine and wax for all manner of priests that will say mass in the said chapel for evermore.

Also, I will that the said two priests be seculars, bachelors of divinity or at the least masters of arts, virtuous and well disposed to learn and for to proceed in degree. And moreover to preach the word of God in relief of simple curates and edification of Christian souls.

And they, in their open sermons, shall pray specially by name for the souls of me, my wife and my ancestors.

And I will that the said two priests every Sunday and double feast, after time the said chapel is belit and fully performed, at five of the bell in the morning begin the matins of the day in my said chapel, and, after matins said, one of them incontinently say the mass of the day, unless they be absent preaching the word of God. And if both be not so absent, then he, that is not so occupied, say the said matins and mass.

And once in the weekday say placebo and dirge with a mass of requiem of me, my wife and my ancestors and of all Christian souls.

Also, I will that the Lord Lovell for the time being name and present the said two priests (so that they be seculars, bachelors of divinity or at the least masters of arts) to the Chancellor of Oxford for the time being. And the said Chancellor, in case he find them by due examination virtuose and of good conversation and diposed to proceed after my will before declared, admit them to sing in my said chapelafter form by me rehearsed. And if by such examination or otherwise, the said two bachelors of divinity or at least masters of art, so named and presented by the Lord Lovell for the time being, be not found of such conditions and virtue as it is in my will before declared, that then they be in no wise admitted to to sing in the said chapel, but then, after notice had thereof, the said Lord Lovell name and present two other in semblance wise to be examined admitted or refused. Wherein I pray and straightly require and (as much as in me is) I charge the said Lord Lovell and chancellor that they, in naming, presenting, examining and admitting the said two priests, put aside all manner of affectuous partiality, favour, service and reward.

Also, I will and declare that in the case the said two priests, or either of them, be promoted to any benefice, college, chantry, or other office of perpetuity, otherwise be of vicious governance or unclean living before the chancellor lawfully convicted, then that their places in my said chapel, and either of them, so promoted or convicted, be void, and the said Lord Lovell name and present other, in manner and form above rehearsed.

Item, I will and bequeath, in this my codicil, to William my son a bed of bawdkin with cushions and the apparell thereto, paying ten pounds.

Also that, where I willed and ordained in my said testament that, anon after nine years after my decease determined, that my feoffees should make estate of all the said manors, lands and tenements with their appurtenance, under form in my said testament contained, I will that my said feoffees be not charged nor in no wise constrained to make any estate unto the term of eleven years after my decease fully determined.

Also, I will and add to my said testament in this my codicil that my servants be rewarded under form and sums that follow:

- First, to Thomas Lesseller and his wife, 5 shillings
- To Henry Normanvyle, 25 shillings, 7 pennies
- To Thomas Stotesbury, 10 shillings
- To John Gyfford, 25 shillings, 7 pennies
- to Drew Streighley, 25 shillings, 7 pennies
- to Bernard Delamere, 25 shillings, 7 pennies
- to Thomas Conyers, 25 shillings, 7 pennies
- to Thomas Ingelfeld, 4 pounds, 7 shillings, 3 pennies
- Also, to Mawt Denham, of fee, so long as she is sole, yearly ten mark. And, if she be worshipfully and well married, to her mariage, 12 pounds, 5 shillings, 7 pennies.
- Also Sybill Fowler, when time she shall be married and worshipfully, 20 pounds to her marriage
- Also, to the servants of John Densell, 3 shillings, 3 pennies
- Also, to Thomas Aunger, 10 shillings
- to John of Chambre,10 shillings
- to John Appynton, 10 shillings
- to Thomas Clerk, 3 shillings, 3 pennies
- to William Aleyn, 10 shillings
- to John Aden, 3 shillings, 3 pennies of fee
- to John Benet, 10 shillings of fee;
- to Richard Whitfeld, 10 shillings
- to John Churche, 32 shillings, 3 pennies
- to William Wynfray, 10 shillings
- to William Skynner, 10 shillings
- to William Grendon, 10 shillings
- to Thomas Ormeston, 20 shillings
- To Thomas Smyth, 10 shillings
- to Thomas Selby, 3 shillings, 3 pennies

- to William Blakbourne, 3 shillings, 3 pennies
- To Thomas Selman,10 shillings
- to Edmund Blakhall, 3 shillings, 3 pennies
- To Iohn Russell, 3 shillings, 3 pennies, of fee;
- to Iohn Barby, 30 shillings, 7 pennies
- To Thomas hunt, 20 sjillings of fee;
- to Richard Milton, 10 shillings
- to William Trumpet, 10 shillings of fee;
- to Geoffrey Taylour, 10 shillings
- to John Woderoff, 30 shillings, 7 pennies
- to Iohn Cransley, 10 shillings
- to John Whighill, 10 shillings of fee.;
- to Henry Yoxhall, 3 shillings, 3 pennies
- to John Donver, 25 shillings, 7 pennies
- to Iohn Gylford, 3 shillings, 3 pennies, in whole fee;
- to Ralph Herrys, for keeping of a wood at Minster Lovell, 25 shillings, 7 pennies of fee;
- to the baily of Minster Lovell, 10 shillings
- To Ralph, gardener of Minster Lovell, 10 shillings of fee yearly, for keeping of the garden there, yearly receiving and keeping the fruites therof to the behoof of the household there;
- To William Kollyng, 20 shillings, of fee;
- to Frank Martyn,32 shillings, 3 pennies
- to John Morayn, 35 shillings, 8 pennies
- to John Culneham, 35 shillings, 8 pennies
- to John Grene, 35 shillings, 8 pennies
- to Derik of the kitchen, 20 shillings
- to Richard of the bakehouse, 25 shillings, 7 pennies
- To Edmund of the bakehouse, 25 shillings, 7 pennies
- To John Skirs of the same, 25 shillings, 7 pennies
- to John Carter, 20 shillings
- to John Lane, 25 shillings, 7 pennies
- to Thomas Blakhalle, 32 shillings, 3 pennies
- to Henry Gaddesby, 25 shillings, 7 pennies
- To William Broyne, 25 shillings, 7 pennies
- To Thomas of the Stable, 25 shillings, 7 pennies

And I again require my wife, sons and heirs, in the way of charity and for the love of Almighty God and eschewing the damnation of their souls, that they help and assist, with all such power as God has given them, my feoffees and my executors to execute my said testament and this my will. And that they in no wise let it nor do for to be letted by no manner of mean nor colour.

Item, I will that all my elder feoffees, if there any be in my said manors, lands and tenements, make a release unto Thomas, Archbishop of Canterbury, and unto his co-feoffees to perform my said testament and will.

Bearing witness hereof: Master Thomas Gascoyne, Doctor of Divinity, Bartholomew Ardern, Thomas Sakvyle, John Grayby, esquires, William Barneville, John Adeen, and John Russell, with other more.

(Second Codicil)

To all true Christian people that this present writing tri-parted intended shall hear or see, William Lord Lovell, Burnell and of Holland, send greeting in our Lord everlasting.

Where that I, the same William Lord Lovell, among other, have enfeoffeed, upon great faith and trust, the right reverend fathers in God, Thomas Bourchier, Archbishop of Canterbury, primate of all England; William, Bishop of Winchester; William Lucy; William Catesby, knights; Robert Danuers (one of the justice of the common place), and other, in and of my manors of Bridelhurst, Obdon, Knoke, Erdescote, Estwamburgh, with the appurtenance, in the shire of Wiltshire and in all my other lands and tenements in the same towns; the manor of Berley with the appurtenance in the shire of Hertford, the manor of Estwycham with the appurtenance in the shire of Kent, and Rotherhith with the appurtenances in the shire of Surrey, the manor of Wodford, with the appurtenance, in the shire of Gloucester, and in all my lands and tenements in Bampton, Little Minster, and elsewhere in the shire of Oxford, with appurtenance, the which were sometimes Eleanor Hill's, and of a fee form of six pounds, five shillings, seven pennies in the shire of Worcester that the prior of Worcester paid to me for Trympley, the manors of Stene, Hynton, Polebroke, with the appurtenance, in the shire of Northampton, the manor of Crawley with the appurtenance in the shire of Buckes, with all my other lands and tenements in the same towns, and in the twon of Banbury in the shire of Oxford, the manors of Wellington and Pycheford, with the appurtenance, in the shire of Salop, the manors of Bidford and Brome with the appurtenance in the shire of Warwick, the moietie of my lordship of Wolverhampton, with the appurtenance, in the shire of Stafford, with all my other lands and tenements in the same towns, and in all my lands and tenements rents and service with the appurtenance in Nantwich and elsewhere in the shire of Chester, late William Brownyng's, to have and to hold them and to their heirs forevermore.

I, the said William Lord Lovell, declare my will and intent of the said enfeoffment in manner and form following:

That is to say, that my said feoffees anon after my decease make estate in and of the said manors of Bridelhurst, Obdon, Knoke, Erdescote, Estwamburgh, Berley, Estwycham, Rotherhith, Wodford, fee-form and in all the said other lands and tenements in the same towns, in all the said lands and tenements in Bampton, Little Minster, and elsewhere in the shire of Oxford that were sometime Eleanor Hill's, with all the appurtenance, to William my second son and to the heirs male of his body lawfully begotten, under the form and conditions following, that of the same William my son or any of the heirs male of his body begotten do or suffer anything to be done by the which the said tail should be discontinued and discontinued, in part or in all, longer or otherwise than for term of the life of the said William my son or of the life of any of his heirs male of his body begotten or during the life of any of the wives of my said son or any of the wives of the heirs male of his body begotten, that then all the said manors of Bridelhurst, Obdon, Knoke, Erdescote, Estwamburgh, Berley, Estwycham, Rotherhith, Wodford, fee-form with all the said other lands and tenements in the same towns, and in the towns of Bampton and Little Minster and elsewhere, specified in the said tail, remain unto the right heirs, and the said estate tailed utterly to be void.

And I pray and require my said feoffees to be helping and assisting my right heirs in the behalf.

And in case the said William my son die without issue male of his body begotten, or else that he or any of his said heirs male (for lack of other issue of me) inherit me and be Lord Lovell, and no such discontinuance made by him nor none of his said heirs male otherwise than is before rehearsed, that then the one half of the said manors, lands, tenements and fee form, with the appurtenance, remain unto Robert Lovell, my third son, and to the heirs male of his body begotten, under semblance form and conditions to be observed and kept by the same Robert and his heirs male as is before rehearsed to be observed and kept by the said William and his heirs male of his body begotten. And in case the said Robert die without issue males of his body begotten, or else that he or any of his said issue males inherit me and be Lord Lovell, and no discontinuance be made by the same Robert nor none of heirs males of his body begotten, of the said halfendell nor of no parcel thereof otherwise than is before rehearsed, that then the said halfendale remain to Henry Lovell my fourth son and to the heir males of his body begotten, under semblance form and conditions to be observed and kept by the same Henry and his heirs male (as is before rehearsed) to be observes and kept by the said William and his heirs male of his body begotten. And for the lack of such issue male of the said Henry, the remainder thereof unto my right heirs. And that the other half of the said manors, lands and tenements with the appurtenance remain unto the same Henry and to the heirs male of his body begotten, under semblance form and conditions to be observed and kept by him and his said heirs male (as is before rehearsed) to be observed and kept by the same William and his heirs male of his body begotten.

And in case the said Henry die without issue males of his body begotten, the remainder thereof unto the same Robert and the heirs male of his body begotten under semblance forme and conditions as if before rehearsed. And for lack of such issue male of the said Robert, the remainder thereof unto my right heirs.

Also I pray and require my said feoffees that they, anon after my decease, make estate unto the said Robert my son in and of the said manors of Stene, Hynton, Polebroke, Crawley, with all their other lands and tenements in the same towns and in the town of Banbury, with the appurtenance, to have and hold to him and to the heirs male of his body begotten, under the form and conditions following:

That of the same Robert or any of the heirs male of his body begotten do or suffer anything to be done by the which the said tail should be discontinued and discontinued, in part or in all, longer or otherwise than for term of the life of the said Robert my son or term of the life of any of his heirs male of his body begotten or term of the life of any of the wives of the said Robert or term of life of any of the wives of the heirs male of the said Robert body begotten, that then all the same manors, lands and tenements remain to my right heirs and the said estate utterly to be void.

And I pray and require my said feoffees to be helping and assisting my right heirs in the behalf.

And in case the said Robert die without issue male of his body begotten then the one half of the same manors, lands and tenements, with the appurtenance, so given to the said Robert, shall remain to the same William my son and to the heirs male of his body lawfully begotten, under semblance form and conditions as if before rehearsed to be observed by the same William and his heirs male. And if the said William die without issue male of his body begotten or else that he or any of his said issue male inherit me and be Lord Lovell and no discontinuance be made by him nor none of his heirs male of the said halfendell nor of no part thereof otherwise than is before rehearsed, that then the said halfendell with the appurtenance shall remain to the same Henry and to the heirs male of his body begotten under semblance form and conditions as is before rehearsed, and, for lack of such issue, the remainder thereof, to my right heirs, and that the other half of the said manors, lands and tenements with the appurtenance shall remain to the same Henry and to the heirs male of his body begotten under semblance form and conditions as if before rehearsed. And in case the said Henry die without such issue of his body begotten the remainder thereof to the same William and to the heirs male of his body begotten, under semblance form and conditions as before rehearsed. And for lack of such issue of the said William, the remainder thereof to my right heirs.

Also I pray and require my said feoffees that they anon after my decease make estate unto the same Henry my son in and of the said manors of Wellington, Pycheford, Bidford, Brome and moietie of the lordship of Wolverhampton and all other lands and tenements in the same towns and in all lands and tenements rents and farms in Nantwich and elsewhere in the shire of Chester, late William Brownyng's, with the appurtenance, to have and to hold to the same Harry and to the heirs male of his body begotten, under form and conditions following: that if the same Henry or any of the heirs make of his body begotten do or suffer any thing to be done by the which the same tail should be discontinued and discontinued, in part or in all, longer or otherwise than for term of life for the same Henry or term of the life of any of his heirs male of his body begotten or for term of the life of the wives of the same Henry or term of the life of any of the wives of the heirs make of his body begotten, that then the said manors, lands and tenements remain to my right heirs, and that the said estate utterly to be void.

And I pray and require my said feoffees to be helping and assisting my right heirs in the behalf.

And in case the said Henry die without issue male of his body begotten, that then the one half thereof remain to the same William my son and to the heirs male of his body begotten, under semblance form and conditions as is before rehearsed. And in case the said William die without issue male of his begotten, or else that he or any of his said issue male inherit me and be Lord Lovell and no discontinuance be made by him nor none of his said heirs male of the said halfendell, nor of no part thereof, other than is before rehearsed, that then the said halfendell with the appurtenance shall remain to the same Robert my son and to the heirs male of his body begotten, under semblance form and conditions as is before rehearsed, and for lack of such issue of the said Robert the remainder thereof to my right heirs. And that the other half of the said manors, moietie, lands, tenements, rents and services with the appurtenance so given to the said Henry shall remain to the said Robert and to the heirs male of his body begotten, under semblance form and conditions as before rehearsed. And for lack of such issue of the said Robert, the remainder thereof to the said William my son and to the heirs male of his body begotten, under semblance form and conditions as before rehearsed, and for lack of such issue of the said William, the remainder thereof to my right heirs.

In witness I have set to my seal of my my arms.'

Letter from John Lovell to John Beaumont, c. 1455

'Right worshipful, and my most best-beloved lord father, I recommend me unto your good lordship; please it you to weet, I have conceived your writing right well, and forasmuch as ye desire the stewardship of Baggeworth for your well-beloved Thomas Everingham, which I trow verily be right a good and a faithful gentleman. Howbeit, my lord, your desire shall be had in all that is in me; and at the instance of your lordship; I, by the advice of my council, shall give it him in writing, under such form as shall please you; wherein I would be glad to do that that might please your good lordship, praying you right heartily ye would be mine especial good lord and father in all such as ye can think should grow to my worship or profit in any wise, as my singular trust is most in you, and I always ready to do you service with God's grace, who have you, my right worshipful and my most best-beloved lord father, ever in his blessed keeping. Written at Rotherfield Gray, the 24th day of July.

Furthermore, my lord, and it like you, my lady my mother recommended her unto your good lordship, in whom her most faith and trust is in, praying you ye will be good brother unto her, for she hath taken you for her chief counsel.

John Lord Lovell.'

Letter from John Lovell and the other Lancastrian lords, July 1460

'Sirs it is yo r saying that ye be the kinges trew liegemen and soo be we wherfore we wul desire of you to wite the cause why ye make us werre And that we may understande how ye may joyne your sayinges and youre dedes togiders, And also what shuld bee the cause that ye take prisouners and we shuld nat defende us ayenst you and of this abovesaid we pray of you an answer for we cast us no more to accomber you w t oure writing, &c.'

Letter to John Lovell and the other Lancastrian lords, July 1460

'Like it your lordshipps to understande and with for certain that according to oure sayn, we have ever bee, nowe we bee, and ever will bee the kinges treu subgettes and humble liegemen And where ye by youre bill desire of us to wite the cause why we make you werre, &c. Therto we answer and seye that ye and your ffelesship have began and n'mde no werre by diverse assault shetyng of gonnez and otherwise by the which the kinges treu liege people aswell the inhabitauntz of this eitee men women and children as over have be murdred slayn maemed and myscheved in sundry wise And soo that at hath be doon by us is onely of youre occasioun in oure defence. And suche as we take for prisouners been for the attemptatz occasiouns and assaultz by theym doon as aforesaid in breche of the kinges peas, and for dispoillyng of the kinges treu people of their vitaillz and goodes without due contentacgn or paiement hadde in that behalve contrary to good equite and all lawe, &c.'

Arrangements for the Surrender of the Lancastrian Lords, July 1460

'Be it rembred that we William Hulyn maire of the citee of London and the aldermen and the comues of the saine agree us by thise presentz to holde ferme and stable and to perform in every pointe in that that in us shall be alle suche appoyntementz touchyng the gyvyng over of the Toute of London by therle of Kendale the lord Scales the lord Lovell the lord Hungerford and Sir Edmond Hampden and others now beyng wtin the saine tour, and the receyving of the tour aforesaid by the erle of Salisbury to the kinges use as be made by the saine erle of his deputees on that one partie, and the said erl of Kendale lord Scales, lord Lovell, lord Hungerford and Sir Edmond Hampdon and others or that othre partie. In witness whereof to thise saine presentz we have put our comon seal writen at London aforesaid the xvi day of July the xxxviiith year of the reign of King Henry the vi.'

Elizabeth Stonor's 1477 Letter to Her Husband

'Ryght reverent and worschypffull and interely best belovyde husbonde, I recomaunde me unto you in the most harteyste wyse hever more desyryng to here off your goode wellfare, the wyche I pray God longe to contune unto your hartys desyr. Syr, I resayved a tokyn ffrom you by Tawbose, my lorde Lovellys sarvant. And Syr, I have sent my lorde Lovell a tokyn and my ladys, as ye comaunde me to do, schuche as schalle plese them. Syr, ye schalle understonde that þe beschope off Bathe ys browthe in to the Towre syne you departyd. Allso Syr, ye schalle understonde that þe wolle hooys departe, as to morw is, ffor as I understonde: I pray Jhesu by thayr goode spede: and Goodard departys allso: and I pray you that ye wylle sende me som off your sarvantys and myne to wayte upone me, ffor now I ame ryght bare off sarvantys, and þat ye know well. Syr, I sent you halffe a honder welkys by Gardenar, and I wollde have sent you som honder desys, but truly I cowde not get none: but and I cane get hony to morow, syr Wylliam salle bryng hyt with hym. Syr, I pray you that I may be recomaundehyde unto my masterys your moder, and unto all goode ffrendys. No more unto you at thys tym, but þe blesyde Trenyte have you in hys kepyng now and hever. Amen. At London þe vj day off Marche.

Cossen, I was crasyd þat the makyng off thys letter, but I thanke God I am ryght well amendyd, blesyd by Jhesu.

By your owen wyff Elysabeth Stonore.

To my ryght reverent and worschypffull Cosyn, syr Wyllm. Stonor, knyght.'

Francis's 1482 Letter to William Stonor

'Cousine Stoner, I commaunde me to yow as hertely as I can, latynge yow have knowledge that I intendide to have bene with the King at the feste of Seynt John Baptist now late passid, to have attende upon his good grace; bot, Cousine, it is said in this contre the King purposes to send Northwardes my lorde of Gloucestre, and my broder Parr and such other folke of worship as hath eny reule in the said northe parties, trustyng we shall have warr of the Scottes: for cause wherof, and yef I shuld as now departe Southwardes it wold be said I withdrew me for the said warre. Bot, Cousine, as hastely as I can have a convenient seasson I purpose to be in the contre. And, Cousine, I pray yow þat ye wull see þat my game be wele kept at Roderfeld. And our lorde ever more have yow in his kepinge. From Tanfeld the xxiiij[th] day of Juyn.

ffraunceys Louell.

To my Cousine William Stonor, knight.'

Text from Oxford University, July 1483

'On the twenty-second day of July, Lord William Waynflete; Bishop of Winchester, revered in Christ the holy father and lord, founder of the college, came to Oxford, and supervised the state of his college and the buildings of the same, and also to respectfully receive the illustrious lord King Richard the Third in its often-named college, making [his way] towards Woodstock.

On the twenty-fourth day of the month, the illustrious lord King Richard the Third was respectfully received at first out[side] the university by the chancellor of the university and by counsilors and non-counsilors. After the respectful reception and the procession into the college of the blessed Mary Magdalen by the said lord founder and by the president and scholars, they spent the night there and the day after, which was the day of St Jacob [James] the Apostel, and the day of St Anne, mother of Mary, until after breakfast, with many spiritual and temporal lords and other nobles, as befitted them.

At the same time as the king, there came to the college the lord bishop of Durham, the lord bishop of Worcester, the lord bishop of St Asaph and master Thomas Langton, bishop-elect of St David's, his lordship the earl of Lincoln, the lord steward the earl of Surrey, the lord chamberlain, lord of Lovell, lord Stanley, lord Audeley, lord Becham, lord Richard Radclyff knight, and several other nobles, who stayed the night in the college, and our lord founder received them with honour.

On the twenty-fifth of the month, commanded and desired by the lord king, there were made in the great hall of the college two disputations; the first being in moral philosophy by master Thomas Kerver, opposing one of the students of the same college. Then, there was another solemn disputation, theological, in the presence of the king, by master John Taylour, professor of sacred theology, and the master William Grocyn answering. All of whom were honourably and greatly rewarded by the lord king, namely, the doctor of theology, with a buck and a hundred shillings, his responder [opponent] with a buck and five marks, the master who disputed in philosophy with one buck and five marks, and the student responding with one buck and forty shillings. Moreover, the noble king gave the president and scholars two bucks with five marks for wine, etc.

May the king live eternally.'

Francis's 1483 Letter to William Stonor

'Cosyn Stoner, y commawnde me to youe as hartely as y cane: for as myche as hit plesyth *þe* Kynges [Richard III's] grace to have warnyd youe and all other to attende upon his grace, and your compeny *þat* ye wolde come in my conysans and my compeny to come with you: and I ame sewre *þat* schall plese his grace beste, and cawse me to thynke *þat* ye lofe my honor, and y trust schalbe to your sewrte. Y pray youe remembyr this, as y schall remembyr youe in tyme to come, by *þe* grace of Jhesu, who ever preserve youe. Wreten at Lyncolne *þe* xj day of Octobyr.

Your hertely lovyng Cosyn ffraunceys Lovell.

Also Cosyn, *þe* kyng hath commawndyd me to sende youe worde to make youe redy, and all your compeny, in all hast to be with his grace at Leyceter *þe* Monday *þe* xx day of Octobyr: for I have sent for all my men to mete me at Bannebery, *þe* Soterday *þe* xviij day of Octobyr.

To my Cosyn [Syr] William Stoner.'

Nicholas von Popplau's report

'There I arrived on the day of Philipp and Jacobi, this is the first of May 1454 [sic] a Saturday, and found the king there, who granted me gracious audience and questioning, in the presence of all princes, earls councils and his whole nobility, in front of which I spoke Latin. This astonished the king almost a lot, because of my eloquence (little though it was), I gave his Majesty King the Imperial Majesty King's letter, next to that of the Duchess of Burgundy, all of which were commendations and promotion letters. These his Majesty King took with great delight very graciously.

After the reading of them the king himself came to me, took me by the hand and pulled me after him. Gave me as an answer, through an interpreter speaking Latin, although not in almost delightful words, that all I wanted and his Majesty King could do he would do with pleasure, because of his Imperial Majesty the Prince of Burgundy and for my person also, in respect of my learning and eloquence, which he would not have looked to me for nor believed me to have had he not heard me himself. Graciously inclined to comply with me, he addressed me three times (as is tradition in England) before I left his Majesty King's presence with the words: "Ick heit Ju willkom, und sit bey mir free willkom." Because the English use these words for persons of high and low standing, if they come from their own country or elsewhere. Use them also in meetings, invitations for meals, or collation (??), also when one blessed the other, they spoke: "Ick heit ju Willkomm." In this way the king's councils princes and lords spoke to me as well when they did me the honour.

When I left the king, he let his nobles and chamberlains accompany me to my inn. This made many people follow us to the house, also women and virgins. Went secretly, with the landlady's permission (so they could look at me alone) into the inn.

The other day the king sent a nobleman to me, that I might go to his church. There I heard the most lovely music, as I had never heard in my life, which, due to the clearness of voices might be compared to the dear angels. After mass the king sent to me the lord of Bergin, Johannem von Zaume (which is a famous town for trade in Brabant). He took me by the right hand in the church when the king wanted to leave the church after mass, and led me first before the king into the chamber or tent, which was erected by the church.

There I saw the king's bed, from top to bottom, with red velvet and a gold piece on top of each other, which the Lombards call Altabass, like adored his Imperial Majesty's bed in like wise. There was in the king's tent also a table, around it with silk cloth and gold embroidered on it, next to the bed adored and prepared. The king went to the table and had a [sash??] of gold on it many and fat pearls, probably of the size of peas with diamonds embroidered beneath them. The [sash??] was about as broad as a large man's hand and went from over his armpits on the left side of his back to beneath his right arm.

With him to the table went his princes and lords. When he had sat at the table, two princes the king's blood-friends and the Earl of Nordhännerland [sic], who is the most powerful in all of England. They did sit very far away from the king though, almost at the end of the table. But when the king saw me, standing for him (because his kingly magnificence, with the wise men of his court had done much hard work so I saw him sit at the table as a king with his kingly jewellery), the king made me sit at the table also with his two blood-friends the abovenamed princes. At which I answered it would be my greatest delight and desire (because I would within a short time have to get up and leave) to see his Kingly Majesty's face and widely-famous virtues rather than sitting at the table with his Majesty's other companions.

Which speech the king much liked, as well as my answers, so that he ate of almost no food, but constantly talked to me. Asked me about his Imperial Highness and all kings and princes of the realm [Holy Roman Empire] which I knew about their habits, happiness, trade and virtues. To which I answered all which would honour them. After that the king was still for a while. Then he began again to trouble me with many questions, of several things and trades, and finally of the Turk. At which I answered the king that Kingly Majesty of Hungary, with the Imperial Majesty with clever people and his Majesty's [delight?], had defeated more than twelve thousand Turks of the Turkish Emperor's.

When the king heard this, he was very happy and answered to it: 'I wished, that this my kingdom and country was in the place of the country and kingdom of Hungary also on the Turkish border. I would certainly cast out, alone with my people without help from other kings, princes and lord, not only the Turk but all my enemies and opponents.' Oh dear God, what a magnanimous lord I recognised in the king.

For eight or more days I stayed there and almost always was at his court for meals. But when I was blessed by the king on the last day he spoke to me: because I was determined to go away, he did not want to irritate nor hinder my determined way. If I on fulfilment of my journey I have decided to make, would like on the way back to visit with his Majesty, I would please his Majesty King far more than now. Wanted to make me feel his grace in all ways. Gave me a golden necklace which he took from the neck of a free or born lord and gave to me in his own person.

Three days before, and before I made goodbye to his majesty, he sent to me Herr Hanßen von Bergin who showed me that Kingly Majesty had for me got fifty nobles [coins] (which are a hundred Rhenish gulden and a half), which his Majesty King gave me as a gift. When I now wanted to sit with His Majesty, I begged his Majesty not to give me such a gift as one undeserving, because I came to His Majesty, not for gifts and presents, but to gain His Majesty's grace [goodwill]. To which the king answered, if I declined for my honour his gifts, which proved his honour, how did I think I could gain his goodwill? Since I desired his goodwill, I should also accept his gracious deference as well and in no way decline. Therefore I thanked the king and finally accepted it, because I regarded the honour higher than the use and in the same way would have chosen the honour, as the highly learned philosopher and orator Marcus Cicero in the third book 'Offitorum' writes and teaches. The [present?] the king have me held in the gold thirteen ounces of londnish weight. One ounce are twelve Rhenish gulden. So I retired also from the princes, lords and councils. Only then the king bade me rent an inn and sent me an open letter, that I might as often travel to His Majesty, safe in land and water, before all his subjects together with my own.

Before that I invited many of the king's chamberlains, along with many of the nobility, with them I had also the king's musicians, pipers [and other musicians]. Also the king have me fifty nobles [coins], which I sent him back and refused to accept. This moved the king and he sent for me again and let me be asked if I was of king's or prince's dynasty that I despised his gifts, to which I answered I had not declined his Majesty's gift and presents because of contempt but only out of honour. So he punished me harshly with words and urged me so I had to take it. To me came also the king's herald, his pipers and [other musicians], which I gave to one and the other crown [coin].

The King Richard is of the dynasty from the land of Gloßcostier, called born prince, three fingers longer but somewhat more slender and not as thick as me, also much leaner. Has very subtle arms and legs, also a great heart.'

Margaret, Countess of Oxford's Letter to John Paston, May 1486

'To my right trusti and welbeloued John Paston, shrieve of Norffolk and Suffolk.

Right trusti and welbiloued, I recommaund me unto you. And for as moche as I ame credebby enformed that Fraunceis, late Lorde Lovell, is now of late resorted into the Yle of Ely to the entente, by alle lykelyhod, to find the wais and meanes to gete him shipping and passage at your costes, or ellis to resorte ageyn to seintuary if he can or maie, I therefor hertily desire and praie you, and neuertheless in the Kinges name streitly chargie you, that ye in all goodly haste endevoire yourself that suche wetche or other meanes be used and hadde in the poortes, creekes, and othre places wher ye thinke necessary by your discrecion to the letting of his seid purpose; and that ye also use all the waies ye can or maie by your wisedom to the taking of the same late Lord Lovell. And what pleasur ye maie doo to the Kinges grace in this matier I am sure is not to you unknowen. And God kepe you.

Wreten at Lauenham the xix day of Maij.

Margaret Oxynford.'

Letter from the Earl of Oxford to John Paston, January 1487

'To my right trusty and welbelouyd councellour John Paston, esquire.

John Paston, I comaund me to you. And as for such tithyngs as ya haue sent, supposyng theym to be gone with the Lord Lovell, they be yitt in England, for he is departyng with xiiii personys and no moo. At the Kyngys coming to London I wold advise you to see his Highnes. And Almyghty God kepe you.

Writen at Wyndesore the xxiiiith day of January.

Oxynford.'

Sir Edmund Bedingfield's Letter to John Paston in May 1487

'Un to my ryght wurshypfull cosyn, John Paston, Esquyer, for the Body.

Ryght wurshypfull cosyn, I recomawnd me un to you as hertly as I can, letyng you wytte I was with my Lorde Stuarde as on Munday laste paste, by the desyir of them that I myght not sey ney to. I herde all that was seyd there, but they gaate non avawntage, wurde, nor promyse off me; but they thought in asmoche as they ware the beste in the shere, that every man owghte to wayte and go with them. Wherto yt was answerd that oure master, nexte the Kynge, havynge hys commysshon, muste nedys have the jentylmen and the contre to a wayte up on hym by the vertu of the same; but yt was thought I owght not to obeye no copy of the commisshon, withoute I had the same under wexe, where in hathe ben gret argument, whyche I understoode by reporte a fortnyte paste, and that causyd me to sende unto my lorde to have the very commysshon, whyche he sente me, and a letter, where off I sende you the copy here in closyd.

As for you, ye be sore takyn in sum place, seying that ye intende swyche thynges as ys lyke to folow gret myscheffe. I seyd I undyrstood non swyche, nor thynges lyke it; and yt ys thoughte ye intende nat to go forthe thys jorneye, nor no jentylman in that quarter but Robert Brandon that hath promysyd to go with them, as they seye.

I understonde Sir Wylliam Bolen and Sir Harry Heydon ware at Thetforde in to Kente ward, but they returnyd in to Norffolk a geyne; I thynke they wull not goo thys jorney, yff the Kynge nede. Ser Harry was at Attylborow on Saterday. I wene he had a vyce there to turne a zen; wher for, cosyn, yt ys good to understonde the sertente what jentylmen intende to goo, and be assuryd to go together, that I may have wurde; my cosyn Hoptun hathe promysyd that he wull be oon. As fore Wysman, he seythe he wull be off the same, but I can have no holde.

Furthermore, cosyn, yt ys seyd that after my lordys departyng to the Kynge ye ware mette at Barkwey, whyche ys construid that ye had ben with the Lady Lovell, but wrathe seyd never well; and in asmoche as we understonde my lordys plesur, yt ys well doon we dele wysly therafter. And, nexte to the Kynge, I answerd pleynly I was bownde to do him service, and to fullfylle hys comaundment to the uttermest off my powere, by the grace off God, Who ever preserve you to Hys plesur.

Wretyn at Oxburgh, the xvj. day of Maye. Your cosyn, E. Bedyngfeld.'

Alice FitzHugh's Letter to John Paston, February 1488

'To my right trusty and welbeloved son, Sir John Paston, be this delyvered.

Jon Paston, I recommaunde me to you in my moste hertely maner. And wher I understande be my doghter Lovell, ye desyre to know whedir I woll have the bargane ye made for me in Norwich or nay, and if I wol, I moste content therefor now in merks. Son, in good faith it is so, I shal receyve no mony of the revenowse of my lyvelod before Mydsommer, and also I have payd accordyng to my promise to Sir William Cabell a great payment, the which ye knoww wel was due to be payde, so that I can not be of power to content therfore, for the which I am right sory, for I know well I shall never have such a bargane.

Also my doghtyr Lovell makith great sute and labour for my sone hir husband. Sie Edwarde Franke hath bene in the North to inquire for hym; he is comyn againe and cane nought understonde wher he is. Wherfore her benevolers willith her to continue his suit and labour, and so I can not departe nor leve hir as ye know well; and if I might be there, I wold be full glad, as knowith our Lorde God, Whoo have you in his blissid kepynge.

From London, the xxiiiith day of February.

Your loving moder, Alise, Lady FitzHugh.'

Francis's Second Attainder, 1495

'For as much as John, late Earl of Lincoln, Francis Lovell late Lord Lovell, and diverse others with them, traitorously imagining and compassing the death and destruction of our sovereign lord the king, assembled them, with other evil-disposed people, to the number of 5000 persons at Stoke, in the county of Nottingham, the 20th day of June [sic], in the second year of the reign of our said sovereign lord the king that now is, and then and there, for the performance of their cursed, mischievous and wretched purpose, in plain field, at the same Stoke, in the said county, with their banners displayed, contrary to their allegiance, against the king, our and their natural sovereign lord, levied and reared war, and made battle against him, for which traitorous and unnatural deed the said John Earl of Lincoln, with diverse others then and there traitorously offending, were late, by authority of Parliament, in a Parliament holden at Westminster in the third year of the reign of the king, our sovereign lord that now is, deemed convicted and attainted of high treason, in which act of attainder the said Francis Lovell was ignorantly left out and omitted, to the most perilous example of others, being of such traitorous mind:

Wherefore be it ordained, enacted and established by the Lord Spiritual and Temporal and the Commons in this present parliament assembled, that the said Francis stand and be deemed, adjudged, convicted and attainted of high treason for his rehearsed traitorous deed, and forfeit to the king our sovereign lord all honours, castles, manners, lordships, hundreds, franchises, liberties, privileges, advowsons, nominations, presentations, knight's fees, lands, tenements, lands, services, reversions, remainders, portions, annuities, pensions, rights, possessions and other hereditaments in England, Wales, Calais, or marches of the same, whereof he, or any other person or persons to his use, were seized of estate of inheritance the 20th of June, the second year of the reign of the king our sovereign lord, or into the which he or any of them had lawful cause of entry the said 20th of June, or any time after, and all other honours, castles, manors, lordships, etc, as above, that the said Francis or his heirs should or might have grown, descended, remained, or reverted, after and by the death of any of his ancestors, as if he had not done nor committed the said heinous treason, and that the said Francis and his heirs were in plain life, when the said descent, remainder or revertory shall move, fall, or grow, and to them or any of them should or might have done, if this present act against him had never been had nor made, saving to every person or persons and their heirs, other than the said Francis and his heirs, and such other person or persons and their heirs, that had any thing in the premises to the use of the said Francis and his heirs, and such persons to whom any of the premises should descend, remain or revert, such right, title, claim, action, entry or interest in, of and upn the premises and every part thereof, as they had, should, or might have had, if this act had never been had nor made.

Provided always, that all letters patent, made by the king's highness to any person or persons of the premises or any part thereof, or of any annuity or office granted by this letters patent to any person or persons out of the same, that now be in strength and force, or that was in strength and force the twelfth of October last past, stand and be good and effectual in the law, after the tenors and purports of this same, this present act in any wise notwithstanding.

Provided also, that by this act the king has no such right and title of any of the premises, that be or hereafter shall descend, remain or revert from any ancestor or cousin of the said Francis, which right and title be or shall be in the said ancestor only in [?] time of his or their decease, whereof their entries, at the time of the same disease, shall be tolled and taken away, by the course of law of this land.

Be it ordered by the said authority, that every of the king's liege people, their successors, heirs and assigns, have and enjoy all manner of rents due and of rights to them, their ancestors or predecessors belonging, before making of this act, of any of the premises, during the time that the same premises remain and abide in the possession of our said sovereign lord or his heirs, and if any of the premises hereafter be granted by the king or any of his heirs, by letters patent, or that it be granted by act of parliament or otherwise, to any person or persons for term of life, in fee simple or in fee tail, that then those persons so seized, hold the same manors, lands and tenements, or other premises, were or should have been holden and charged with, and that they may distrain for the same rents and services, and have all other lawful remedy for recovery or non-payment or non-doing of the same, as they or any of them might have had, before the making of this present act, homage of tennants for term of life only except.

Provided always, that this act of attainder, nor any act or acts made or hereafter to be made in this present parliament extend not, nor be in no wise prejudical nor hurtful to Anne Viscountess Lovell, late wife of the said Francis late Viscount Lovell, to or for any estate made of any of the premises to the said late viscount and the said Anne, nor to any other person or persons to or for any estate made of any of the premises by the said late viscount or any other to the use of the said Anne; but that the same Anne, or such other person or persons to whom any such estate or estates has been made of, as they should have done had this act, or any other act in this present Parliament, had never been had nor made.'

Notes

Introduction

1. For a history of the Lovell family, see, for example: Monika E. Simon, *The Lovells of Titchmarsh: An English Baronial Family, 1297–148?* (York: Department of History, University of York, 1999)

1 'The Lord Lovell ys son'

1. Annales Monastrii S Albanes, Volume I, p. 62
2. Monika E. Simon, *The Lovells of Titchmarsh: An English Baronial Family, 1297–148?* (York: Department of History, University of York, 1999), p. 142
3. Calendar of Patent Rolls, Henry VI, Volume V, AD 1446–1452, p. 385, Calendar of Patent Rolls, Henry VI, Volume V, AD 1441–1446, p. 333
4. Matthew Lewis, *Richard, Duke of York: King by Right* (Stroud: Amberley Publishing, 2016), Position 3881
5. Ibid
6. For example in: Monika E. Simon, *The Lovells of Titchmarsh*
7. Anthony Emery, *Greater Medieval Houses of England and Wales, 1300–1500: Volume 3, Southern England* (Cambridge: Cambridge University Press, 2006) pp. 117–119
8. Who eventually became the nurse of Henry VI's only son, Edward of Westminster
9. She is mentioned in William Lovell's Last Will and Testament, see Appendix 2 for full text
10. Monika E. Simon, *The Lovells of Titchmarsh*, p. 67. Though Monika E. Simon points out that letters of denization were issued for a 'John Lovell born in the duchy of Normandy' in 1452, and that it is possible they referred to William's son, which would put his birth before 1432, the age given in the IPM is almost certainly correct. A preliminary inquisition into William's lands on 13 August 1455 stated that John had turned twenty-two 'on the morrow of Easter last past'. (Inquisition post mortem on William Lovell, held by the Shakespeare Birthplace Trust. ER 101/31. Partially quoted in: *The Thirty-Seventh Annual Report of the Deputy Keeper of the Public Records* (London: George E. Eyre and William Spottiswoode, 1876) p. 479.) Such an exact date suggests that

a proof of age had been requested for John, and means that the letters of denization must have referred to someone else.

11. Calendar of Patent Rolls, Henry VI, Volume V, AD 1441–1446 p. 443

12. Joan was mentioned in her grandmother Joan Phelip's will as unmarried on the former date.

13. Inquisition Post Mortem on Joan Lovell, National Archive, C140_40_7_001, C140_40_7_002, C140_40_7_003, C140_40_7_004, C140_40_7_005, C140_40_7_006, C140_40_7_007, C140_40_7_008

14. Joanna M. Williams, 'The Political Career of Francis, Viscount Lovell 1456–1487(?)', *The Ricardian* (1990) p. 383

15. See Appendix 2 for the full text of the will.

16. Which is most definitely not the only instance of John being apparently scorned by his family, see further down.

17. Inquisition post mortem on William Lovell, held by the Shakespeare Birthplace Trust. ER 101/31. Partially quoted in: Ed. Thomas Stapleton, *De Antiquis Legibus Liber. Cronica Maiorum et Vicecomitum Londoniarum et quedam, que contigebant temporibis illis ab anno MCLXXVIII; cum appendice* (London: Camden Society, 1846)

18. Matthew Lewis, *Richard, Duke of York*, Position 3881

19. Inquisition post mortem on William Lovell, held by the Shakespeare Birthplace Trust. ER 101/31. Partially quoted in: Ed. Thomas Stapleton, *De Antiquis Legibus Liber. Cronica Maiorum et Vicecomitum Londoniarum et quedam, que contigebant temporibis illis ab anno MCLXXVIII; cum appendice* (London: Camden Society, 1846)

20. Monika E. Simon, 'Who is buried in the Tomb in St Kenelm's Church, Minster Lovell?', *The Ricardian* (2009)

21. Ibid

22. Calendar of Fine Rolls, Henry VI, AD 1452–1461, p. 155

23. Inquisition Post Mortem on Joan Lovell, National Archive, C140_40_7_001, C140_40_7_002, C140_40_7_003, C140_40_7_004, C140_40_7_005, C140_40_7_006, C140_40_7_007, C140_40_7_008

24. Calendar of Patent Rolls, Henry VI, Volume III, AD 1436–1441 p. 569

25. Ibid p. 880

26. John Watts, 'Beaumont, John, first Viscount Beaumont', *Oxford Dictionary of National Biography* (Oxford University Press, 2004)

27. Calendar of Patent Rolls, Henry VI, Volume V, AD 1441–1446 p. 596

28. Ibid

29. On which date Joan is mentioned as unmarried in her grandmother Joan Phelip's will. She was left 100 pounds and Joan Phelips "best gold girdle" as well as a "buckle set with pearls". This will is partly quoted in quoted: Ed. Thomas Stapleton, *De Antiquis Legibus Liber*

30. On which date William Lovell granted her and his son John some land, see footnote 13

31. John Watts, 'Beaumont, John, first Viscount Beaumont'

32. Ibid

33. Ibid

34. Matthew Lewis, *Richard, Duke of York*, position 3881

35. John Watts, 'Beaumont, John, first Viscount Beaumont'

36. When the appointment was made is uncertain. A reference to her having held the post is found in the Calendar of Patent Rolls, Henry VI, Volume VI, AD 1452–1461 p. 567

37. See Appendix for its full text. James Gairdner, *The Paston Letters, AD 1422–1509. Volume III.* New Complete Library Edition (London: Chatto & Windus, Exeter: James G. Commin, 1904) p. 143

38. This would have been just after John Lovell became 8th Baron Lovell.

39. The Last Will and Testament of John Beaumont, Viscount Beaumont. National Archives, E211_281. All translations from this document are my own.

2 *Francis's Early Years and the Wars of the Roses*

1. See chapter 10.

2. For the typical birth and name orders of the Lovell family see, for example: Monika E. Simon, *The Lovells of Titchmarsh: An English Baronial Family, 1297–148?* (York: Department of History, University of York, 1999)

3. Calendar of Patent Rolls, Edward IV, Edward V, Richard III. AD 1476–1485 p. 14

4. Ibid p. 62

5. Inquisitions Post Mortem on John Lovell, National Archives, C140/13/27.

6. Nicholas Orme, *Medieval Children* (New Haven and London: Yale University Press, 2001) pp. 35–43

7. Ibid pp. 52/3

8. Josephine Wilkinson, *Richard the Young King to Be* (Stroud: Amberley Publishing, 2014) p. 65

9. Josephine Wilkinson, *The Princes in the Tower* (Stroud: Amberley Publishing, 2013) pp. 14/5

10. Monika E. Simon, *The Lovells of Titchmarsh*, p. 211

11. Paul Murray Kendall, *Richard the Third* (London: George Allan & Unwin, 1955, 1956.) p. 51

12. Josephine Wilkinson, *Richard the Young King to Be*, pp. 52–57

13. See several appointments and rewards granted to them, recorded in the Calendar of Patent Rolls, Henry VI, Volume VI, AD 1452–1461.

14. John Watts, 'Beaumont, John, first Viscount Beaumont', *Oxford Dictionary of National Biography* (Oxford University Press, 2004)

15. Ed. John Silvester Davies, *An English chronicle of the reigns of Richard II, Henry IV, Henry V, and Henry VI written before the year 1471; with an appendix, containing the 18th and 19th years of Richard II and the Parliament at Bury St. Edmund's, 25th Henry VI and supplementary additions from the Cotton. ms. chronicle called "Eulogium"* (London: Camden Society, 1856) pp. 94/5

16. Calendar of Patent Rolls, Henry VI, Volume VI, AD 1452–1461 p. 534

17. Ed. John Silvester Davies, *An English chronicle*, p. 95

18. Charles Ross, *Edward IV* (New Haven and London: Yale University Press, 1974) pp. 26/7

19. Ed. John Silvester Davies, *An English chronicle*, pp. 95/6

20. Ibid, p. 96

21. Ibid

22. Reginald R Sharpe, *London and the kingdom: a history derived mainly from the archives at Guildhall in the custody of the corporation of the city of London. Volume III* (London: Longmans, Green & Co, 1895). p. 384

23. Ibid, pp. 384/5

24. The original text of these letters is in appendix 2.

25. Reginald R Sharpe, *London and the kingdom*, p. 385

26. Matthew Lewis, *Richard, Duke of York: King by Right* (Stroud: Amberley Publishing, 2016), position 5020

27. Matthew Lewis, *Richard III: Loyalty Binds Me* (Stroud: Amberley Publishing, 2018), position 684

28. Ibid, position 709–723

29. Mike Ingram, *10 July 1460: The Battle of Northampton* (Northampton: Northampton Battlefield Society, 2015) pp. 128–130

30. Ibid, pp. 12–15

31. Matthew Lewis, *Richard III: Loyalty Binds Me*, positions 462–476

32. Ed. Paul Brand, Anne Curry, Chris Given-Wilson, Rosemary Horrox, Geoffrey Martin, Mark Ormrod, *Henry VI: November 1459*, in *Parliament Rolls of Medieval England* (Woodbridge, Boydell, 2005) (https://www.british-history.ac.uk/no-series/parliament-rolls-medieval/november-1459) Last accessed 13/10/2018, 14:24)

33. Ed. John Silvester Davies, *An English chronicle*, pp. 83–85

34. Mike Ingram, *10 July 1460*, pp. 69–85

35. Ed. John Silvester Davies, *An English chronicle*, pp. 94–96

36. Ibid, p. 97

37. Ibid

38. Ibid

39. Ibid

40. Ibid

41. Mike Ingram, *10 July 1460*, pp. 97/8

42. Ed. John Silvester Davies, *An English chronicle*, p. 97

43. William Beaumont's proof of age, quoted in Ed. Thomas Stapleton, *De Antiquis Legibus Liber. Cronica Maiorum et Vicecomitum Londoniarum et quedam, que contigebant temporibis illis ab anno MCLXXVIII; cum appendice* (London: Camden Society, 1846). P. ccvii. Translations are my own.

44. Ed. John Silvester Davies, *An English chronicle*, p. 96

45. Ibid, p. 97

46. Reginald R Sharpe, *London and the kingdom: a history derived mainly from the archives at Guildhall in the custody of the corporation of the city of London. Volume III* (London: Longmans, Green & Co, 1895) pp. 385/6

47. Ed. John Silvester Davies, *An English chronicle*, p. 98

48. Reginald R Sharpe, *London and the kingdom*, pp. 385/6

49. Ed. John Silvester Davies, *An English chronicle*, p. 98

50. Ibid, p. 99/100

51. The fact of his illegal seizures of some manors is recorded in the Calendar of Patent Rolls, Edward IV, AD 1461–1467 pp. 549/550

52. Francis later claimed some of these manors in his mother's right, see chapter 10.

53. William Beaumont's proof of age, quoted in: Ed. Thomas Stapleton, *De Antiquis Legibus Liber*, p. ccvii. Translations are my own.

54. The last will and testament of John Beaumont, Viscount Beaumont. National Archives, E211_281
55. Ed. John Silvester Davies, *An English chronicle*, pp. 102–106
56. Calendar of Patent Rolls, Edward IV, AD 1461–1467, pp. 549/550
57. Ibid, pp. 43/4
58. Ibid, p. 87
59. Blomefield Collections Canterbury, as quoted in John Mason Neale, *Illustrations of Monumental Brasses No V* (Cambridge: T Stevenson, 1842) p. 173
60. Monika E. Simon, *The Lovells of Titchmarsh*, p. 304
61. Calendar of Close Rolls, Edward IV, AD 1461–1468, p. 139
62. Monika E. Simon, *The Lovells of Titchmarsh*, p. 92
63. Ibid
64. Calendar of Patent Rolls, Edward IV, AD 1461–1467, p. 222
65. Ibid, p. 346

3 '... *during the minority of the said Francis*'

1. Inquisitions Post Mortem on John Lovell, National Archives, C140/13/27.
2. There is no indication where in the chapel John was buried.
3. See chapter 10.
4. As above.
5. See chapter 3.
6. Ed. James Gairdner, *Testamenta Eboracensia, A Selection of Wills from the Registry at York, Volume 3* (London: Whittaker and Co., 1865), pp. 132/3
7. Ibid
8. Ibid
9. James Gairdner, *The Paston Letters, AD 1422–1509. Volume IV.* New Complete Library Edition. (London: Chatto & Windus, Exeter: James G. Commin, 1904), pp. 216/7
10. Ibid. Stephen David's recent book, *Last Champion of York: Francis Lovell, Richard III's Truest Friend* gives the date as 1466.
11. K. L. Clark, *The Nevills of Middleham. England's Most Powerful Family in the Wars of the Roses* (Stroud: The History Press, 2016), pp. 294/5
12. See chapter 5.
13. Josephine Wilkinson, *The Princes in the Tower* (Stroud: Amberley Publishing, 2013), p. 28
14. There is no evidence the king attended the wedding.
15. Several instances of this are found in the Calendar of Patent Rolls, Edward IV, AD 1461–1467
16. Thomas Penn, *Winter King: Henry VII and the Dawn of Tudor England* (London: Penguin Books Ltd, 2011) p. 2
17. F. Devon, *Issues of the Exchequer* (London: John Murray, 1837), p. 409. Quoted in Caroline Halsted, *Richard III as Duke of Gloucester and King of England, Volume I* (London: Longman, Brown, Green and Longman, 1844) pp. 118/9
18. F. Devon, *Issue Rolls of the Exchequer*, p. 409
19. Charles Ross, *Edward IV* (New Haven and London: Yale University Press, 1974), p. 93
20. Ibid
21. Calendar of Patent Rolls, Edward IV, AD 1461–1467 p. 474

22. Ibid
23. Joanna M. Williams, 'The Political Career of Francis, Viscount Lovell 1456–1487(?)', *The Ricardian* (1990), p. 385
24. Calendar of Patent Rolls, Edward IV, Henry VI. AD 1467–1477 p. 215
25. What little is known about Sir William's son and why I come to the conclusion that he was Joan Beaumont's is discussed in Appendix 1
26. Alice Deincourt died in 1474, her husband a year before that
27. K. L. Clark, *The Nevills of Middleham*, p. 295
28. Paul Murray Kendall, *Richard the Third* (London: George Allan & Unwin, 1955, 1956.) p. 51
29. Josephine Wilkinson, *Richard the Young King to Be* (Stroud: Amberley Publishing, 2014) pp. 105–120
30. For example in Paul Murray Kendall, *Richard the Third*, p. 275, and Charles Ross, *Richard III* (York: Eyre Methuen Ltd, 1981), p. 49
31. Paul Murray Kendall, *Richard the Third*, p. 51
32. Calendar of Patent Rolls, Edward IV, Henry VI. AD 1467–1477 p. 51
33. Ibid, p. 215

4 In the Lord FitzHugh's Household

1. Charles Ross, *Edward IV* (New Haven and London: Yale University Press, 1974) p. 117
2. Ibid, pp. 131–135
3. Ibid, pp. 149–152
4. Ibid, p. 145
5. Ibid
6. Ibid, p. 147
7. This is mentioned, for example, in Anthony J. Pollard, *Lord FitzHugh's Rising in 1470* (Bulletin of the Institute of Historical Research, 1979) p. 1
8. James Gairdner, *The Paston Letters, AD 1422–1509. Volume IV.* New Complete Library Edition. (London: Chatto & Windus, Exeter: James G. Commin, 1904) p. 80
9. Anthony J. Pollard, *Lord FitzHugh's Rising in 1470*, p. 1
10. Ibid
11. Calendar of Patent Rolls, Edward IV, Henry VI. AD 1467–1477 p. 215
12. Among them was Edward Franke, who would in later years be a close associate of Francis's
13. Charles Ross, *Edward IV*, p. 152
14. Ibid, p. 136
15. Ibid, pp. 156–160
16. Ed. James Balfour Paul, *The Register of the Great Seal of Scotland. AD 1424–1513* (Edinburgh: HM General Register House, 1882) p. 213. See footnote 167.
17. Charles Ross, *Edward IV*, p. 161
18. Ed. John Bruce, *Historie of the Arrivall of Edward IV in England and the Finall Recouerye of his Kingdomes from Henry VI AD M.CCCC.LXXI.* (London: John Bower Nichols and Son, 1838) p. 3
19. Ibid, pp. 9–12
20. Ibid, p. 8

21. Ibid, pp. 16–18
22. Ibid, pp. 18/9
23. Ibid, p. 20
24. Cora L Scofield, *The Life and Reign of Edward IV, King of England and France and Lord of Ireland: Volume 2*. (London: Longmans, Green & Co, 1923), p. 8
25. Ibid
26. It is, for example, stated as a fact that he left in Charles Ross, *Edward IV*, p. 152
27. Ed. James Balfour Paul, *The Register of the Great Seal of Scotland*, p. 213 The translation from Latin is my own.
28. Ed. John Bruce, *Historie of the Arrivall of Edward IV*, p. 30
29. Charles Ross, *Richard III* (York: Eyre Methuen Ltd, 1981), p. 28
30. Charles Ross, *Edward IV*, p. 175. Also, Matthew Lewis, *Richard III: Loyalty Binds Me* (Stroud: Amberley Publishing, 2018), position 2812

5 In the Duke and Duchess of Suffolk's Household

1. Calendar of Patent Rolls, Edward IV, Henry VI. AD 1467–1477 p. 261
2. Michael Hicks, 'Pole, John de la, second duke of Suffolk', *Oxford Dictionary of National Biography* (Oxford University Press, 2004)
3. Ibid
4. Michael J. Bennett, 'Stanley, Sir William', *Oxford Dictionary of National Biography* (Oxford University Press, 2004)
5. Some of their interactions are found in the Calendar of Patent Rolls, Edward IV, Henry VI. AD 1467–1477 and Calendar of Patent Rolls, Edward IV, Edward V, Richard III. AD 1476–1485.
6. For the Duke of Suffolk's lifestyle, see J. A. F. Thomson, 'John De La Pole, Duke of Suffolk', *Speculum* (1979)
7. Document from the National Archives, C1/66//341
8. Document from the National Archives, C1/48/436
9. See further down in this chapter
10. Calendar of Patent Rolls, Edward IV, Henry VI. AD 1467–1477, p. 312
11. For example, both Ewelme and Minster Lovell Hall are in Oxfordshire, only 30 miles apart
12. Anne Lovell was Anne Neville's first cousin, the daughter of her father's sister
13. See chapter 6
14. *The Register of the Guild of Corpus Christi in the City of York; with an Appendix of Illustrative Documents, containing some account of the Hospital of St. Thomas of Canterbury, without Micklegate-Bar, in the suburbs of the city* (Durham: Andrews and co., London: T. and W. Boone, Edinburgh: Blackwood and Sons, 1872), pp. v–xix
15. Ibid
16. Ibid
17. See chapter 10.
18. *The Register of the Guild of Corpus Christi in the City of York*, pp. v–xix
19. Ibid, p. 86
20. Ibid, p. 134

21. One such example is the parish church of Wyke Rusyngdon, which is noted in the Calendar of Patent Rolls, Edward IV, Henry VI. AD 1467–1477, on 22 March 1474 as 'in the king's gift by reason of the minority of Francis son and heir of John Lovell, late lord Lovell', without any explanation as to why it was not in the Suffolks' hands.

22. Inquisitions Post Mortem on Alice Deincourt, National Archives, C140/47/64

23. Calendar of Patent Rolls, Edward IV, Henry VI. AD 1467–1477, p. 421

24. Ibid, p. 440

25. Ibid, p. 468

26. Inquisitions Post Mortem on William Lovell, Lord Morley, National Archives, C140/47/64

27. Calendar of Close Rolls, Edward IV, Henry VI. AD 1468–1477 p. 433, quoted in *The Thirty-Seventh Annual Report of the Deputy Keeper of the Public Records* (London: George E. Eyre and William Spottiswoode, 1876), p. 479

28. Charles Ross, *Edward IV* (New Haven and London: Yale University Press, 1974), pp. 367–369

29. Charles Ross, *Richard III* (York: Eyre Methuen Ltd, 1981), p. 34

30. Josephine Wilkinson, *Richard the Young King to Be* (Stroud: Amberley Publishing, 2014), pp. 265–277

6 *In His Own Household*

1. Anthony Emery, *Greater Medieval Houses of England and Wales, 1300–1500: Volume 3, Southern England* (Cambridge: Cambridge University Press, 2006), pp. 119/120

2. See chapters 7 and 8.

3. Calendar of Close Rolls, Edward IV, Edward V, Richard III 1476–1485, p. 413

4. Ed. Charles Lethbridge Kingsford, *The Stonor letters and papers, 1290–1483 Vol III* (London: Offices of the Society, 1919), p. 41

5. See chapter 12

6. See chapter 10

7. See chapters 7 and 10

8. See chapter 10 for its full text

9. Peter W. Hammond, Anne F. Sutton, *The Coronation of Richard III: The Extant Documents* (Middlesbrough: A Sutton Publishing, 1984), p. 23

10. For evidence of Richard favouring this keep: For example, Paul Murray Kendall, *Richard the Third* (London: George Allan & Unwin, 1955–1956), pp. 150, 177

11. See chapter 11

12. *The Register of the Guild of Corpus Christi in the City of York; with an Appendix of Illustrative Documents, containing some account of the Hospital of St. Thomas of Canterbury, without Micklegate-Bar, in the suburbs of the city* (Durham: Andrews and co., London: T. and W. Boone, Edinburgh: Blackwood and Sons, 1872) p. 101

13. See chapter 10

14. See chapters 10 and 11.

15. See chapter 11.

7 *Francis, Lord Lovell*

1. Calendar of Patent Rolls, IV, Henry VI. AD 1467–1477, p. 62
2. Calendar of Close Rolls, Edward IV, Edward V, Richard III, AD 1476–1485, p. 76
3. Ibid, pp. 84/5
4. Ibid
5. *Rotuli Parliamentorum, ut et petitiones, et placita in Parliamento, Ab Anno Duodecimo R. Edwardi IV. ad Finem eiusdem Regni Volume VI* (London, 1777), p. 256
6. Ibid, p. 212
7. Calendar of Patent Rolls, Edward IV, Henry VI. AD 1467–1477, p. 81
8. Josephine Wilkinson, *The Princes in the Tower* (Stroud: Amberley Publishing, 2013), pp. 28–30
9. *Rotuli Parliamentorum, ut et petitiones, et placita in Parliamento, Ab Anno Duodecimo R. Edwardi IV. ad Finem eiusdem Regni Volume VI* (London, 1777), p. 172
10. Ed. C. A. J. Armstrong, *The Usurpation of Richard III by Dominic Mancini* (Middlesbrough: A. Sutton Publishing, 1984) pp. 62/3
11. John Ashdown-Hill, *The Third Plantagenet* (Stroud: The History Press, 2014), p. 161
12. For example, such an opinion is expressed in Charles Ross, *Edward IV* (New Haven and London: Yale University Press, 1974), p. 244
13. Calendar of Patent Rolls, Edward IV, Henry VI. AD 1467–1477, p. 213
14. L. C. Attreed, *The York House Books, Volume I* (Middlesbrough: A Sutton Publishing, 1991), pp. 30, 81
15. As done by Edward I and his wife Eleanor for their daughter Elizabeth
16. Joanna M. Williams, 'The Political Career of Francis, Viscount Lovell 1456–1487(?)', *The Ricardian* (1990), p. 388
17. Virginia Davies, *William Wayneflete: Bishop and Educationalist* (Woodbridge: The Boydell Press, 1993), pp. 143–144
18. Ibid, p. 143
19. Ibid
20. Ibid, pp.143–144
21. Ibid
22. Ibid
23. Ibid
24. Ibid
25. Ibid
26. Wendy E. A. Moorhen, 'Such was his Renown in Warfare', *Ricardian Bulletin* (2004) http://www.richardiii.net/2_3_0_riii_leadership.php#military
27. See further down in this chapter
28. Ed. G. E. C. Cokayne, *The Complete Peerage* (London, Cokayne, 1932) pp. 224–225
29. Ibid
30. Ibid
31. Joanna M. Williams, 'The Political Career of Francis, Viscount Lovell 1456–1487(?)', *The Ricardian* (1990), p. 387
32. Calendar of Patent Rolls, Edward IV, Henry VI. AD 1467–1477 p. 343

33. Ed. Charles Lethbridge Kingsford, *The Stonor letters and papers, 1290–1483* (London: Offices of the Society, 1919) p. 418

34. Wendy E. A. Moorhen, 'Such was his Renown in Warfare'

35. Ibid

36. 24 June

37. Wendy E. A. Moorhen, 'Such was his Renown in Warfare'

38. Ibid

39. Ed. Charles Lethbridge Kingsford, *The Stonor letters and papers*, p. 418

40. Joanna M. Williams, 'The Political Career of Francis, Viscount Lovell 1456–1487(?)', p. 399

41. Ibid

42. *Rotuli Parliamentorum VI*, pp. 204–5

8 'Visconte Lovell, sieur de Holland, de Burnell, Deygnecort et de Grey de Rotherfilde'

1. Ibid

2. Ed. G. E. C. Cokayne, *The Complete Peerage* (London: Cokayne, 1932), pp. 224–5

3. This is referred to in *Rotuli Parliamentorum, ut et petitiones, et placita in Parliamento, Ab Anno Duodecimo R. Edwardi IV. ad Finem eiusdem Regni Volume VI* (London, 1777), p. 483

4. Ibid

5. Joanna M. Williams, 'The Political Career of Francis, Viscount Lovell 1456–1487(?)', *The Ricardian* (1990)

6. Charles Ross, *Edward IV* (New Haven and London: Yale University Press, 1974), p. 402

7. Calendar of Patent Rolls, Edward IV, Henry VI. AD 1467–1477, p. 568

8. *Rotuli Parliamentorum VI* (London, 1777), p. 256

9. Ibid

10. Joanna M. Williams, 'The Political Career of Francis, Viscount Lovell 1456–1487(?)', p. 391

11. Ibid

12. Ibid

9 'Our entierly beloved cousin'

1. Charles Ross, *Edward IV* (New Haven and London: Yale University Press, 1974), p. 415

2. See, for example Charles Ross, *Edward IV* (New Haven and London: Yale University Press, 1974), p. 415; Paul Murray Kendall, *Richard the Third* (London: George Allan & Unwin, 1955–1956), pp. 181–185

3. Annette Carson, *Richard III: The Maligned King* (Stroud: The History Press, 2008), p. 16

4. Ibid

5. Charles Ross, *Edward IV*, pp. 415–417

6. Ibid, pp. 415–423

7. Ed. C. A. J. Armstrong, *The Usurpation of Richard III by Dominic Mancini* (Middlesbrough: A Sutton Publishing, 1984) p. 69

8. Ibid p. 71

9. Ibid

10. Ibid
11. Charles Ross, *Edward IV* (New Haven and London: Yale University Press, 1974) p. 197
12. Ibid pp. 417–418
13. John Ashdown-Hill, *Richard III's "Beloved Cousyn": John Howard and the House of York* (Stroud: The History Press, 2009), p. 112
14. Paul Murray Kendall, *Richard the Third* (London: George Allan & Unwin, 1955–1956), pp. 194–197
15. Ed. C. A. J. Armstrong, *The Usurpation of Richard III by Dominic Mancini* (Middlesbrough: A Sutton Publishing, 1984) p. 79
16. Ibid
17. Ibid
18. Charles Ross, *Edward IV*, p. 424–426
19. Ed. C. A. J. Armstrong, *The Usurpation of Richard III by Dominic Mancini*, p. 79
20. Thomas More, *The History of King Richard the Third*. pp. 13–15 http://www.thomasmorestudies.org/docs/Richard.pdf
21. Ed. C. A. J. Armstrong, *The Usurpation of Richard III by Dominic Mancini*, pp. 79–80
22. The first documents are dated to 14 May
23. Ibid, p. 83
24. Ibid
25. Annette Carson, *Richard III: The Maligned King* (Stroud: The History Press, 2008), p. 72
26. Ed. C. A. J. Armstrong, *The Usurpation of Richard III by Dominic Mancini*, p. 83
27. Ibid
28. Ibid
29. Those are the ones named by Mancini, and also later by Polydore Vergil
30. Calendar of Patent Rolls, Edward IV, Edward V, Richard III. AD 1476–1485, p. 553
31. Ibid, pp. 555, 560, 569, 579
32. Harleian Manuscripts 433 Vol 3, p. 4
33. Ibid, p. 5
34. Ibid
35. James Gairdner, *The Paston Letters, AD 1422–1509. Volume VI.* New Complete Library Edition (London: Chatto & Windus, Exeter: James G. Commin, 1904), p. 73
36. Ibid
37. Ed. Charles Lethbridge Kingsford, *The Stonor letters and papers, 1290–1483* (London: Offices of the Society, 1919), p. 400
38. Ibid
39. Joanna M. Williams, 'The Political Career of Francis, Viscount Lovell 1456–1487(?)', *The Ricardian* (1990), p. 389
40. R. Davies, *Extracts from the Municipal Records of the City of York* (London, 1843), pp. 149–150
41. Ibid
42. This letter is quoted in Paul Murray Kendall, *Richard the Third* (London: George Allan & Unwin, 1955–1956), p. 246
43. Ed. C. A. J. Armstrong, *The Usurpation of Richard III by Dominic Mancini*, p. 91

44. Thomas More, *The History of King Richard the Third*, pp. 18–22 http://www.thomasmorestudies.org/docs/Richard.pdf

45. John Ashdown-Hill, *Richard III's "Beloved Cousyn"*, pp. 128–133

46. Ed. C. A. J. Armstrong, *The Usurpation of Richard III by Dominic Mancini*, p. 91

47. See for example, Charles Ross, *Richard III* (York: Eyre Methuen Ltd, 1981), pp. 81–84

48. See for example, Paul Murray Kendall, *Richard the Third*, pp. 247–251

49. Ed. C. A. J. Armstrong, *The Usurpation of Richard III by Dominic Mancini*, p. 91

50. Annette Carson, *Richard Duke of Gloucester as Lord Protector and High Constable* (Horstead: Imprimis Imprimatur, 2015), position 1417–1552

51. Matthew Lewis, *Richard III: Loyalty Binds Me* (Stroud: Amberley Publishing, 2018), position 5747

52. H. T. Riley, *Ingulph's Chronicle of the Abbey of Croyland* (London: George Bell and Sons, 1908), p. 485–488

53. Ed. C. A. J. Armstrong, *The Usurpation of Richard III by Dominic Mancini*, pp. 92/3

54. Ibid, p. 95

55. Thomas More, *The History of King Richard the Third*, pp. 51–53 http://www.thomasmorestudies.org/docs/Richard.pdf

56. Ibid, pp. 59 http://www.thomasmorestudies.org/docs/Richard.pdf

57. See chapter 10

58. As above.

10 *The King's Kinsman and Chamberlain*

1. Charles Ross, *Richard III* (York: Eyre Methuen Ltd, 1981), pp. 49–50

2. Rosemary Horrox, 'Lovell, Francis, Viscount Lovell (b. c.1457, d. in or after 1488)', *Oxford Dictionary of National Biography* (Oxford University Press, 2004)

3. L. G. Wickham Legg, *English Coronation Records* (Edinburgh: Archibald Constable & Co, 1901), p. 196

4. Peter W. Hammond, Anne F. Sutton, *The Coronation of Richard III: The Extant Documents* (Middlesbrough: A. Sutton Publishing, 1984) p. 41, 96, 218, 249, 277

5. Ibid

6. Ibid

7. Ibid

8. Joanna M. Williams, 'The Political Career of Francis, Viscount Lovell 1456–1487(?)', *The Ricardian* (1990) p. 399

9. Peter W. Hammond, Anne F Sutton, *The Coronation of Richard III*, pp. 41, 96, 218, 249, 277

10. Joanna M. Williams, 'The Political Career of Francis, Viscount Lovell 1456–1487(?), p. 389

11. L. G. Wickham Legg, *English Coronation*, p. 197

12. See, for example, Paul Murray Kendall, *Richard the Third* (London: George Allan & Unwin, 1955–1956), p. 275

13. John Ashdown-Hill, *Richard III's "Beloved Cousyn": John Howard and the House of York* (Stroud: The History Press, 2009), pp. 135–143

14. Ibid
15. John Rous, *Joannis Rossi antiquarii Warwicensis Historia regum Angliae*, p. 217
16. This letter is quoted in Charles Ross, *Richard III* (York: Eyre Methuen Ltd, 1981), p. 151
17. David Baldwin, *Stoke Field: The Last Battle of the Wars of the Roses* (Barnsley, Pen & Sword Military, 2006), chapter 3
18. Ibid
19. Ibid
20. John Ashdown-Hill, *Richard III's "Beloved Cousyn"*, p. 133
21. Ed. William Dunn Macray, MA FSA, *A register of the members of St Mary Magdalen College, Oxford, from the foundation of the college* (London: Henry Frowde, 1894), pp. 11–12, Vol. I. All translations from this source are my own.
22. Ibid
23. Ibid
24. John Ashdown-Hill, *Richard III's "Beloved Cousyn"*, p. 133
25. Ibid, pp. 133–4
26. H. T. Riley, *Ingulph's Chronicle of the Abbey of Croyland* (London: George Bell and Sons, 1908) p. 496
27. Ibid
28. Annette Carson, *Richard III: The Maligned King* (Stroud: The History Press, 2008), p. 168
29. Rosemary Horrox, 'Lovell, Francis, Viscount Lovell (b. c.1457, d. in or after 1488)', *Oxford Dictionary of National Biography* (Oxford University Press, 2004)
30. Ibid
31. Ibid
32. Calendar of Patent Rolls, Edward IV, Edward V, Richard III. AD 1476–1485. P.365
33. Ibid
34. See chapter 10
35. See chapter 1
36. J. A. F. Thomson, 'John De La Pole, Duke of Suffolk', *Speculum* (1979)
37. L. C. Attreed, *The York House Books, Volume I* (Middlesbrough: A. Sutton Publishing, 1991), p. 80
38. Ed. Eric E. Barker, *The Register of Thomas Rotterham, Archbishop of York, 1480–1500* (York: Canterbury and York Society, 1976), pp. 42, 113
39. Calendar of Patent Rolls, Edward IV, Edward V, Richard III. AD 1476–1485, p. 386
40. Peter Hammond, *The Children of Richard III* (Stroud: Fonthill Media, 2018), p. 22
41. Joanna M. Williams, 'The Political Career of Francis, Viscount Lovell 1456–1487(?)', *The Ricardian* (1990) p. 400
42. John Ashdown-Hill, *The Third Plantagenet* (Stroud: The History Press, 2014) p. 172
43. John Rous, *Joannis Rossi antiquarii Warwicensis Historia regum Angliae*, p. 217. All translations from this book are my own.

Notes

44. Ibid

45. Paul Murray Kendall, *Richard the Third*, pp. 150–161

46. L. C. Attreed, *The York House Books, Volume II* (Middlesbrough: A Sutton Publishing, 1991), p. 718

47. Ibid

48. Charles Ross, *Edward IV* (New Haven and London: Yale University Press, 1974), pp. 84–103

49. Paul Murray Kendall, *Richard the Third*, p. 282. I have not been able to locate Kendall's source for this 'reward'.

50. John Rous, *Joannis Rossi antiquarii Warwicensis Historia regum Angliae pp. 217/8*

51. L. C. Attreed, *The York House Books, Volume I*, p. 292

52. Ibid.

53. David Baldwin, *Richard III* (Stroud: Amberley Publishing, 2013), position 1865

54. For example, see Annette Carson, *Richard III*, pp. 234–260

55. The letter is quoted in Paul Murray Kendall, *Richard the Third*, p. 325

56. H. T. Riley, *Ingulph's Chronicle of the Abbey of Croyland* (London: George Bell and Sons, 1908) p. 491

57. Thomas More, *The History of King Richard the Third*, p. 76 http://www.thomasmorestudies.org/docs/Richard.pdf

58. See note 102 below

59. Ed. Charles Lethbridge Kingsford, *The Stonor letters and papers, 1290–1483* (London: Offices of the Society, 1919) p. 467

60. James Gairdner, *The Paston Letters, AD 1422–1509. Volume VI.* New Complete Library Edition. (London: Chatto & Windus, Exeter: James G. Commin, 1904) p. 73

61. Joanna M. Williams, 'The Political Career of Francis, Viscount Lovell 1456–1487(?)', p. 400

62. Calendar of Patent Rolls, Edward IV, Edward V, Richard III. AD 1476–1485 p. 382

63. John Ashdown-Hill, *Richard III's "Beloved Cousyn*, p. 149

64. H. T. Riley, *Ingulph's Chronicle*, pp. 490–493

65. Ibid

66. See, for example, Paul Murray Kendall, *Richard the Third*, pp. 326–330 and Matthew Lewis, *Richard III: Loyalty Binds Me*, positions 6753–7154

67. Calendar of Patent Rolls, Edward IV, Edward V, Richard III. AD 1476–1485 p. 371

68. *Rotuli Parliamentorum, ut et petitiones, et placita in Parliamento, Ab Anno Duodecimo R. Edwardi IV. ad Finem eiusdem Regni Volume VI* (London, 1777) pp. 245/6

69. Ibid

70. Matthew Lewis, *Richard III*, position 7206

71. For example, Rosemary Horrox, *Richard III: A Study of Service.* (Cambridge: Cambridge University Press, 1989), pp. 28–88

72. Annette Carson, *Richard III*, p. 258–260

73. Calendar of close Rolls, Edward IV, Edward V, Richard III. AD 1477–1485 pp. 413/4

74. Ibid

75. Rosemary Horrox, *Richard III*, pp. 28–88
76. Joanna M. Williams, 'The Political Career of Francis, Viscount Lovell 1456–1487(?)', p. 390
77. Paul Murray Kendall, *Richard the Third*, p. 334
78. Ibid
79. Harleian Manuscripts 433, Vol 2, p. 53
80. David Baldwin, *Stoke Field: The Last Battle of the Wars of the Roses*, chapter 3
81. H. T. Riley, *Ingulph's Chronicle*, p. 498
82. Joanna M. Williams, 'The Political Career of Francis, Viscount Lovell 1456–1487(?)', p. 400
83. Anne F. Sutton, Livia Visser-Fuchs, *Richard III 1452–1485: His Book of Hours.* (Leicester Cathedral, 2016) p. 12, http://leicestercathedral.org/wp-content/uploads/2018/01/RIII_V3.pdf
84. Ibid
85. Ibid pp. 221/2
86. Monika E. Simon, *The Lovells of Titchmarsh: An English Baronial Family, 1297–148?* (York: Department of History, University of York, 1999), p. 211
87. Ibid
88. James Gairdner, *History of the Life and Reign of Richard the Third, to which is added the story of Perkin Warbeck: from original documents* (Cambridge: Cambridge University Press, 1898) pp. 161/2
89. Audrey Williamson, *The Mystery of the Princes.* (Gloucester: Alan Sutton Publishing Limited, 1978), pp. 109–113
90. Ibid, p. 112
91. Matthew Lewis, *Richard III*, positions 7168–7608
92. Ibid
93. Ibid
94. Charles Ross, *Edward IV*, p. 291
95. Rosemary Horrox, 'Lovell, Francis, Viscount Lovell (b. c.1457, d. in or after 1488)'
96. *Rotuli Parliamentorum VI*, p. 256
97. G. V. Belenger, 'Francis Viscount Lovel or The Life of a "Dog" in the Fifteenth Century' (Bachelor Thesis from Keele University, 1980), p. 26
98. Ibid
99. Ibid
100. Calendar of Patent Rolls, Edward IV, Edward V, Richard III. AD 1476–1485 p. 386
101. Ibid
102. For example, it is stated to have been so in Charles Ross, *Richard III*, p. 101
103. Annette Carson, *Richard III*, p. 276–279
104. Ibid pp. 70, 277
105. For example, see Charles Ross, *Richard III*, p. 101
106. Annette Carson, *Richard III*, p. 273
107. Harleian Manuscripts 433, vol 3
108. Document from the National Archives, E_40_4790_001
109. Ibid
110. Ibid

111. H. T. Riley, *Ingulph's Chronicle*, pp. 496–7
112. Paul Murray Kendall, *Richard the Third*, pp. 349–350
113. Annette Carson, *Remembering Edward of Middleham*, http://www.annettecarson.co.uk/357052365/4685305/posting/remembering-edward-of-middleham
114. John Rous, *Joannis Rossi antiquarii Warwicensis Historia regum Angliae*, pp. 217–8
115. Annette Carson, *The Death of Edward of Middleham, Prince of Wales*, http://www.annettecarson.co.uk/357052362
116. Ed. Piotr Radzikowsk, *Reisebeschreibung Niclas von Popplau, Ritters, bürtig von Breslau* (Kraków, 1998), pp. 44–61. All translations are my own.
117. Ibid
118. Ibid
119. Ibid
120. Peter Hammond, *The Children of Richard III* (Stroud: Fonthill Media, 2018), p. 50
121. Paul Murray Kendall, *Richard the Third*, pp. 386–7
122. Ibid
123. Charles Ross, *Richard III*, p. xlvii
124. H. T. Riley, *Ingulph's Chronicle*, p. 500
125. Peter Hammond, *The Children of Richard III*, pp. 24–5
126. Ibid p. 24
127. Ibid p. 46
128. Calendar of Patent Rolls, Edward IV, Edward V, Richard III. AD 1476–1485, p. 478
129. Ibid
130. H. T. Riley, *Ingulph's Chronicle*, pp. 497–8
131. Paul Murray Kendall, *Richard the Third*, pp. 360/1
132. Ibid, p. 361
133. Calendar of Patent Rolls, Edward IV, Edward V, Richard III. AD 1476–1485. p. 518
134. Matthew Lewis, *Richard III*, Position 7137
135. Paul Murray Kendall, *Richard the Third*, pp. 362–3
136. Ibid, p. 366
137. H. T. Riley, *Ingulph's Chronicle*, pp. 498–9; Polydore Vergil, *Anglica Historica* (1534); Raphael Holinshed, *Chronicles of England, Scotland and Ireland* (1577)
138. H. T. Riley, *Ingulph's Chronicle*, pp. 498–99
139. Polydore Vergil, *Anglica Historica* (1534), http://www.philological.bham.ac.uk/polverg/26eng.html
140. H. T. Riley, *Ingulph's Chronicle*, pp. 498–9
141. Matthew Lewis, *Richard III*, positions 7929–7942
142. Annette Carson, *Richard III*, pp. 298–303
143. H. T. Riley, *Ingulph's Chronicle*, p. 499
144. Ibid
145. Paul Murray Kendall, *Richard the Third*, pp. 150–161
146. Ibid
147. Annette Carson, *Richard III*, pp. 289–303

148. Calendar of Patent Rolls, Edward IV, Edward V, Richard III. AD 1476–1485, p. 505

149. H. T. Riley, *Ingulph's Chronicle*, pp. 498/9

150. Ibid, p. 498

151. Calendar of Patent Rolls, Edward IV, Edward V, Richard III. AD 1476–1485, p. 505

152. Edward Norris appears to have had more Lancastrian leanings, while his wife was clearly favoured by Richard

153. Calendar of Patent Rolls, Edward IV, Edward V, Richard III. AD 1476–1485, p. 506

154. Ibid

155. Monika E. Simon, *The Lovells of Titchmarsh*, p. 89

156. H. T. Riley, *Ingulph's Chronicle*, pp. 497–499

157. Ibid

158. Ed. Jean Alexandre C. Bouchon, *Chroniques de Jean Molinet, vol 3* (Paris: Verdière, 1828) pp. 151–154. All translations from this text are my own.

159. John Ashdown-Hill, *The Mythology of Richard III* (Stroud: Amberley Publishing, 2015), position 1975

160. H. T. Riley, *Ingulph's Chronicle*, p. 499

161. Ibid

162. Alison Weir, *Richard III and the Princes in the Tower* (London: Random House, 1992), pp. 202–213

163. See, for example: Caroline Halsted, *Richard III as Duke of Gloucester and King of England, Volume I* (London: Longman, Brown, Green and Longman, 1844), pp. 413–414

164. H. T. Riley, *Ingulph's Chronicle*, p. 499

165. *Acts of the Court of the Mercers' Company* (Cambridge: Cambridge University Press, 1936), pp. 155–156

166. Ibid

167. H. T. Riley, *Ingulph's Chronicle*, p. 500

168. John Ashdown-Hill, *The Mythology of Richard III* (Stroud: Amberley Publishing, 2015), position 1975

169. Ibid

170. David Baldwin, *Stoke Field: The Last Battle of the Wars of the Roses* (Barnsley, Pen & Sword Military, 2006), chapter 3

171. Ibid

172. Ibid

173. Ibid

174. Paul Murray Kendall, *Richard the Third*, pp. 386–7

175. Document from the National Archives, E40_4790_001. The translation is my own.

176. Document from the National Archives, E211_281

177. The appointment is found in the Calendar of Patent Rolls, Edward IV, Edward V, Richard III. AD 1476–1485, p. 375

178. H. T. Riley, *Ingulph's Chronicle*, pp. 500–1

179. Ibid

180. Thomas Penn, *Winter King: Henry VII and the Dawn of Tudor England* (London: Penguin Books Ltd, 2011), p. 1

181. Matthew Lewis, *Richard III*, Positions 8156–8169

182. Ibid
183. Ibid
184. Polydore Vergil, *Anglica Historica* (1534), http://www.philological.bham.ac.uk/polverg/26eng.html
185. Matthew Lewis, *The Survival of the Princes in the Tower. Murder, Mystery and Myth* (Stroud: The History Press, 2017), pp. 68–81
186. E.g. Polydore Vergil, *Anglica Historica* (1534)
187. *Rotuli Parliamentorum VI*, pp. 275–278

11 '... convicted and attainted of high treason'

1. Thomas Penn, *Winter King: Henry VII and the Dawn of Tudor England* (London: Penguin Books Ltd, 2011), p. 95
2. Ibid
3. Terry Breverton, *Henry VII: The Maligned Tudor King* (Stroud: Amberley Publishing, 2016), chapter 5
4. Edward Hall, *The Union Of The Two Noble And Illustre Famelies Lancastre & Yorke Beeyng Long In Continual Discension For The Croune Of This Noble Realme With All The Actes Done In Bothe The Tymes Of The Princes, Bothe Of The One Linage And Of The Other, Beginnyng At The Tyme Of Kyng Henry The Fowerth, The First Aucthor Of This Deuision, And So Successiuely Proceadyng To The Reigne Of The High And Prudent Prince Kyng Henry The Eight, the Undubitate Flower And Very Heire Of Both The Sayd Linages* (1548), p. 421
5. H. T. Riley, *Ingulph's Chronicle of the Abbey of Croyland* (London: George Bell and Sons, 1908), p. 492
6. John Ashdown-Hill, *The Dublin King* (Stroud: The History Press, 2015), position 2219
7. The will is quoted in its entirety in Daniel Williams, 'The Hastily Drawn-Up Will of William Catesby, Esquire, 25 August 1485', *Leicestershire Archaeological and Historical Society Transactions* (1975/6), https://www.le.ac.uk/lahs/downloads/1975-76/1975-76%20(51)%2040-55%20Notes.pdf
8. Ibid
9. Ibid
10. Matthew Lewis, *Richard III: Loyalty Binds Me* (Stroud: Amberley Publishing, 2018), position 5804
11. See William Lovell's will in Appendix 2
12. Calendar of Patent Rolls, Edward IV, Edward V, Richard III, AD 1476–1485, p. 510
13. Ibid
14. Matthew Lewis, *The Survival of the Princes in the Tower. Murder, Mystery and Myth* (Stroud: The History Press, 2017), p. 74
15. Ibid, p. 76
16. David Baldwin, *The Lost Prince: The Survival of Richard of York* (Stroud: The History Press, 2016), pp. 87–101
17. Ashdown-Hill, *The Dublin King* (Stroud: The History Press, 2015), position 2340
18. Ibid, position 2355
19. Ibid

20. E.g. Annette Carson, *Richard III: The Maligned King* (Stroud: The History Press, 2008), p. 325

21. Audrey Williamson, *The Mystery of the Princes* (Gloucester: Alan Sutton Publishing Limited, 1978), p. 158

22. Ibid

23. Ibid

24. Ibid

25. For the dangers of a rising by the FitzHugh family, see chapter 4

26. See chapter 11

27. L. G. Wickham Legg, *English Coronation Records* (Edinburgh: Archibald Constable & Co, 1901)

28. Ibid

29. Hannes Kleineke, 'Richard III and the Origins of the Court of Requests', *The Ricardian* (2007)

30. *Rotuli Parliamentorum, ut et petitiones, et placita in Parliamento, Ab Anno Duodecimo R. Edwardi IV. ad Finem eiusdem Regni Volume VI* (London, 1777), pp. 275–278

31. Calendar of Patent Rolls, Henry VII, Vol I AD 1485–1494, p. 119

32. Ibid

33. John Ashdown-Hill, The Dublin King, positions 1803–2005

34. See further down in this chapter

35. Calendar of Patent Rolls, Henry VII, Vol I. AD 1485–1494, pp. 39–40

36. *The Manuscripts of His Grace the Duke of Rutland K.G, preserved at Belvoir Castle* (London: Mackie & Co. Ltd, 1905), vol I, p. 8

37. See further in this chapter

38. See further in this chapter

39. L. C. Attreed, *The York House Books, Volume I* (Middlesbrough: A Sutton Publishing, 1991), p. 395

40. W. Gurney Benham, *The Red Paper Book of Colchester* (Colchester, Essex County Stand, 1907), p. 158

41. Audrey Williamson, *The Mystery of the Princes* (Gloucester: Alan Sutton Publishing Limited, 1978), p. 144

42. Ibid

43. See above in this chapter

44. Ed. Thomas Stapleton, Esq., FSA *Plumpton Correspondence. A Series of Letters, Chiefly Domestick, written in the reigns of Edward IV, Richard III, Henry VII and Henry VIII* (London: John Bowyer and Son, 1839), pp. 49–50

45. Ibid

46. Calendar of Patent Rolls, Henry VII, Vol I. AD 1485–1494, p. 64

47. H. T. Riley, *Ingulph's Chronicle*, p. 512

48. C. H. Williams, 'The Rebellion of Humphrey Stafford 1486', *The English Historical Review* (1928), p. 183

49. Ibid, p. 185

50. Ibid

51. Ibid, p. 183

52. H. T. Riley, *Ingulph's Chronicle*, pp. 522–523

53. See for example: Charles Ross, *Richard III* (York: Eyre Methuen Ltd, 1981) p. 112 or Annette Carson, *Richard III: The Maligned King* (Stroud: The History Press, 2008), pp. 253–255

54. Ed. James Gairdner, *Letters and Papers Illustrative of the Reigns of Richard III and Henry VII Volume I* (London: Green, Longman, Roberts, and Green, 1863), pp. 234/5

55. See above

56. H. T. Riley, *Ingulph's Chronicle*, p. 513

57. Charles Ross, *Edward IV* (New Haven and London: Yale University Press, 1974), pp. 118, 151

58. Matthew Lewis, *Richard, Duke of York: King by Right* (Stroud: Amberley Publishing, 2016), positions 2737–2906

59. Ed. James Gairdner, *Letters and Papers Illustrative of the Reigns of Richard III and Henry VII Volume I*, p. 198

60. C. H. Williams, 'The Rebellion of Humphrey Stafford 1486', *The English Historical Review* (1928), p. 181

61. Polydore Vergil, *Anglica Historica* (1534), http://www.philological.bham.ac.uk/polverg/26eng.html

62. Calendar of Patent Rolls, Henry VII, Vol. I AD 1485–1494, pp. 86/7

63. H. T. Riley, *Ingulph's Chronicle*, p. 513

64. Polydore Vergil, *Anglica Historica*

65. C. H. Williams, 'The Rebellion of Humphrey Stafford 1486', p. 188

66. Polydore Vergil *Anglica Historica*

67. Ibid

68. Ibid

69. Ibid

70. Ibid

71. C. H. Williams, 'The Rebellion of Humphrey Stafford 1486', p. 186

72. Several of the lands which had belonged to their father were distributed among men loyal to Henry VII.

73. L. C. Attreed, *The York House Books, Volume II* (Middlesbrough: A Sutton Publishing, 1991), p. 542

74. Ibid

75. Joanna M. Williams, 'The Political Career of Francis, Viscount Lovell 1456–1487(?)', p. 394

76. Ibid

77. H. T. Riley, *Ingulph's Chronicle*, pp. 513/4

78. Ibid

79. Polydore Vergil, *Anglica Historica*

80. British Library Manuscript Cotton *Julius BXII, f. 9r*

81. Polydore Vergil, *Anglica Historica*

82. L. C. Attreed, *The York House Books, Volume II*, pp. 484–484

83. H. T. Riley, *Ingulph's Chronicle*, pp. 513/4

84. Polydore Vergil, *Anglica Historica*

85. Ibid

86. L. C. Attreed, *The York House Books, Volume I*, p. 552

87. Ibid

88. Ibid

89. Thomas Penn, *Winter King*, p. 23

90. H. T. Riley, *Ingulph's Chronicle*, p. 514

91. Ibid

92. C. H. Williams, 'The Rebellion of Humphrey Stafford 1486'

93. Thomas Penn, *Winter King*, p. 23

94. C. H. Williams, 'The Rebellion of Humphrey Stafford 1486', p. 186
95. Document from the National Archives, KB9/138
96. C. H. Williams 'The Rebellion of Humphrey Stafford 1486', p. 186
97. They may have hoped for support there, since the abbey had ties to Francis, see chapter 10
98. C. H. Williams 'The Rebellion of Humphrey Stafford 1486', p. 187
99. Ibid
100. Ibid, p. 189
101. Ibid
102. Ibid
103. E.g. Charles Ross, *Richard III*, p. 87, addressing such accusations
104. Polydore Vergil, *Anglica Historica*
105. Ibid
106. James Gairdner, *The Paston Letters, AD 1422–1509. Vol VI*, pp. 92–3
107. Ibid
108. John Ashdown-Hill, *The Dublin King*, Positions 2284
109. See further down in this chapter
110. British Library Julius BXII, f. 17r
111. Polydore Vergil, *Anglica Historica*
112. Ibid
113. Ibid
114. Ibid
115. They were later noted to be involved in the Simnel rebellion, see further down in this chapter
116. James Gairdner, *The Paston Letters, AD 1422–1509. Vol VI*, p. 95
117. Thomas Penn, *Winter King*, pp. 21–28
118. Ibid, p. 60
119. They were in Burgundy by February 1487
120. See further down in this chapter
121. Polydore Vergil, *Anglica Historica*
122. Ibid
123. Ibid
124. Ibid
125. Ibid
126. David Baldwin, *Elizabeth Woodville: Mother of the Princes in the Tower* (Stroud: Sutton Publishing Limited, 2002), p. 121
127. Ibid
128. Terry Breverton, *Henry VII*, chapter 6
129. David Baldwin, *Elizabeth Woodville*, p. 121
130. Elizabeth Woodville's will, in which she complains about having nothing but her blessing to pass on to her children, is mentioned in David Baldwin, *Elizabeth Woodville*, p. 132–3
131. Polydore Vergil, *Anglica Historica*
132. Thomas Penn, *Winter King*, p. 54
133. David Baldwin, *Elizabeth Woodville*, pp. 132–3
134. Thomas Penn, *Winter King*, p. 24
135. See above in this chapter
136. E.g. Matthew Lewis, *The Survival of the Princes in the Tower*, pp. 99–100
137. W. Gurney Benham, *The Red Paper Book of Colchester*, p. 158

138. Ed. James Gairdner, *Memorials of King Henry VII* (London: Camden Society, 1858), pp. 49–52

139. Ibid

140. See above in this chapter

141. This is detailed in Christine Weightman: *Margaret of York: Diabolical Duchess* (Stroud: Amberley Publishing, 2012, first published 1989)

142. Ibid

143. Ibid

144. Ibid

145. Audrey Williamson, *The Mystery of the Princes* (Gloucester: Alan Sutton Publishing Limited, 1978), p. 162

146. See Polydore Vergil *Anglica Historica*; Jean Alexandre C. Bouchon, *Chroniques de Jean Molinet, vol 3* (Paris: Verdière, 1828); and Ed. Andrew R. Scoble, Esq., *The Memoirs of Philippe de Commines, Lord of Argenton, containing the histories of Louis XI and Charles VIII Kings of France and of Charles the Bold, Duke of Burgundy. To which is added the scandalous chronicle, or secret history of Louis XI, by Jean de Troyes* (London: George Bell and Sons, 1877)

147. See Charles Ross, *Edward IV*, p. 203

148. Matthew Lewis, *The Survival of the Princes in the Tower*, pp. 82–83

149. Ibid

150. Alexandre C. Bouchon, *Chroniques de Jean Molinet, vol 3*, pp. 151–154

151. Ibid

152. Ibid

153. Polydore Vergil, *Anglica Historica*

154. See Jean Alexandre C. Bouchon, *Chroniques de Jean Molinet, vol 3* and Ed. Andrew R. Scoble, Esq, *The Memoirs of Philippe de Commines*

155. Jean Alexandre C. Bouchon, *Chroniques de Jean Molinet, vol 3*, pp. 151–154

156. Ibid

157. Matthew Lewis, *Richard, Duke of York: King by Right* (Stroud: Amberley Publishing, 2016), positions 2299–2324

158. Jean Alexandre C. Bouchon, *Chroniques de Jean Molinet, vol 3*

159. Ibid

160. Ibid

161. Ibid

162. Gordon Smith, 'Lambert Simnel and the King from Dublin', *The Ricardian* (1996)

163. Ibid p. 11

164. Ed. James Gairdner, *Memorials of King Henry VII*, p. 52

165. E.g. John Ashdown-Hill, *The Dublin King*, positions 2298–2310

166. Matthew Lewis, *The Survival of the Princes in the Tower*, p. 81

167. E.g. John Ashdown-Hill, *The Dublin King*, positions 2992–3095

168. See Trans. and intro. Daniel Hobbins, *The life of Henry VII/Bernard Andrés* (New York: Italica Press, 2011); Polydore Vergil, *Anglica Historica*; Jean Alexandre C. Bouchon, *Chroniques de Jean Molinet, vol 3*; and Ed. Andrew R. Scoble, Esq, *The Memoirs of Philippe de Commines*

169. John Ashdown-Hill, *The Dublin King*, positions 2779–2793

170. Polydore Vergil, *Anglica Historica*

171. Alexandre C. Bouchon, *Chroniques de Jean Molinet, vol 3*, pp. 151–154

172. Ibid
173. Ibid
174. James Gairdner, *The Paston Letters, AD 1422–1509. Vol VI*, pp. 99–100
175. Charles Ross, *Richard III*, p. 56
176. Being her second cousin
177. John Ashdown-Hill, *The Dublin King*, Position 3248. However, Ashdown-Hill states that the rebels were greeted by Thomas Broughton and his family, which is certainly incorrect, given that Broughton was identified as having joined Francis's flight to Burgundy.
178. Ibid
179. Ed. Angelo Raine, *York Civic Records* (York: Wakefield Society, 1939), p. 22
180. Ibid
181. Ibid
182. Ibid
183. Ibid
184. Ibid, p. 23
185. Ibid
186. Ibid
187. Ibid
188. Polydore Vergil, *Anglica Historica*
189. Thomas Penn, *Winter King*, p. 23
190. Ibid
191. John Ashdown-Hill, *The Dublin King*, positions 3235–3422
192. Polydore Vergil, *Anglica Historica*
193. John Ashdown-Hill, *The Dublin King* (Stroud: The History Press, 2015), positions 3235–3422
194. Thomas Penn, *Winter King*, p. 23
195. Ibid
196. Ed. Angelo Raine, *York Civic Records*, pp. 23–4
197. Ed. James Gairdner, *Memorials of King Henry VII*, p. 52
198. John Ashdown-Hill, *The Dublin King*, positions 3484–3617
199. Ibid

12 'Discomfited and fled'

1. Polydore Vergil, *Anglica Historica* (1534), http://www.philological.bham.ac.uk/polverg/26eng.html
2. James Gairdner, *The Paston Letters, AD 1422–1509. New Complete Library Edition. Vol VI* (London: Chatto & Windus, Exeter: James G. Commin, 1904), pp. 91–92
3. See Raphael Holinshed, *Chronicles of England, Scotland and Ireland* (1577) and Edward Hall, *The Union Of The Two Noble And Illustre Famelies Lancastre & Yorke Beeyng Long In Continual Discension For The Croune Of This Noble Realme With All The Actes Done In Bothe The Tymes Of The Princes, Bothe Of The One Linage And Of The Other, Beginnyng At The Tyme Of Kyng Henry The Fowerth, The First Aucthor Of This Deuision, And So Successiuely Proceadyng To The Reigne Of The High And Prudent Prince Kyng Henry The Eight, the Undubitate Flower And Very Heire Of Both The Sayd Linages* (1548)

Notes

4. Ed. Rev. J. Rawson Lumby, D.D., *Bacon's History of the Reign of Henry VII* (Cambridge: Cambridge University Press, 1885), p. 37

5. Anthony Emery, *Greater Medieval Houses of England and Wales, 1300–1500: Volume 3, Southern England* (Cambridge: Cambridge University Press, 2006), pp. 117–119

6. https://murreyandblue.wordpress.com/2017/07/16/is-francis-lovell-lying-at-rest-in-gedling-church/

7. Ibid

8. Ed. James Balfour Paul, *The Register of the Great Seal of Scotland. AD 1424–1513* (Edinburgh: HM General Register House, 1882), p. 370

9. Christine Weightman, *Margaret of York: Diabolical Duchess* (Stroud: Amberley Publishing, 2012, first published 1989), chapter 6

10. David Baldwin, 'What Happened to Lord Lovel?', *The Ricardian* (1985)

11. Ed. James Balfour Paul, *The Register of the Great Seal of Scotland*, p. 370

12. Ed. Angelo Raine, *York Civic Records Vol. II* (York: Wakefield Society, 1939), p. 87

13. James Gairdner, *The Paston Letters*, pp. 91/01

14. Ibid, p. 91

15. Ibid

16. See the treatment of her grandmother Alice, Countess of Salisbury, for committing treason, for example in Matthew Lewis, *Richard III: Loyalty Binds Me* (Stroud: Amberley Publishing, 2018), position 764

17. James Gairdner, *The Paston Letters*, p. 91

18. Calendar of Patent Rolls, Henry VII, Vol I AD 1485–1494, p. 304

19. Ibid

20. The younger son, George, apparently named one of his many children after her, as well as after his aunt Frideswide and after Francis

21. Inquisitions Post Mortem on William Beaumont, partly quoted in John Mason Neale, *Illustrations of Monumental Brasses No V* (Cambridge: T. Stevenson, 1842), p. 181

Appendix 1: Sir William Stanley's Son

1. John Seacome, *The History of the House of Stanley* (Preston: E. Sergent, 1793)

2. Ed. G. E. C. Cokayne, *The Complete Peerage*, Vol XII (London, Cokayne, 1932), p. 846

3. Barbara Coulton, 'The Wives of Sir William Stanley', *The Ricardian* (1992)

4. J. M. Gidman, 'The Wives and Children of Sir William Stanley of Holt', *The Ricardian* (1992)

5. Joanna M. Williams, 'The Political Career of Francis, Viscount Lovell 1456–1487(?)', *The Ricardian* (1990), p. 384

6. John Seacome, *The History of the House of Stanley*

7. Ibid

8. Inquisition Post Mortem on Elizabeth Hopton, National Archives, E150/832/8

Appendix 2: Full Text of Original Letters and Wills

1. Lincoln Diocese Documents, https://quod.lib.umich.edu/c/cme/LinDDoc/1:1.8?rgn=div2;view=fulltext

Bibliography

Primary Sources

Acts of the Court of the Mercers' Company (Cambridge: Cambridge University Press, 1936)

Annales Monastrii S Albanes, Volume I

Ed. C. A. J. Armstrong, *The Usurpation of Richard III by Dominic Mancini* (Middlesbrough: A. Sutton Publishing, 1984)

L. C. Attreed, *The York House Books, Volume I* (Midddlesbrough: A Sutton Publishing, 1991)

Ed. Eric E. Barker, *The Register of Thomas Rotterham, Archbishop of York, 1480–1500* (York: Canterbury and York Society, 1976)

W. Gurney Benham, *The Red Paper Book of Colchester* (Colchester, Essex County Stand, 1907)

Ed. Jean Alexandre C. Bouchon, *Chroniques de Jean Molinet, vol 3* (Paris: Verdière, 1828)

Ed. Paul Brand, Anne Curry, Chris Given-Wilson, Rosemary Horrox, Geoffrey Martin, Mark Ormrod, *Henry VI: November 1459*, in *Parliament Rolls of Medieval England* (Woodbridge, Boydell, 2005)

(https://www.british-history.ac.uk/no-series/parliament-rolls-medieval/november-1459) Last accessed 13/10/2018, 14:24)

British Library Manuscript Cotton *Julius BXII, f. 9r*

British Library *Julius BXII*, f. 17r

Ed. John Bruce, *Historie of the Arrivall of Edward IV in England and the Finall Recouerye of his Kingdomes from Henry VI AD M.CCCC.LXXI (*London: John Bower Nichols and Son, 1838)

Calendar of Close Rolls, Edward IV, AD 1461–1468

Calendar of Close Rolls, Edward IV, Edward V, Richard III 1476–1485

Calendar of Fine Rolls, Henry VI, AD 1452–1461

Calendar of Patent Rolls, Henry VI, Volume III, AD 1436–1441

Calendar of Patent Rolls, Henry VI, Volume V, AD 1441–1446

Calendar of Patent Rolls, Henry VI, Volume V, AD 1446–1452

Calendar of Patent Rolls, Henry VI, Volume VI, AD 1452–1461

Calendar of Patent Rolls, Edward IV, AD 1461–1467

Calendar of Patent Rolls, Edward IV, Henry VI. AD 1467–1477

Calendar of Patent Rolls, Edward IV, Edward V, Richard III. AD 1476–1485

Calendar of Patent Rolls, Henry VII, Vol I. AD 1485–1494

Ed. G. E. C. Cokayne, *The Complete Peerage* (London, Cokayne, 1932)

Ed. John Silvester Davies, *An English chronicle of the reigns of Richard II, Henry IV, Henry V, and Henry VI written before the year 1471; with an appendix, containing the 18th and 19th years of Richard II and the Parliament at Bury St. Edmund's, 25th Henry VI and supplementary additions from the Cotton. ms. chronicle called "Eulogium* (London: Camden Society, 1856)

R. Davies, *Extracts from the Municipal Records of the City of York* (London, 1843)

F. Devon, *Issues of the Exchequer* (London: John Murray, 1837)

Document from the National Archives, C1/48/436

Document from the National Archives, C1/66//341

Document from the National Archives, E_40_4790_001

Document from the National Archives, E211_281

Document from the National Archives, KB9/138

Ed. James Gairdner, *Memorials of King Henry VII* (London: Camden Society, 1858)

Ed. James Gairdner, *Letters and Papers Illustrative of the Reigns of Richard III and Henry VII Volume I* (London: Longman, Green, Longman, Roberts, and Green, 1863)

Ed. James Gairdner, *Testamenta Eboracensia, A Selection of Wills from the Registry at York, Volume 3* (London: Whittaker and Co., 1865)

James Gairdner, *The Paston Letters, AD 1422–1509. Volume III.* New Complete Library Edition (London: Chatto & Windus, Exeter: James G. Commin, 1904)

James Gairdner, *The Paston Letters, AD 1422–1509. Volume IV.* New Complete Library Edition (London: Chatto & Windus, Exeter: James G. Commin, 1904)

James Gairdner, *The Paston Letters, AD 1422–1509. Volume VI.* New Complete Library Edition (London: Chatto & Windus, Exeter: James G. Commin, 1904)

Edward Hall, *The Union Of The Two Noble And Illustre Famelies Lancastre & Yorke Beeyng Long In Continual Discension For The Croune Of This Noble Realme With All The Actes Done In Bothe The Tymes Of The Princes, Bothe Of The One Linage And Of The Other, Beginnyng At The Tyme Of Kyng Henry The Fowerth, The First Aucthor Of This Deuision, And So Successiuely Proceadyng To The Reigne Of The High And Prudent Prince Kyng Henry The Eight, the Undubitate Flower And Very Heire Of Both The Sayd Linages* (1548)

Harleian Manuscripts 433 Vol. 2

Harleian Manuscripts 433 Vol. 3

Trans. and intro. Daniel Hobbins, *The life of Henry VII/Bernard Andrés* (New York: Italica Press, 2011)

Raphael Holinshed, *Chronicles of England, Scotland and Ireland* (1577)

Illustrations of Monumental Brasses No V (Cambridge: T Stevenson, 1842)

Inquisitions Post Mortem on Alice Deincourt, National Archives, C140/47/64

Inquisition Post Mortem on Elizabeth Hopton, National Archives, E150/832/8

Inquisition Post Mortem on Joan Lovell, National Archive, C140_40_7_001, C140_40_7_002, C140_40_7_003, C140_40_7_004, C140_40_7_005, C140_40_7_006, C140_40_7_007, C140_40_7_008

Inquisitions Post Mortem on John Lovell, National Archives, C140/13/27

Inquisition Post Mortem on William Lovell, held by the Shakespeare Birthplace Trust. ER 101/31

Inquisitions Post Mortem on William Lovell, Lord Morley, National Archives, C140/47/64

Ed. Charles Lethbridge Kingsford, *The Stonor letters and papers, 1290–1483 Vol. III* (London: Offices of the Society, 1919)

The Last Will and Testament of John Beaumont, Viscount Beaumont. National Archives, E211_281

The Last Will and Testament of William Lovell

Lincoln Diocese Documents: https://quod.lib.umich.edu/c/cme/LinDDoc/1:1.8?rgn=div2;view=fulltext

L. G. Wickham Legg, *English Coronation Records* (Edinburgh: Archibald Constable & Co., 1901)

Ed. Rev. J. Rawson Lumby, D.D., *Bacon's History of the Reign of Henry VII* (Cambridge: Cambridge University Press, 1885)

Ed. William Dunn Macray, MA FSA, *A register of the members of St Mary Magdalen College, Oxford, from the foundation of the college*, vol. I (London: Henry Frowde, 1894)

The Manuscripts of His Grace the Duke of Rutland K.G, preserved at Belvoir Castle (London: Mackie & Co. Ld, 1905)

Thomas More, *The History of King Richard the Third*, http://www.thomasmorestudies.org/docs/Richard.pdf

Ed. James Balfour Paul, *The Register of the Great Seal of Scotland AD 1424–1513* (Edinburgh: HM General Register House, 1882)

Ed. Piotr Radzikowsk, *Reisebeschreibung Niclas von Popplau, Ritters, bürtig von Breslau* (Kraków, 1998)

Ed. Angelo Raine, York Civic Records (York: Wakefield Society, 1939)

H. T. Riley, *Ingulph's Chronicle of the Abbey of* Croyland (London: George Bell and Sons, 1908)

Rotuli Parliamentorum, ut et petitiones, et placita in Parliamento, Ab Anno Duodecimo R. Edwardi IV. ad Finem eiusdem Regni Volume VI (London, 1777)

John Rous, *Joannis Rossi antiquarii Warwicensis Historia regum Angliae*

Ed. Andrew R. Scoble, Esq., *The Memoirs of Philippe de Commines, Lord of Argenton, containing the histories of Louis XI and Charles VIII Kings of France and of Charles the Bold, Duke of Burgundy. To which is added the scandalous chronicle, or secret history of Louis XI, by Jean de Troyes* (London: George Bell and Sons, 1877)

John Seacome, *The History of the House of Stanley* (Preston: E. Sergent, 1793)

Reginald R. Sharpe, *London and the kingdom: a history derived mainly from the archives at Guildhall in the custody of the corporation of the city of London*, vol. III (London: Longmans, Green & Co., 1895)

Ed. Thomas Stapleton, Esq., FSA, *Plumpton Correspondence: A Series of Letters, Chiefly Domestick, written in the reigns of Edward IV, Richard III, Henry VII and Henry VIII* (London: John Bowyer and Son, 1839)

The Register of the Guild of Corpus Christi in the City of York; with an Appendix of Illustrative Documents, containing some account of the Hospital of St. Thomas of Canterbury, without Micklegate-Bar, in the suburbs of the city (Durham: Andrews and Co., London: T. and W. Boone, Edinburgh: Blackwood and Sons, 1872)

Polydore Vergil, *Anglica Historica* (1534) http://www.philological.bham.ac.uk/polverg/26eng.html

Secondary Sources

John Ashdown-Hill, *Richard III's "Beloved Cousyn": John Howard and the House of York* (Stroud: The History Press, 2009)

John Ashdown-Hill, *The Third Plantagenet* (Stroud: The History Press, 2014)

John Ashdown-Hill, *The Dublin King* (Stroud: The History Press, 2015)

John Ashdown-Hill, *The Mythology of Richard III* (Stroud: Amberley Publishing, 2015)

Bibliography

David Baldwin, 'What Happened to Lord Lovel?', *The Ricardian* (1985)

David Baldwin, *Elizabeth Woodville: Mother of the Princes in the Tower* (Stroud: Sutton Publishing Limited, 2002)

David Baldwin, *Stoke Field: The Last Battle of the Wars of the Roses* (Barnsley, Pen & Sword Military, 2006)

David Baldwin, *Richard III* (Stroud: Amberley Publishing, 2013)

David Baldwin, *The Lost Prince: The Survival of Richard of* York (Stroud: The History Press, 2016)

G. V. Belenger, 'Francis Viscount Lovel or The Life of a "Dog" in the Fifteenth Century' (Bachelor Thesis from Keele University, 1980)

Michael J. Bennett, 'Stanley, Sir William', *Oxford Dictionary of National Biography* (Oxford University Press, 2004)

Terry Breverton, *Henry VII, The Maligned Tudor King* (Stroud: Amberley Publishing, 2016)

Annette Carson, *Richard III, The Maligned King* (Stroud: The History Press, 2008)

Annette Carson, *Richard Duke of Gloucester as Lord Protector and High Constable* (Horstead: Imprimis Imprimatur, 2015)

Annette Carson, 'Remembering Edward of Middleham', http://www.annettecarson.co.uk/357052365/4685305/posting/remembering-edward-of-middleham

Annette Carson, 'The Death of Edward of Middleham, Prince of Wales', http://www.annettecarson.co.uk/357052362

K. L. Clark, *The Nevills of Middleham: England's Most Powerful Family in the Wars of the Roses* (Stroud: The History Press, 2016)

Barbara Coulton, 'The Wives of Sir William Stanley', *The Ricardian* (1992)

Virginia Davies, *William Wayneflete: Bishop and Educationalist* (Woodbridge: The Boydell Press, 1993)

Anthony Emery, *Greater Medieval Houses of England and Wales, 1300–1500: Volume 3, Southern England* (Cambridge: Cambridge University Press, 2006)

James Gairdner, *History of the Life and Reign of Richard the Third, to which is added the story of Perkin Warbeck: from original documents* (Cambridge: Cambridge University Press, 1898)

J. M. Gidman, 'The Wives and Children of Sir William Stanley of Holt', *The Ricardian* (1992)

Caroline Halsted, *Richard III as Duke of Gloucester and King of England, Volume I* (London: Longman, Brown, Green and Longman, 1844)

Peter W. Hammond, Anne F. Sutton, *The Coronation of Richard III: The Extant Documents* (Middlesbrough: A Sutton Publishing, 1984)

Peter W. Hammond, *The Children of Richard III* (Stroud: Fonthill Media, 2018)

Michael Hicks, 'Pole, John de la, second duke of Suffolk', *Oxford Dictionary of National Biography* (Oxford University Press, 2004)

Rosemary Horrox, *Richard III: A Study of Service* (Cambridge: Cambridge University Press, 1989)

Rosemary Horrox, 'Lovell, Francis, Viscount Lovell (b. *c.* 1457, d. in or after 1488)', *Oxford Dictionary of National Biography* (Oxford University Press, 2004)

Mike Ingram, *10 July 1460: The Battle of Northampton* (Northampton: Northampton Battlefield Society, 2015)

Paul Murray Kendall, *Richard the Third* (London: George Allan & Unwin, 1955–1956)

Hannes Kleineke, 'Richard III and the Origins of the Court of Requests', *The Ricardian* (2007)

Matthew Lewis, *Richard, Duke of York: King by Right* (Stroud: Amberley Publishing, 2016)

Matthew Lewis, *The Survival of the Princes in the Tower: Murder, Mystery and Myth* (Stroud: The History Press, 2017)

Matthew Lewis, *Richard III: Loyalty Binds Me* (Stroud: Amberley Publishing, 2018)

Wendy E. A. Moorhen, 'Such was his Renown in Warfare', *Ricardian Bulletin* (2004) http://www.richardiii.net/2_3_0_riii_leadership.php#military

John Mason Neale, *Illustrations of Monumental Brasses No V* (Cambridge: T. Stevenson, 1842)

Nicholas Orme, *Medieval Children* (New Haven and London: Yale University Press, 2001)

Thomas Penn, *Winter King: Henry VII and the Dawn of Tudor England* (London: Penguin Books Ltd, 2011)

Anthony J. Pollard, *Lord FitzHugh's Rising in 1470* (Bulletin of the Institute of Historical Research, 1979)

Charles Ross, *Edward IV* (New Haven and London: Yale University Press, 1974)

Charles Ross, *Richard III* (York: Eyre Methuen Ltd, 1981)

Cora L. Scofield, *The Life and Reign of Edward IV, King of England and France and Lord of Ireland: Volume 2* (London: Longmans, Green & Co, 1923)

Monika E. Simon, *The Lovells of Titchmarsh: An English Baronial Family, 1297 – 148?* (York: Department of History, University of York, 1999)

Monika E. Simon, 'Who is buried in the Tomb in St Kenelm's Church, Minster Lovell?', *The Ricardian* (2009)

Gordon Smith, 'Lambert Simnel and the King from Dublin', *The Ricardian* (1996)

Ed. Thomas Stapleton, *De Antiquis Legibus Liber. Cronica Maiorum et Vicecomitum Londoniarum et quedam, que contigebant temporibis illis ab anno MCLXXVIII; cum appendice* (London: Camden Society, 1846)

David Stephen, *Last Champion of York: Francis Lovell, Richard III's Truest Friend* (Marlborough: The Crowood Press, 2019)

Anne F. Sutton, Livia Visser-Fuchs, *Richard III 1452–1485: His Book of Hours* (Leicester Cathedral, 2016), p. 12, http://leicestercathedral.org/wp-content/uploads/2018/01/RIII_V3.pdf

The Thirty-Seventh Annual Report of the Deputy Keeper of the Public Records (London: George E. Eyre and William Spottiswoode, 1876)

J. A. F. Thomson, 'John De La Pole, Duke of Suffolk', *Speculum* (1979)

John Watts, 'Beaumont, John, first Viscount Beaumont', *Oxford Dictionary of National Biography* (Oxford University Press, 2004)

Christine Weightman, *Margaret of York: Diabolical Duchess* (Stroud: Amberley Publishing, 2012, first published 1989)

Alison Weir, *Richard III and the Princes in the Tower* (London: Random House, 1992)

C. H. Williams, 'The Rebellion of Humphrey Stafford 1486', *The English Historical Review* (1928)

Daniel Williams, 'The Hastily Drawn-Up Will of William Catesby, Esquire, 25 August 1485', *Leicestershire Archaeological and Historical Society Transactions* (1975/6)

Audrey Williamson, *The Mystery of the Princes* (Gloucester: Alan Sutton Publishing Limited, 1978)

Josephine Wilkinson, *The Princes in the Tower* (Stroud: Amberley Publishing, 2013)

Josephine Wilkinson, *Richard the Young King to Be* (Stroud: Amberley Publishing, 2014)

Joanna M. Williams, 'The Political Career of Francis, Viscount Lovell 1456–1487(?)', *The Ricardian* (1990), p. 383

Acknowledgements

This book has been a long time in the making, and would never have been finished without the help of many, to whom I am now indebted and owe gratitude.

First of all, my thanks go to everyone at Amberley Publishing who agreed to take me on, and most especially to my editor Shaun Barrington, who patiently answered even the most stupid questions about the publishing process I put to him.

I'm also grateful to the librarians working for the Goethe Universität in Frankfurt and the Technische Universität in Darmstadt, for helping me navigate their libraries and finding books I needed, often just for one tiny tidbit of information.

Thanks to Alice, Carla, Marie and Zuzanna, who were supportive from the first, encouraged me even to attempt writing this book and have cheered me every step of the way. I owe you all!

Robin Kaye's help has been wonderful, as he was always happy to help and to listen, didn't complain when I sent him questions at the strangest times, and offered advice in a humorous way.

I'd also like to thank Nathen Amin, who, despite our frequently differing opinions, has offered nothing but support and encouragement, and Matthew Lewis, whose kindness and willingness to help me make contact with Amberley Publishing has been invaluable.

I'm especially indebted, of course, to my family. My parents, who never stopped believing I could write this book. My sister, who read and offered advice on it as it developed. My brother-in-law, who stepped up to help whenever there was a problem with my computer. And naturally my niece, who I hope will grow up to enjoy this book one day.

Finally, to my grandparents. I hope you would be proud.

Index

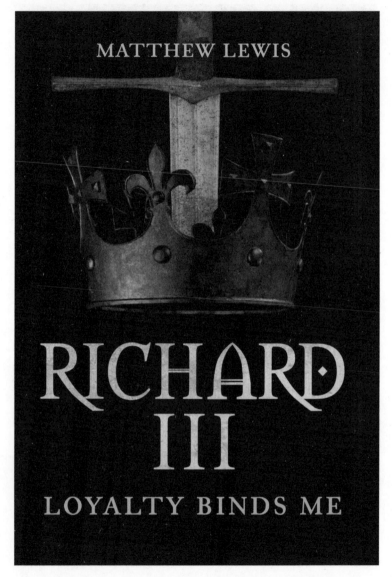